Corporations In Evolving Diversity:
Cognition, Governance, and Institutions

The Clarendon Lectures in Management Studies are jointly organized by Oxford University Press and the Saïd Business School. Every year a leading international academic is invited to give a series of lectures on a topic related to management education and research, broadly defined. The lectures form the basis of a book subsequently published by Oxford University Press.

Clarendon Lectures in Management Studies:

Corporations in Evolving Diversity

Cognition, Governance, and Institutions

By
MASAHIKO AOKI

OXFORD
UNIVERSITY PRESS

OXFORD
UNIVERSITY PRESS

Great Clarendon Street, Oxford OX2 6DP

Oxford University Press is a department of the University of Oxford.
It furthers the University's objective of excellence in research, scholarship,
and education by publishing worldwide in

Oxford New York

Auckland Cape Town Dar es Salaam Hong Kong Karachi
Kuala Lumpur Madrid Melbourne Mexico City Nairobi
New Delhi Shanghai Taipei Toronto

With offices in

Argentina Austria Brazil Chile Czech Republic France Greece
Guatemala Hungary Italy Japan Poland Portugal Singapore
South Korea Switzerland Thailand Turkey Ukraine Vietnam

Oxford is a registered trade mark of Oxford University Press
in the UK and in certain other countries

Published in the United States
by Oxford University Press Inc., New York

British Library Cataloguing in Publication Data

Data available

Library of Congress Cataloging in Publication Data

Data available

Typeset by SPI Publisher Services, Pondicherry, India
Printed in Great Britain
on acid-free paper by
Clays Ltd, St Ives Plc

ISBN 978–0–19–921853–0

1 3 5 7 9 10 8 6 4 2

Preface

One afternoon in mid-October of 2008, I landed at London Heathrow Airport, and then headed for Oxford to deliver the Clarendon Lectures in Management Studies. The shock wave cast by the bankruptcy of Lehman Brothers a month before was still palpable in the air, in Oxford as much as in London. The themes of the lectures that I had prepared over the course of the previous year appeared to be more relevant than I had anticipated. Do corporations exist primarily for the accumulation of investors' wealth? Will, or should, the global corporate landscape become ever flatter under the sovereign leadership of financial power? If there is no space left to debate these issues, are we facing the End of History for corporate law?

This book—based on my 2008 Clarendon Lectures, but also incorporating some new facts and thoughts collected since then—attempts to question these assumptions. It does so by going back to the basics beyond practical business/policy prescriptions and by making an effort to develop a systematic framework for understanding the nature and behavior of business corporations as one of evolving diversity. By focusing on the associational-cognitive aspect of organizational architecture and its corporate governance implications, my argument may sometimes be at odds with the orthodox views of corporate law and finance, as well as the neoclassical theory of the firm. However, it is more broadly consistent with recent contributions from (epistemic) game theory, the theory of knowledge, and the cognitive sciences, as well as a reason for the historical genesis of corporations in general. The book also deals with the interactions of business corporations with other agents not only in the domain of economic-exchange, but also political- and social-exchange in society. These interactions taken together can be considered as forming the institutional context of society, which is itself an evolving system. Thus, I hope that, although focusing on business corporations, this book may be read more generally as a treatise on institutions. In fact, Chapter 4 provides a synthetic perspective of institutional analysis that hopefully goes beyond my previous work on the subject, *Toward a Comparative Institutional Analysis* (2001).

Needless to say, I owe a great deal to my teachers, fellow scholars, colleagues, students, editors, and others, for the research leading up to the Lectures and for the completion of this book. Without naming them all here, I hope that the extensive yet selective references I make to many of their works throughout this book will acknowledge their contributions to this project and demonstrate my indebtedness albeit in a humbled and incomplete way. I would expressly like to mention a few names, however, that I owe specifically in completing this project. Dean Colin Mayer and Professor Mari Sako, both of the Saïd Business School of Oxford University, and David Musson of Oxford University Press, extended to me the kind invitation to present the prestigious Clarendon Lectures in Management Studies, and offered help at various stages leading up to the publication of this book. I am most grateful to them. My great thanks also go to Professors Gregory Jackson and Hideaki Miyajima for allowing me to cite extensively from their research results in Chapter 5.1; Professors Simon Deakin, Herbert Gintis, Colin Mayer, and Douglass North for reading the entire manuscript and writing generous endorsements from varied disciplinary perspectives; Mr Yusuke Narita, Takuya Onoda, Kazuhiro Taniguchi, and Ben Self for useful suggestions, as well as editorial and research assistance. Finally, my wife, Reiko, who accompanied me on the literal and spiritual journey to Oxford, and afterwards, by offering companionship, loving encouragement, care, and empathy, leading to the completion of this book: Thank you.

February 2010
Stanford

Contents

Contents

List of Figures

List of Tables

1

Introduction:
What Do Corporations Do?

What do business corporations do and how? Are they becoming more alike everywhere, between the Anglo-American and the Continental Europe, between the West and the East? Is that the way that should be? Or is there any virtue in there being some diversity between corporate organizations on the global scale? How do, or should, financial corporations serve non-financial business corporations?

Until the recent financial crisis, the answers to these questions were generally considered to be obvious and easy. That is, the objective of business corporations is to maximize profits. They are then to be organized and governed to maximize share value that supposedly represents the present value sum of expected future profits. Artificial barriers to this goal should be removed. The shareholders are then motivated to, and can therefore effectively, govern business corporations for the benefit of society as a whole. The reason being that share-price maximizing can act to remove any wasteful element in corporate activities, discipline the behavior of the workers, control the illegitimate attempt of management to accumulate their personal wealth at the sacrifice of others, and so on. And, we were told, the world is moving in that direction because of the mighty competitive pressure of globalized financial markets.

Whenever events occurred in the past that shook the corporate economy, however, the orthodox view of shareholder sovereignty was exposed to public scrutiny. This happened after the Great Depression and it happened again in the 1980s in the USA when the industrial competitiveness of the US economy was perceived to be threatened by Germany and Japan. The first occasion led to the introduction of the legal debate between the stakeholder-oriented view of corporate governance and the shareholder-oriented view.[1] The later occasion brought together for the first time

1

economists to earnestly engage in discussions on the topic of corporate governance that previously had been almost exclusively a subject for lawyers. In the debate, interests in national differences in corporate governance arose and their implications were discussed. The so-called "Varieties of Capitalism" paradigm eventually emerged out of this debate as a variant of the stakeholders-oriented view.[2]

However, the pendulum was soon to swing back to an orthodox view with the period around 1990 marking a turning point in hindsight. The ideological and political-economy battle between the planned economy and the corporate-market economy, which had raged over most of the last century, finally came to an end with the demise of the Soviet Union, and (former) communist countries—including China—were set to explore the transition to a market economy. State enterprises, which were essentially nothing but administrative units of communist states, were to be transformed into market-oriented corporate firms, either privately-owned or state-owned. To facilitate the transition, the crucial roles of various institutional supports, such as the legal enforcement of property rights and contracts, social norms of trust, the transparency of corporate information, and the accountability of management were highlighted. Every economist seems to have agreed on that much. However, two subtly differentiated views gradually grew out of this general consensus. One view, a more institutionalist-oriented one, posited that the institutional supports may not be automatically implemented merely by an act of the legislature and that the transition path may therefore be diverse and could be even an uneasy one, depending on the historical, social, and political factors of each economy.[3] The other view was premised on a deeper faith in the universalistic value of markets and the market-oriented governance of corporate firms. If appropriate legal arrangements are provided and enforced after the privatization of state-owned enterprises, it was held, the corporate economy can thrive autonomously.[4] Faith in the market- and shareholder-oriented governance model gained momentum from the mid-1990s on, and it looked uncontestable.

Indeed, from the 1990s up to 2007, share prices registered spectacular growth except for interim dents during the currency crisis in 1997 and the burst of the dot-com bubble in 2001 accompanied by the disclosure of Enron and WorldCom scandals. The growth of the world economy, including the so-called emergent market economies, made the orthodox view of business corporations more credible. Resonant with the Zeitgeist of the time, prominent scholars of corporate law proclaimed "the end of history for corporate law" (Hansmann and Kraakman 2001), arguing that the ideological or normative battle over corporate law was over. "The management-oriented model of America, the labor-oriented model of Germany, the state-oriented model of France and Japan" were all claimed to have failed and there was no longer any serious competitor to the shareholder-oriented model.

However, in less than a decade a credit crisis erupted in Wall Street and the City, in September 2008. It revealed that the spectacular growth of financial assets had been to a great extent engineered by financial intermediaries whose incentives were distorted toward endogenously generating higher risks.[5] Trillions of dollars worth of shareholder wealth disappeared within a matter of one month. The impact immediately spread to the real sector of the corporate economy on a global scale, as symbolized by the failure of two of the Detroit Three (once the Big Three).

What went wrong? Is it that the basic tenet of the shareholder-oriented model of the corporate economy is basically right, but that the crisis was created by the "*A*rrogance, *I*ncompetence and *G*reed" (AIG) of the financial intermediaries so that it can be cured by regulatory reform? Or ought it be taken more seriously as a symptom of a mismatch in the ways that financial markets and intermediaries relate to non-financial business corporations? Do we therefore need an alternative model of business corporations and the corporate economy so that the single-minded shareholder-oriented model will not ideologically mislead the global corporate economy again? If so, what form would such a model take? Is it sufficient to resurrect the familiar, albeit humbled, stakeholder-society view scorned by the orthodox shareholder-oriented view for its lack of solid logic (e.g. Tirole 2001)? Does the "varieties of capitalism" view have still something to offer in spite of the globalization of markets, organizations, and information, as well as rising concern over the sustainability of the global commons (the natural environment, etc.)?

In this treatise, I will try to attempt a new look at "what (non-financial) business corporations do," and their relationships with financial markets as well as societies. As a way of introducing such an agenda, let me briefly go back to the basics: namely, I will ask the ontological question of what the generic nature and *raison d'être* of corporations is, business corporations being nothing more than one species of corporation. Corporations are undoubtedly one of the most important societal devices that human beings have ever invented. Although the legal concept of corporations has arguably been said to have originated in the Roman era,[6] it was in medieval Europe that the incorporation was initiated for various social functions and started to flourish in a variety of domains: religion, learning, politics, philanthropy, trades, and crafts. Access to the corporate form was limited at this time to elites of various types. But this decentralized institutional innovation prepared "doorstep conditions" (North, Wallis, and Weingast 2009) for Europe, allowing it to get one step ahead of other regions and to make an earlier transit to the modern democratic state and corporate economy.[7]

Needless to say, contemporary business corporations are a highly developed form of the corporation that are both historically unparalleled and still evolving. Their special features, such as the pooling of a large sum of financial capital and the transferability of its shares through markets, the capital market control of management, limited liability, the organization of operational activities through various types of contracts, and so on need to be understood in their own light and indeed understanding has been sought through the disciplines of economics, jurisprudence, finance theory, business studies and so on. At the same time, however, business corporations share some generic features with other species of corporations that pursue different objectives than business and perform diverse social functions. This point is so obvious that it may appear not worthwhile mentioning it. But reflecting a little on the generic features of corporations may help to shed light on some aspects of business corporations that are often left behind in specialized professional inquiries. As a reference point, let me try to verbalize a minimalist conceptualization of corporations as follows: *Corporations are voluntary, permanent associations of natural persons engaged in some purposeful associative activities, having unique identity, and embodied in rule-based, self-governing organizations.*[8] It is expected that contemporary business corporations satisfy all these generic characteristics in unique, substantive forms and possibly more.

Among these characteristics, let us first consider the generic nature of corporations as a "permanent" entity or having perpetual life.[9] The great jurist of eighteenth-century England, Blackstone, began the first modern treatment of the corporations by characterizing it as "a person that never dies; in like manner as the river Thames is still the same river, though the parts which compose it are changing every instant" (Blackstone 1765–9/ 2005, Bk 1, ch. 18). Indeed, it is obvious that corporations can do what individuals with limited biological longevity cannot do. For one thing, the corporate ability to own property, backed up by the institution of shared ownership and share transferability, makes the permanence of business corporations secure. Its advantage is made very clear if we consider the consequence of limits on it. For example, the argument of Kuran (2005) who examined "[t]he absence of the corporation in Islamic Law" makes a point. Under a relatively egalitarian inheritance system of Islamic Law, the fragmentation of the estates of merchants hindered the durability of their businesses over generations. Therefore successful merchants converted their wealth into real estate and reconverted it into the corpus of a *Waqf*, the unique Islamic corporate body that emerged in the eighth to ninth centuries. The founder could appoint himself or his successor to the position of manager-trustee (*mutawalli*). Endowed real estates were leased to commercial facilities in the short term by the corporate body, and revenues from them were spent on creating and sustaining communal and religious goods such as drinking water supply, assistance to religious and commercial travelers, road maintenance, mosques and so on. But the growth of *waqf* was limited because of its individual nature, for it had to be founded by an individual and the leasing conditions were controlled by him even after his death through the enforceable, enduring founding deed. Incentives for the dynamic accumulation of corporate property were lacking, because of the incomplete separation of natural individuals and the corporate body.[10]

However, what an individual cannot do but corporations can is not limited to owning and using real estate and other physical property beyond his or her life. Actions, physical and cognitive, are also relevant. Corporations can organize associative activities among its members by distributing cognitive actions among members. Corporations as a corporate body can cognize and store what a mere collection of individuals cannot. Indeed it is worthwhile recalling that the first prominent types of corporations that emerged in the early medieval period and became legal models preceding later-day business corporations were those "founded *ad studendum et orandum* [for study and prayer], for the encouragement and support of religion and learning" (Blackstone 1765–9). The Roman Catholic Church was established as a legal corporate body under canon law through the Gregorian Reformation (1075–1122). A law school which had been started in Bologna around 1087 by an individual teacher named Irnerius survived after his death and was incorporated into two bodies as *universitas* by students. The universities of Paris and Oxford were also incorporated as early as the thirteenth century (In the New World as well, one of the first corporations was Harvard University, chartered in 1636).

The primary functions of these types of corporations were to understand or interpret the world, accumulate, theorize, and bestow knowledge for future uses and advancement, sustain culture as common knowledge and so on—although property issues were not unimportant for them either.[11] Some historians argue that the initial organization of European universities, as mentioned above, were actually influenced by the structure of *waqf*-financed colleges (*madrasas*), but the former quickly developed into higher learning institutions because of the flexibility made possible by legal personhood. One innovation made possible by this arrangement was the ability of the universities as organizations to grant degrees rather than awarding certificates from individual teachers.[12] Indeed, great universities became great as a result of "incorporating" scholars and students who had diverse, but complementary, cognitive competence and interests.

The primary purpose of business corporations is to make money, not to learn. But even for them, the reasons why incorporation are vital for religious and learning activities are not entirely irrelevant. As knowledge use and creation (that is, innovation) becomes a more and more important resource for the competitiveness of business corporations, this point cannot be overlooked. However, in England where the corporate economy first emerged on a substantive scale, the traditional legal view was to formally limit membership to the shareholders. But business corporations also have the dimension of the economic concept of the "firm" *à la* Coase (1937), that is, as the enduring producing organization that cannot be decomposed to a bundle of short-term contracts. Production and other activities taking place within the corporate firm may appear on the surface as a mere assemblage of individual physical actions, with physical externalities among them (e.g. congestion in the use of corporate physical assets, the common use of digital files, etc.). However, as expounded further in the next chapter, all physical actions of human beings are coordinated by cognitive actions, while the physical actions and assets provide extended resources for the latter.[13] But the orthodox economic theory of contracts is premised on the idea that cognition can take place only within the mind of individuals. Thus people may hide their intentions, information, and so on to their individual advantage, unless they are provided with the proper incentives to reveal them. This presumption indeed lies at the heart of micro economics (the economics of information) that theoretically supported the shareholder-oriented view in past decades. However, the recent development of experimental economics, cognitive neuro-science, and related areas increasingly provides evidence and theories that human cognition also takes place in more interactive ways at the group level in some contexts. Therefore, the way in which business corporations are organized as *systems of associational cognition* deserves no less attention than the financial aspects of the corporation.

However, the orthodox contract theory of the firm considers the human aspects of business corporations only in terms of authority relationships between the management and the workers. The philosophy and substance of corporate governance laws, following the English common law tradition, certainly embrace this approach. One of the reasons why such a view permeated in the law in the first place may have been a reflection of the timing of the first modern corporate law in England: the Joint Stock Companies Act (1844). Ahlering and Deakin (2007) argued that the passing of this act was preceded by Britain's Industrial Revolution and the master–servant regime was imported from the previous practice and transplanted into the company law. One authoritative textbook published in 1969 of the company law in the UK criticized the state of the legal theory at that time as follows:

In so far as there is any true association in the modern public company it is between them and workers rather than between the shareholders *inter se* or between them and the management. But the fact that the workers form an integral part of the company is ignored by the law. In legal theory the relationship between a company and its employees is merely the contractual relationship of master and servant and the servants no more form part of the company than do its creditors. ... This orthodox legal view is unreal in that it ignores the undoubted fact that the employees are members of the company for which they work to a greater extent than are the shareholders whom the law persists in regarding as its proprietors. (Gower 1969, 1979: 10–11)

Since then, the situation has been slightly changed in terms of formal statute. Even in the UK, the Companies Act 1985 obliges corporate directors in the execution of their functions to have regard to "the interest of employees in general, as well as the interests of its members." However, the philosophy and ideology of those who subscribe to the shareholder-oriented model does not seem to have been affected much.

Treating the workers merely as hands was deeply rooted in Industrial America as well. During the Second World War, Peter Drucker, who had emigrated from Vienna via England to the USA, was invited by Alfred Sloan to visit the offices, factories, and archives of General Motors (GM) and research how great the GM management style was. His study culminated in a classical treatise, the *Concept of the Corporation* (1946/1972). In that book, he praised the inventiveness of GM's multidivisional organization and so on, but at the same time urged GM to treat the workers as a resource rather than as a cost. He observed on the shop floors that when workers experienced and understood the whole facets of work processes (i.e. the entire assembly job), rather than being confined to a single compartmentalized job, they were better able to solve together emergent complex problems arising to meet highly delicate requirements of military procurements.

The workers can become more productive by "standing the assembly-line technique on its head," said Drucker (1946/1972: 156). This idea eventually led him to the notion of "knowledge workers" who can supply brains, not merely hands. But GM banned their employees and managers from reading the book, while Japanese managers studied it ardently during the 1950s and 1960s. This difference may eventually have taken a heavy toll on GM.

One thing that I intend to do in this book is to attend to the cognitive aspect of "what business corporations do." That is, inside business corporations, cognitive activities, such as information collections, processing, uses and storage, are systematically distributed and interrelated between the management and the workers, as well as among the workers, while the investors, in effect, supply cognitive tools to them. Let us refer to the hither-to-rather-neglected cognitive relations between the management and the workers inside the corporate organizations as associational cognition. The reason why we need to look into this aspect of business corporations is somewhat related to the famous question raised by Coase. He wanted "to discover why a firm emerges at all in a specialized exchange economy" (1937: 335). As is well known, his answer was that the firm emerged and expanded to the extent that it was able to save on transaction costs by replacing authority relationships for markets. Within the firm the employed workers obey the entrepreneur's discretion within the bounds of "indifference" set by contracts. He pointed out two situations under which such transaction cost saving could occur. One is where it is difficult to find relevant prices and the other is where it is troublesome to negotiate repeated market contracts. If the permanent association of the body of employees is beneficial for any reason, then the repetition of contract negotiations is certainly without merit. The difficulty of finding appropriate prices manifests itself most prominently when multilateral externalities (and economies of scale) are involved. And, the associational cognition inherently involves lots of externalities. Cognition can be shared across members and over time to organizational advantage, and sometimes to its disadvantage (e.g. too much cognitive assimilation is not always good in an organizational context; organizational inertia overriding new information may become detrimental to adapting to new environments and so on).

If we thus recognize the potential importance of associational cognition, then questions follow such as: How are cognitions (to be) distributed and related among the members of its system? How are they related to the system of tools of cognition such as computers, the Internet, robotics, machines, digital files, and so on? Whose cognitive assets are "essential" in an economically meaningful sense? Are the workers simply the bodily extension of the manager's brain in associational cognition? Focusing on this aspect of corporate architecture appears to be particularly important in the era of information technology. I will discuss in Chapter 2 the fact that there are actually discrete forms of architecting the corporate system of associational cognition that are not limited to the Coasian "authority relationship." And they can be subjected to selection by various factors that are not limited to efficiency. Just as there is diversity, as well as similarity, among individuals in their cognitive competence, interests, and contents, so there is among business corporations viewed as a system of associational cognition.

Besides the cognitive aspect, is there any other dimension of the corporation as generically defined previously that may suggest for us a way to revisit the nature of contemporary business corporations as a species? Contemporary jurists characterize business corporations above all by such properties as legal personality (i.e. the capacity to become the subject of contracts, property ownerships, and formal legal dispute), limited liabilities, shared ownerships and their transferability, and delegated management. These characteristics may be regarded as business-specific substantive representations of the "unique identity" and "self-organizing" dimensions of the corporation, on which I will discuss shortly.

The question of what represents the "purposeful activities" specific to the contemporary business corporation may appear obvious at a general level: that is, to be engaged in market-oriented business activities. However, if we pursue this question more specifically, it turns out to constitute the crux of the matter that we are concerned with: "what do corporations do?", that is, "exclusively for profit" as the shareholder-oriented view dictates or for something broader as the stakeholder-oriented view claims. I submit that a proper answer theoretically depends on ways in which a system of associational cognition is architected in corporate organizations. Yes, the shareholder-oriented model could be one viable model under certain conditions. But I intend to develop an argument that there can also be another model that was not even mentioned in the aforementioned, simplistic classification by Hansmann and Kraakman (2001) either as "management-oriented" (traditional American), "labor-oriented" (traditional German), or "state-oriented" (traditional French, Japanese) in their terminology. This model involves rather novel three-way relationships between the management, the workers, and the investors, whose presence may grow with the rising importance of human cognitive assets in business. This book attempts to contribute to an understanding of this new emergent phenomenon.

The characteristics "rule-based" and "self-governing" in the generic defi-nition of the corporation may at first sound somewhat contradictory. If the rules for corporate governance are to be specified by an outsider, say government, is the governance by corporate insiders according to those rules truly self-governing? It can be so, but then what are relationships between them? Some historically notable corporations, such as the East India Company and many of the public corporations engaged in public works during the seventeenth- and early nineteenth-century America, were chartered by the king or states. It was not until the mid nineteenth century that England finally made it possible for companies to be organized by the mere act of a registration without getting a special charter. But almost a century before that, Blackstone had already offered the following insight: "BUT, with us in England, the king's consent is absolutely necessary to the erection of any corporation, either impliedly or expressly given. The king's implied consent is to be found in corporations which exist by force of the common law, to which our former kings are supposed to have given their concurrence; common law being nothing else but custom, arising from the universal agreement of the whole community" (1765–9: ch. 18.I).

Also, in the first systemic treatise on corporations in the USA written in the late nineteenth century and published in the following century, Davis referred to "the creation by the state" as one of their basic attributes, but then quickly added such things as "voluntary inception-compulsory endurance," "autonomy, self-sufficiency, self renovation"(Davis 1905/2000: 13) to qualify the characterization. Even now, there is a heated debate among scholars with regards to the question of which is the more critical determinant of corporate governance, law, politics or spontaneous evolution.[14] How do we understand (or reconcile) the dual aspects (the opposing views, respectively) of business corporations as expressed by these authors or in the debate?

It is telling that pre-business corporations, such as the Roman Catholic Church and municipalities, were not the immediate creation of the modern nation state. They were voluntarily created, even though some of them needed the explicit or implicit approval of the rulers. As members of *voluntary* organizations, corporate participants must basically have con-sented to obey its own rather than any external authority. It is considered that under Gregorian Reform in the eleventh century the Roman Catholic Church set an important precedent in this respect. The assignments of jobs in their organizations, including the election of Popes, were made on the assumed capacity of the appointed persons to carry out ecclesiastical mis-sions. In this way, the separation of office and person was made complete and the Church was able to free itself of the interference of secular power (Berman 1983). The authority of the Pope's decrees was made absolute, even above any interpretative writings of the Bible by the saints (Genka 2009). The same, self-generating, self-governing nature can be seen in city communes, as well as within the Law Merchants, established as a neutral dispute-judgment organization in Champaigne Fair.[15]

This has implications for our inquiry into the nature of business corporations. As a starting point, we may inquire what kind of general rules for governance can be agreeable to and consented to by the constituent members of the corporation. Then, we may ask whether those endogenous rules can be consistent with general rules prevailing in society. Without the first property, people would not participate in corporations voluntarily, while without the second property, corporations would not be sustainable in society. They are interrelated.[16]

Let us first consider the self-governing question. All the constituent members of business corporations, or equivalently the holders of constituent assets, human, financial, and physical, can potentially benefit from participating in corporate associative activities in one way or another. However, their interests in the division of economic benefits from their associative activities are, at the same time, partly in opposition. Thus, concomitant with an evolving architectural convention, there ought to be basic agreeable rules about how the interests of the holders of contributing corporate assets are to be mediated and regulated in terms of their respective rights and duties. What could the nature of such rules be? In my view, this is the essence of the corporate governance problem, broadly conceived. I will discuss in the second half of the next chapter that the general characteristics of such rules are to be co-determined with a conventional mode of organizational architecture and that it may be characterized as a latent "agreement" among the contributing asset holders with their respective bargaining power being conditional on their positions in the architecture. By an agreement, I imply a solution that would satisfy such fundamental requirements as competitive sustainability of associative activities, consistency with a shared sense of fairness/justice, and a cognitive economy independent of irrelevant information. As informed readers easily recognize, these requirements are fundamentally equivalent to the basic axioms of a Nash bargaining solution (Nash 1953)[17].

Beyond an agreement on the basic principle, however, the governance rules may need to be further specified and formalized to become effective and workable by generating secure expectations among the people. This can partly be the role of formal statutes. However, I contend that legislative rules need to be consistent with the basic principle as conceptualized above. If not, they would not be enforceable and would have a detrimental effect on the competitive working of the associative activities of business corporations by distorting the incentives of constituent members. One of the most influential theories of corporate governance at the present time, the legal origin theory, identifies a difference in the legal origin of corporate laws as the most important variable that can explain variations in corporate performance across different economies.[18] However, it is debatable whether a desirable as well as a workable pattern of legal provisions can be uniquely identified and made durable over time.[19] I will argue in this book that different modes of corporate associational cognition call for different forms of governance in order to satisfy the fundamental requirement of self-governance as mentioned above.

I plan to deal with the second, consistency issue as follows. While pursuing their own business objectives under self-governing relationships among their members, corporations in general are overtly or implicitly exerting significant social and public impacts. Thus, for business corporations to become an institutionalized element of a social order, stable expectations need to be both generated and sustained in society in terms of the patterns of corporate behavior. In other words, corporate governance must be such as to generate corporate behavior that is largely consistent and coherent with societal institutional arrangements. Even if business corporations are not literally created by the state—either through a state charter, state ownership, or otherwise—are they still "state-created" in some other sense? More broadly, do they have to secure some kind of "a franchise from society" (Hannah 1976)? In spite of their self-governing nature in the sense discussed above, I answer these questions in the affirmative in a particular sense. I consider that the governance rules prevailing in the corporate field where business corporations cluster and compete must be in a "stable state" in the broader spectrum of *societal rules* that include enforceable statutory laws but are not limited to them.

Societal rules, or institutions, are not imposed on business corporations simply as external constraints. While business corporations attempt to behave in a coherent manner with existing market demands and societal rules, they are also active players in the formation of societal rules through their market and other behaviors. What is needed then is a framework for conceptualizing and analyzing such two-way interplays between business corporations and other social actors, including individuals, governments, non-business corporations, interest groups, non-governmental organizations (NGOs), and so on. These social actors mutually interact with some intentions. They aim to achieve some goals—economic, political, or social by their own actions, but in doing so they have to form expectations as to how the others will act and react to their own actions (which in turn is based on others' expectations about their own expectations and so on). In that sense, social interactions are all games, regardless of whether payoffs are exclusively self-regarding, material-oriented, hedonistic, or otherwise.[20] I call those games recursively played in society the *societal games*, although there are different kinds of domains of play. Indeed, viewing the societal order as stable patterns of game playing, and seeing it as generated through the recursive play of games, has been expounded by many authors— prior to the birth of, as well as outside the realm of, formal game theory as founded by von Neumann and Morgenstern (1944). Besides Huizinga, who said "play creates order, is order" in a book entitled *Homo Ludens* (*Man, as the One Who Plays*), many great authors, including Plato, Hume, Adam Smith, Hayek, Braudel, and possibly many more, employed analogies of the game as a means of understanding the nature of society.[21]

I follow this tradition, but try to go beyond a mere analogy by differentiating the discrete domains of societal games that embed corporate organizations— commons, economic, social, and polity—by discerning mutually distinct game forms and examining the interrelationships between those games and organization games played internally within business corporations by their members including workers. However, I may add in advance that, in doing so, I am not to be bound by the severe notion of substantive rationality and that of exclusively material-oriented, self-regarding payoffs (i.e. what individuals seek to achieve). I recognize that individuals are limited in their cognitive competence, and for this reason, they need societal rules, as well as corporate organizations, as extended cognitive resources. I will formulate primitive models of societal games in the mentioned domains and examine how different societal rules can evolve in each of those domains together with, and corresponding to, discrete modes of corporate architecture and governance. One great advantage of the application of game theory is its ability to analyze mutual relationships between embedding societal rules and corporate self-governing rules as stable, fit outcomes of play, that is as (multiple) equilibrium phenomena, of the societal and organizational games as linked. Those societal rules include the structure of public governance (that is, the political state), social norms and social status, legal rules and so on.

I have just referred to "equilibrium" in order to capture stable and mutually reinforcing aspects of the societal order and its impacts on the architectural and governance structure of business corporations. However, nothing in the societal order is static in a strict sense. Business corporations adapt their associative activities in response to evolving market and societal environments, while evolving corporate behavior impacts on the latter. But under what conditions can these mutually reinforcing processes generate a stable co-evolving path? Can it be understood as the aggregate outcome of rational choices by individual persons, natural and corporate, who are strong enough to possess their own unshakable tastes/objectives, beliefs, values, cognitive capacities, and so on, formed prior to the processes of societal interactions? The recent contributions of epistemic game theory and other disciplines suggest that in order for a stable societal order to evolve, something more may be needed, say, common backgrounds in information and inference, as well as various social cognitive categories such as social symbols carrying some meanings, public propositions such as laws and regulations acting as focal points for cognition, culture as common priors, and so on. In other words, in order to understand the basic nature of institutional evolution, the ironclad methodological individualism needs to be laid to rest. Arrow, one of the greatest economists of our time, stated in his Ely Lecture at the American Economic Association that: "I do conclude that social variables, not attached to particular individuals, are essential in studying the economy or any other social system and that, in particular, knowledge and technical information have an irremovably social component, of increasing importance over time" (Arrow 1994: 8). Chapter 4 of this book presents a coherent framework for understanding how the rules of societal games can be formed and evolve, what the role of business corporations in this process can be, how the above mentioned social categories can be generated and become cognitive environments to which cognitively-limited individual agents including corporations can offload their cognitive burdens.

Finally, toward the end of the book I provide data which depicts the corporate landscape of Japan that emerged out of the so-called "Lost Decade" triggered by the 1992 burst of the financial bubble. I regard the naming of the "Lost Decade" as a more meaningful reference to the societal cognitive crisis rather than just to the economic consequences of macro-policy and banking failures: that is, the state in which traditional rules could not be taken for granted any more. But no consensus has yet emerged as regards what the new rules could be. Yet, behind the crisis, the Japanese corporate landscape had undergone a tremendous change and it can no longer be characterized by a single stereotype of the "Japanese model." Beside with the traditional corporate structure, it now includes architectural hybrids featuring both increasingly indispensable human cognitive assets and market monitoring, on one hand, and those absorbing a more mobile, often disadvantaged, workforce combined with traditional bank financing, on the other. I interpret the causes, nature, and political implications of the evolving diversity, using the framework developed by that point. I suggest then that this diversifying phenomenon is not necessarily an isolated event limited to Japan, but there is a suggestion of similar phenomena evolving globally, albeit each one in a path-dependent, unique manner.

Evolving corporate diversity is thus not so much exactly a diversity due to national characteristics as the "varieties of capitalism" literature suggests, but a ubiquitous phenomenon across economies, exhibiting to differing degrees. In that sense it can be considered as a product of the global integration of economies. The global corporate landscape will never become flat, but it will exhibit varied modes of architectural structure that are built into it. In order to derive the potential gains from the global process of a "convergence to diversities", however, the global financial markets need to co-evolve as an infrastructure that will accommodate this evolutionary path of diversifying corporate architecture rather than exercise sovereign control over non-financial business corporations of all types. The 2008 credit crisis revealed that relationships between financial intermediaries and non-financial business corporations are still uneasy. The painful process of corporate recovery from the recession is to become the process of a search for a mutual fit between the two.

Notes

1. The shareholder-oriented view was prominently presented by Berle and Means (1932) out of concerns arising from their findings of the widespread share ownerships and the consequential separation of management and ownership in the USA. In his earlier writing Berle maintained that corporate powers were held in trust not only for the corporation per se but also for individual members of it (Berle 1931). Dodd (1932) challenged this view by arguing that the directors of a corporation must (if they had not already) become trustees, not merely for shareholders but also for other constituents of corporation, such as employees, customers, and particularly the entire community. Later, Berle conceded to Dodd, and admitted that modern directors act *de facto* and *de jure* as administrators of a community system, although he remained rather cautious about admitting this as the "right disposition" (Berle 1959: xii).
2. For a systematic exposition of the "varieties of capitalism" position, see Hall and Soskice (2001) and Amable (2003). Around this period, I also wrote about

Japanese and German corporate organizations and governance in a comparative perspective (e.g. Aoki 1984, 1988, 1990). However, as is to be clarified in this book, my theory and approach are to be distinguished from those in the so-called "Varieties of Capitalism" literature.

3. See, for example, Aoki (1994c) in which a mixture of bank-oriented governance and securities market-oriented governance was proposed as an option for evolutionary selection on the transition path.

4. Boycko *et al* (1996). Also see Shleifer and Vishny (1997).

5. Financial engineering—designing various financial derivatives to hedge risks—relies on mathematical tools, such as the Black–Scholes formula as an extension of Ito's Lemma, that can be applied to calculus of stochastic processes (say, securities prices) involving a random Brownian movement of variables. However, in the practical performance-evaluation of financial engineers the tail risks (extreme events with small probability) are not properly accounted for. If events occur in the lower tail, the loss is largely born by client investors who are less well-informed, while financial engineers are generously rewarded when events occur in the high tail. However a large proportion of the revenue increase in the latter case is not a real gain, but should be set-aside as a reserve for future risks (i.e. as costs). Such misalignment of incentives has induced financial engineers and fund managers to gamble on excessive tail risks, which was bound to result in a great crash.

6. The term "corporation" (*universitas*; also *corpus* or *collegium*) was derived from Roman law. Romans formed associations of families as *societatis* and *corpora*. The former were engaged in various types of colonial management such as tax farming, while the latter was a kind of guild. Although they had the notion of collective ownership, it has been pointed out that the Roman jurists, "with their intense hostility to definitions and theories," rarely used or analyzed the phrase "legal person" (Berman 1983: 85–8). North, Wallis, and Weingast (2009: 159–60) also point out that the Romans lacked a clear notion of "legal person" and a corporate body had to be represented by and act through individuals (2009: 160).

7. Also see Davis (1905/2000), Berman (1983), Rosenberg and Birdzell, Jr. (1986), Micklethwait and Wooldridge (2003), Greif (2008). Although more constrained in design and application, however, various institutional devices sharing certain aspects of corporations evolved elsewhere even before the development of capitalist economies, and those organizational experiences left path-dependent impacts on the nature of their transition to corporate market economies. For example, one may cite *Waqf* under the Ottoman Empire, referred to below, and various quasi-corporate organizations, such as *Han* governments, merchant houses, cultural schools, and so on in Edo Japan (e.g. Sugeno 1931; Murakami 1984, 1985; Ikegami 1995; Kasaya 1988). These Japanese organizations were formally dynastically controlled, but equipped with a professional administrative/management apparatus. Incompetent rulers/heads were forced to retire

early by the bureaucrats and the lack of any proper successors in kinship was dealt with by the practice of the adoption of, or arranged marriage with, able men. Although it is beyond the scope of this book, I consider historical comparative studies of the evolution of corporations and quasi-corporations in various cultural regions will have a significant contribution to our understanding of diverse evolutionary paths of the institutional arrangements of business corporations.

8. The eighteenth-century jurist, Blackstone gave the following classical characterizations which he said applied to "every corporation": (1) perpetual succession; (2) the ability to sue and be sued by its corporate name; (3) to purchase lands, and hold them; (4) to have a common seal; and (5) to make by-laws or private statutes (Blackstone 1765–9/2005, Bk 1, ch. 18, II). The first systemic treatise of corporation in the USA by Davis conceptualized the corporation as "a group of natural persons embodied in a certain class of the many forms of organization within or through which certain classes of social functions are exercised" (1905/2000: 13). Then, as its delimitations, he referred to the following attributes: (1) associative activity; (2) creation by the state; (3) voluntary inception–compulsory endurance; (4) autonomy, self-sufficiency, self renovation; (5) compulsory unity; (6) having its motives in private interest; (7) functioning in the public domain and in a manner appropriate for associative activity. Greif (2008) also gives a similar definition of corporations, supposedly consistent with their historical meanings, as "intentionally created, voluntary, interest-based, and self-governed permanent associations". (2008: 8) My definition does not explicitly refer to the "motivational" or "incentive-based" aspect. But for a while let it be implicit in the "voluntary" nature of association.

9. Needless to say, even corporations may cease to exist by their own choice or by law. But its life is not defined by the identity of its members.

10. Under the Ottoman rule, the number of *waqf*-owned commercial facilities amounted to 5,400 in the central market and port districts of Istanbul. By the middle of the nineteenth century most of them had become de facto owned by the lessees and in the twentieth century were transferred to them at a low price (Hayashi 2000).

11. Incorporating the property rights over real estate and prohibiting private ownership of them was a contested issue even for the Gregorian Reformation, and its establishment had to overcome fierce resistance from local priests (Berman 1983). For universities as well, issues of property ownership, even of prisons, became sources of enduring disputes with neighboring communities, sometimes involving severe physical confrontation leading to the deaths of students and residents (e.g. Davis 1905/2000, ch. 7).

12. Makdisi (1981) referred to by Kuran (2005: n.50).

13. This is a growing view of cognitive science; see Clark (1997, 2008).

14. See the debate discussed in chapter 3.

15. See Milgrom, North, and Weingast (1990) for the Law Merchant.

16. North, Wallis, and Weingast (2009) classify two types of organizations: "An *adherent organization* is characterized by self-enforcing, incentive compatible agreements among its members... *Contractual organizations*, in contrast, utilize both third-party enforcement of contracts and incentive compatible agreements among members." (p.16) Clearly business corporations are considered to belong to the second category. In contrast, I premise that the deep structure of internal "agreements" defines the fundamental self-governing nature of business corporations, while the third-party enforcement by the state complements them. They co-evolve as discussed in Chapter 3.

17. Binmore (1994, 1998, 2005) provides a comprehensive, general theory of the deep structure of social order based on a Nash bargaining solution. Aoki (1984) is an early treatment of business corporations from a similar perspective.

18. See La Porta *et al* (1998, 1999, 2008).

19. For critical examinations of the legal-origin theory and empirical methodology, see Ahlering and Deakin (2007), Armour *et al.* (2009).

20. A numerical measure thought to underlie observed behavior is referred to as "a decision utility" by Kahneman (1994). That is, the action chosen is inferred to have the highest numerical decision utility not limited to hedonistic experience associated with the consumption of a good or an event but reflecting other motives, say social, altruism, public concern, and so on.

21. Plato believed that playing games according to the rules is essential for educating children to follow societal rules. "I say that in states generally no one has observed that the plays of childhood has a great deal to do with the permanence or want of permanence in legislation. For when plays are ordered with a view to children having the same plays, and amusing themselves after the same manner, and finding delight in the same playthings, the more solemn institutions of the state are allowed to remain undisturbed" (2000, Book VII, 797: 154). Contrast this view with an analogy by McMillan (2002: 22) of the evolutionary development of the rules of folk football to the institutional evolution of market institutions (to be discussed later in Chapter 4(A)(iii)). The famous analogy of "the great chessboard of human society" by Adam Smith is found in (1759: 234). See Hayek (1988, Appendix E: 154) for a reference to "insufficiently appreciated" work by Huizinga. Braudel, the great historian of the French *École des Annales*, discusses the possibility of fruitful interactions between the historic observation of social reality and a model based on "social mathematics", particularly "the language of conditional facts, neither determined nor contingent but behaving under certain constraints, tied to the rules of a game, to the 'strategic' axis in the game of Von Neumann and Morgenstern" (Braudel 1969/1980: 42). He argued that through such interactions, the model can attempt "at an explanation of the structure, and instrument of control and comparison, able to verify the solidity and the very life of a given structure" (1969/1980: 44–5). But the models are of varying duration as the structures are subjected to swift or slow deterioration under the effect of contradictory pressures.

2

Varied Frames of Corporate Cognition and Self-Governance

2.1 Integrating architectural and governance perspectives

Traditionally there have been two major perspectives to an economic approach to business corporations: one focusing on their financial aspects and the other on their organizational aspects. The former deals with corporate attributes such as: the ability to raise a large sum of capital to implement a large scale investment that is not possible for individual or family enterprises; the ability to undertake risky ventures while providing opportunities for risk-averse investors to diversify their investment across shares with different risk characteristics,[1] as well as to limit investors' exposure to risk through the institutional device of limited liability. This approach regards the interests of the shareholders, as the supplier of financial capital, to be sovereign in the design of corporate governance and its ethos is to assure "proper returns to investments" (Shleifer and Vishny 1997: 737), that is to say, to maximize share values.

The second approach may be considered to have originated in the famous thesis of Adam Smith that the division of labor within the factory can exploit economies of specialization. Further, the corporate firm serves as a device to collectively preserve and re-combine knowledge, expertise, know-how, etc. and make use of these attributes for the production of new knowledge that can be useful for businesses and ultimately for society (e.g. Schumpeter 1934; Penrose 1959; Nonaka 1991). The modern literature also abounds in works dealing with the extent to which organizations can save on the costs of market transactions (e.g. Coase 1937; Williamson 1975, 1996); the ways corporate activities are structured as the internal organization (e.g. Doeringer and Piore 1971; Chandler 1977, 1990); contractual methods that incentivize the members of the internal organization (e.g. Holmstrom 1979, 1982; Milgrom and Roberts 1990); and unique functions of management such as entrepreneurship, strategy-making, cognitive leadership (e.g. Drucker 1985; Roberts 2004); and so on.

These two aspects of corporate firms, large scale finance by transferable shares and a large-scale internal organization, result in the so-called separation of control and management. Thus, as already noted in Chapter 1, its implications for corporate governance have become the object of heated discussions on corporate governance since the publication of a seminal book by Berle and Means (1932). One view holds that the presence of the internal organization may not be inconsistent with the shareholder-value view of business corporations, if it is run to maximize the surplus accruable to the investors after contractual payments have been made to all the internal members. In this view, management is nothing but the share-holders' agent. If management pursues their own class interests in terms of higher compensation, perks, social prestige, empire building and the like, they ought to be checked. An alternative view regards the role of the board as striking a balance between the interests of the investors and the members of the internal organization—the workers—and possibly beyond, including benefits to the community, by serving as the trustees for all these stake-holders.[2]

In this chapter I present a simple framework for synthesizing the two aspects of the corporate firm, external finance and internal organization, into a coherent whole, and consider its implications for corporate architec-ture and governance. Very simply, I regard the corporate body as being composed of three basic constituents: the investors, the manager, and the workers (as a general reference to all corporate employees except top management) and see how they interact in corporate activities and the disposition of their outcomes. However, it does so from a different angle than both the conventional shareholder-oriented view and the stake-holders' society view. I begin my argument by focusing on the aspect of the corporate body as an associational cognitive system. I identify five generic modes of organizational architecture viewed in this way, each of which is distinguished by specific combinations of human cognitive assets, management's and workers', together with their unique relation-ships to physical assets as extended cognitive resources. Then, I examine the governance structure that can equilibrate each of those architectural modes by distributing the rights and duties among the holders of those assets in a matching manner. Each model is kept as simple as possible and may not be immediately paralleled to corporate structures in practice.

However, the generic features of these modes may be latent in varied combination underneath the much more complex, nested, and animated structures of business corporations. I hope that because of its simplicity, the logic of multiple equilibria becomes theoretically transparent and easy to grasp, which will in turn clarify why architectural-governance combination becomes diverse in practice across economies and industries.

In the past, discrete modes of cognitive and governance structure of business corporations tended to appear as national or regional clusters for social, political, and cultural reasons that I will explore in this and following chapters. However, each of those clusters appears to have served comparatively well in markets with certain specific characteristics, but not necessarily well in markets of all possible characteristics. It is intuitively clear that Silicon Valley clustering of small start-up firms is not so competitive in markets for standard mass-products as in high-tech products design, while the clustering of firms emergent in the free-economic zones of South-East China in the 1980s and 1990s might have been so in those markets. Do such observations suggest that some kind of geographical diversity in a corporate architecture–governance combination will continue and be more efficient in ever-complex global markets? Is there any reason to believe that globalization will somehow lead to a better arrangement of corporate diversity? Or alternatively is the corporate landscape becoming ever more flatter and alike everywhere due to the force of globalization? My journey throughout this book is essentially devoted to exploring these issues.

2.2 A cognitive perspective: why and how?

In principal–agency theory and mechanism design theory, the management and the worker are assumed to enter the business corporation as the agent of the investors and that of the management respectively. They communicate with each other, using only encoded messages and overt actions. It is assumed that there is no means for them to know the tastes, intentions, beliefs, and information of the other party except through those means of representation, and, for the same reason, no means of detecting possible misrepresentations. Therefore, organizational communications need to be designed under the constraint that each member will reveal his/her true state and position on these matters only to the extent compatible with his/her hidden motives. The basic purpose of mechanism design theory is thus to inquire how to design a mechanism for exchanging messages under the condition of "privacy-preserving" (Hurwicz and Reiter 2006), while the purpose of contract theory is to investigate how to design a second-best contractual form subject to the "incentive compatibility" constraints. Organizational design is thus viewed as essentially conditioned by individual motivational factors.

However, cognition and motivation may not be entirely private and self-serving in some societal contexts. Recent advances in various disciplines suggest that there are much richer possibilities within human cognition and communication in general. We human beings not only communicate with each other using formal languages, but we also seem to have some ability to infer someone's intentions or thinking by observing their actions (the so-called "theory of mind," naïve-psychology[3]) or from the context (e.g. linguists' theory of relevancy[4]); to detect misrepresentations by others (e.g. neural science, evolutionary psychology[5]); to exhibit tendency of reciprocity (e.g. experimental economics, cultural psychology[6]); to participate with others in collaborative activities with shared goals (e.g. philosophy, cultural psychology, cognitive neuro science[7]); to infer the social-exchange implications of one's own actions on others (e.g. cognitive science[8]); and so on. Although those empirical and experimental results and the theoretical claims based on them would not warrant the immediate overhaul of the individualistic premise on which economics has been built, we would do well to pay heed to the latent implications they have for organizational behavior, particularly the possibility of associational (or group-level) cognition.

Therefore, I will start with the system of associational cognition, or the organizational architecture, as a basis for my analysis. If cognitions are organized within the organization in some systematic way, then reasonably coherent decisions may be made for collective action. One of the most important *raisons d'être* of the corporation is precisely to facilitate and exploit this possibility. By intentional design as well as through conventions and routines evolving during overlapping generations of its members, cognitions are systematically distributed among the managers and the workers, and their contents are extended, assimilated, or encapsulated among them; reasoning and judgment (decision-making for action) are also distributed among them and made by them according either to coded rules, informal conventions, routines, or on broadly agreeable ad hoc methods. Memories can be collectively stored beyond the biological longevity of individual members for future use, while distorted misrepresentations (hiding, lying, intentionally misleading, and the like) may be detected and controlled to reasonable degree, although not completely.

By this I do not intend to imply that associational cognitions can be perfectly organized, and "opportunism" (Williamson 1975) can be completely controlled in the organizational context. However, human beings can organize to do together what each of us cannot do as individuals. But, because there is inevitably an element of incompleteness in this, there can be varied ways of organizing, and the problems of moral hazard, misrepresentations, opportunism, and so on would arise accordingly. Opportunism is ubiquitous. However, I posit that the organizational mode is not selected primarily in order to control people's opportunistic behavior, but in order to benefit from working together. We then worry about the architecture-specific problem of opportunism.[9]

But under what kind of organizational arrangement can all the above become feasible? Surely each individual has his or her own interests in voluntarily participating in the corporate organization. Thus, the organizational process of the cognitive and physical actions of its members may be considered as a "game" in that their actions, as well as their consequences, matter to the interests of each member (whatever they may be). If the organization cannot implement any of the above possibilities in one way or another in a systematic and expected fashion, the playing of the game would become chaotic and, sooner or later, its sustainability would be seriously impaired. On the other hand, if a pattern governing these processes becomes common knowledge among the members of an organization, it can constitute a frame of the organizational game for the players. It provides to each of them "much of the information, assumptions, goals, and attitudes that enter into his decisions, and provides him also with a set of stable and comprehensible expectations as to what the other members are doing and how they will react to what he or she says and does" (Simon 1957: xvi). Simon called such a pattern "an organization." Then the members of the organization act more like "team" members than as individuals engaged in solely individualized cognition with exclusively self-regarding motives.[10] And it is to this framework that a substantial amount of the problem-solving tasks of individual members can be off-loaded.

Then, what kind of architectural mode of associational cognition and its motivational support can become common knowledge in corporate and societal contexts? Why can there be varied modes? I will proceed to understand this based on the following four ideas.

First, I examine the nature and forms of corporate organizational architecture as *systems of associational cognition*. There have been a fair number of works on the cognitive aspect of the business corporation in business studies, but they usually identify corporate cognitive action either as management strategy-making (e.g. Witt 1998, 2000; Gavetti and Rivikin 2007) or as collective organizational learning (e.g. Nonaka 1991; Nonaka *et al.* 2008; Greve and Taylor 2000; Gavetti and Levinthal 2000).[11] Instead, as already noted above, I focus on the aspect of corporate cognition as a system of associational cognition composed of the management and other internal members of the organization (dubbed simply as the workers) and inquire how it can be architected in varied forms. As Hayek (1945) once persuasively argued regarding the use of knowledge in society, useful information for the organization as well cannot be completely centralized and made use of by the manager as a central planner.[12] Management macroscopic cognition about the world and the corporate position in it, on one hand, and workers' microscopic cognition on-site, on the other, may be either hierarchically ordered, mutually assimilated, or made reciprocally indispensable, and so on. Such distinction provides the elementary units for classifying generic modes of organizational architecture (see Section 2.4 below).

Secondly, if varied modes of corporate architecture of associational cognition are possible, each of them must be able to anticipate the availability of a fit type of human resources in terms of cognitive disposition, attitudes toward associational cognition, the type and level of integrated cognitive and action skills and so on. It is this availability that provides an overall societal framework for possible architectural modes. However, this availability is conditioned by the strategic decisions taken by individuals on investment in types of *cognitive assets* through education, training, etc., while individual investment decisions are affected by their perceptions about which mode of corporate architecture is to prevail and accordingly which cognitive assets are likely to be profitable and so on. In other words, a prevailing mode of corporate architecture and fit type of human cognitive assets may be said to co-evolve (see Section 2.5 below). Thus, the nature and qualities of human cognitive assets relevant to corporate organizations are not entirely exogenous to the corporate field, even if they may appear to be so to individual corporations. And this is one of the major reasons why an optimal portfolio of organizational architectures is not likely to be immediately available in any individual economy.

Thirdly, human cognition, individual and collective, is not an isolated activity of individual brains, but uses bodily actions, physical tools and instruments, and human-made environments including societal rules as extended resources (e.g. Hutchins 1996; Clark 1997, 2008). For associational cognitions in business corporations, the system of non-human, physical assets as *cognitive tools* made up of computers, networks, machines, robots, digitally-stored files, and so on play particularly important roles. The ways in which the members of corporate associational cognition, the management and the workers, relate to those physical assets are another aspect of the modes of organizational architecture. In other words, if we refer to the personification of these physical assets as the investors (alternatively, the "capitalists" as the owner of physical capital goods), three-way relationships among the managers, the workers, and the investors become an essential defining factor of organizational architecture. According to the neoclassical folklore, in which the firm is represented by the production function with capital and labor as symmetric inputs exhibiting constant returns to scale, "it does not matter whether capital hires labor or labor hires capital." On the other hand, the basic stance of orthodox corporate governance theory is that the investors hire the management as instruments for their own share-value maximization and the management hire the workers as instruments for the implementation of their strategies. In a way my approach may be considered to reverse the goal–instrument relationship of this view. But, as seen below, it does not imply that the investors are merely passive and voiceless suppliers of cognitive tools. They can assert their own position and interests, depending on the role of the capital goods—which they control—as tools of associational cognition.

Fourthly, re-focusing on the cognitive aspect of business corporations does not imply that the motivational factor may be set aside. As mentioned above, a basic framework of organizational architecture needs to become common knowledge among its (internal) members in the sense that every one of them knows and follows the basic rules of organizational architecture, and that every one of them knows that everyone else knows this. For this to become possible and a corresponding architectural mode to become viable and sustainable, potential conflicts of interest among the members of associational cognition, as well as between them and the owner of the cognitive tools, must be settled by a "binding agreement." Above all, it must specify basic matters such as how their assets are to be deployed and rewarded, under what kinds of event they are to be withdrawn from cooperation, and so on. Such agreement ought to be endogenous to the prevailing mode of architecture and constitute the above-mentioned *cognitive frame* for the game that they play in associational cognition. It determines the fundamental "self-governing" nature of business corporations (cf. Chapter 1, pp. 11–2). The next chapter goes further and introduces institutional frames of political and social origins that embed corporate associational cognition. Although the internal, endogenous frame is supported and reinforced by them, it is not unilaterally derived from them, however. Unless it possesses essentially self-governing and self-sustaining properties, the sustainability of a business corporation as an institution would be fragile. Politics and social norms can support the ways that business corporations are organized and governed, but cannot create those ways from the outside.

In the next section, I begin with a simple, yet exhaustive, classification of possible modes of associational cognition between the two agents and examine their comparative cognitive properties. These are then used as generic building blocks for corporate architecture, together with physical cognitive tools (i.e. capital goods), in a variety of ways. The above four factors are then introduced one by one in order to make the model of business corporations both realistic and diverse, to illustrate the merits of a cognitive perspective.

2.3 Building blocks of organizational architecture

2.3.1 *Elemental modal units of associational cognition*

The organizational architecture of corporations is extremely complex and diverse, and its complexity might defy any realistic formalization. Therefore, I adopt the following simple expository strategy: first, I begin with an outrageously simple, in fact the simplest, form of associational cognition, that is a cognitive connectedness between two agents. I use this later as a possible building block for the design of an organizational architecture composed of the management and the workers. I identify three basic "modes" for associational cognition that are possible between two agents for achieving a common goal and examine what factors determine the comparative cognitive advantages of these basic modes. The discussion reveals two important points for organizational design—that there are two ways of assimilating cognitions between the two agents with different performance qualities and that more communication is not always better than less. For now, I do not explicitly consider the use of physical assets as tools of associational cognition that may become a possible determinant of architectural type. In the next two subsections I will do so, and this will bring us a step closer to the reality of corporate organizational architecture.

A mode of associational cognition between the two agents may be identified with a pair of rules: one for the distribution of cognition regarding the work environments, and the other for action by each of them, based on available information, to achieve the common goal (assuming such a goal exists for now). Let me describe this somewhat formally. Suppose that two agents, denoted by I $= 1$, 2, cooperate to achieve a certain common goal. Suppose that their goal is represented by the maximization of the real-valued function, $F(X_1, X_2; \tilde{\theta}_1, \tilde{\theta}_2, \tilde{\sigma})$, where X_1, X_2 represent the level of actions taken by the respective agents; $\tilde{\theta}_1$ and $\tilde{\theta}_2$ are stochastic parameters representing the states of local environments affecting the respective impacts of X_1, X_2 on the goal; and $\tilde{\sigma}$ is the stochastic parameter representing the state of common environment affecting the impact of both X_1 and X_2 on the goal. Although the stochastic parameters $\tilde{\theta}_1$ and $\tilde{\theta}_2$ are observed only by respective agents with some imprecision, the common stochastic parameter $\tilde{\sigma}$ can be observed directly by both agents jointly, separately, or either one of the agents, each with some imprecision. Decision-making by each agent regarding his/her own action choice is assumed to depend on his/her cognized values of the environmental parameters: that is, $X_1 = f(\hat{\theta}_1, \hat{\sigma}_1)$ and $X_2 = g(\hat{\theta}_2, \hat{\sigma}_2)$ where the symbol ˆ indicates the value of the relevant parameter recognized by the agent denoted by the subscript.[13] The cognitive competence of each agent is measured by the expected (normalized) deviations of its observations from true values.[14]

The tasks of the two agents are complementary to the achievement of the goal F (otherwise there is no need for cooperation) but they are competitive at the same time in their use of the cognitive resources (tools) in the common pool.[15] It is known that if they are relatively more competitive than complementary, it is better for the cognitions of the agents to be differentiated or *encapsulated*. That is to say, they should not communicate with each other about their cognition. This will make it more likely that the situation can be avoided whereby the inevitable cognitive errors are synchronized in the same direction with the consequence that there is congestion in the use of the resources in the common pool. More communication is not better for the organization in this case. On the other hand, if the decision variables are relatively more complementary than competitive, it is better for the organizational architecture to be designed in such a way that decision choices are coordinated on the basis of assimilated cognitions ($\hat{\sigma}_1 = \hat{\sigma}_2 = \hat{\sigma}_{12}$, say). This is because divergent choices can be detrimental to the achievement of the common goal in this case (cf. Aoki 1986, 2001, Cremer 1990, Pratt 1996, Alonso *et al.* 2008).

How can observations of the common stochastic variable be assimilated among the agents? Put simply, there can be two modes for this: one is for two agents to pool their observations and reach a consensus in their decision-making possibly through the sharing of observational context, mutual communications and discussions both formal and informal, and so on. The costs involve the time and effort needed for communication and consensus-making, the discarding of idiosyncratic but potentially useful observations, etc. I will refer to this method as *cognitive sharing* or simply *assimilated cognition*. The second method is for one agent to specialize in observing the common environment and transmit its observed value to the other using formal codes. This method involves the costs caused by a sender's failure to encode his observation precisely, noise in the process of information transmission, a receiver's mistake in decoding (misunderstanding), the missing of subtle information that cannot be easily codified, any time-lag between an observation by one agent to recognition by the other and so on. I will refer to this assimilative mode as *hierarchical cognition*.

The question of which mode of associational cognition is better in the case of strong complementarities depends on the characteristics of the environments of the agents and various costs specific to each mode indicated above. If the difference between the task environments of the two agents is greater, then cognition sharing may not be worth the communication costs, because the available information is relatively unrelated and they ought to be used as such. On the other hand, if the environments are very much alike (and if there is a disparity of cognitive skills among the agents), then it is on average better for organizational costs to be saved in such a way that one of the agents (the one possessed with a higher cognitive skill) is specialized in observing the common environment and hierarchically transmit its own specialized observation to the other. For situations between these two extremes, cognitive sharing is expected to perform better, provided that the cognitive competence of both agents are alike. In this case, possible bad consequences arising from individual cognitive errors about the common environment can be mitigated by the pooling of observations.[16]

For example, imagine that two industrial laboratories try to develop new generations of batteries and motors, respectively, for modular parts of a future electric car. At an early stage of development, the required research fields (e.g. chemical engineering, material science on one hand and mechanical engineering on the other) have less in common and their development efforts may be done fairly independently in the interests of cost savings, etc. (encapsulated cognition). However, as the development processes progress, there must be more intense coordination so that their respective modular designs will be compatible, requiring them to resolve any inconsistency problems (common environment) together (cognitive-sharing). On the other hand, in a situation where a computer network is to be designed, maintained and used within a firm, design and maintenance can be centralized, while operational uses are decentralized at the terminal level. In this case, once cognitive tasks relevant to the whole system are fulfilled, subsequent operations require less demanding, standard cognitive tasks. This is a simple example of hierarchically specialized cognition, but note that, at this level of abstraction, the word hierarchy does not imply any authority relationship among the agents.

Table 2.1. Comparative advantage of the elemental modal units of associational cognition

Tasks	Environments		
	Distinct	Intermediate	Alike
Complementary	(E) Encapsulated	(S) Assimilated	(H) Hierarchical
Competitive	(E) Encapsulated	(E) Encapsulated	(E) Encapsulated

The described comparisons of the three basic modes of bilateral cognition are summarized in Table 2.1. An interesting question quite relevant throughout this book is whether the summarized theoretical results can indeed predict and/or explain some essential aspects of observed societal portfolios of organizational architecture. The answer will be partly yes, and partly no. In order to discuss this issue, however, I still have to introduce a classification of types of human assets—cognitive assets—that fit and carry the respective modes of associational cognitions and inquire into the nature of the societal process by which they are accumulated and accordingly make the corresponding architectural modes feasible. Then the information summarized in Table 2.1 can be utilized as a guide for diagnosing the consequences of such a process. It will turn out that a non-optimal architectural configuration is a likely possibility, although there may be a general tendency for the process to climb (evolve) toward a local optimum (Section 2.5 below).

2.3.2 Human cognitive assets, and physical assets as extended cognitive resources

Now let me make a modicum of further progress towards a model of corporate organizational architecture by distinguishing two types of human agents as the carriers of associational cognition—the management and the workers. They are distinct in terms of the role of associational cognition: the former is primarily responsible for cognizing the systemic and common environment (the world, so to speak) and the position of the corporation in it, while the latter is responsible for the local environment in which their tasks take place, although their cognition can be connected in various ways that will be specified in Section 2.4 below. The management and the workers each possess particular cognitive skills characterized by certain orientations, attributes, dispositions, abilities, and so on to do their cognitive tasks. Those skills also serve as sources for their holders to derive shares in the organizational gain. Therefore I refer to them as (human) *cognitive assets*. There are two reasons for adopting this term.

Of course human actions in the context of the organization involve not only mental activities (e.g. perceiving, imaging, guessing, theorizing, deciding, etc.) but also physical ones (e.g. operating machines, uttering speech, typing an e-mail, etc.). However, the latter is not only impossible without conscious or unconscious control by the former, but the latter also constitute important resources for the former (consider economists' notion of learning-by-doing; Arrow 1962). Thus cognitive and physical actions are inseparable. The cognitive scientist Andy Clark views the workings and states of the mind broadly in terms of the complex, continued interplay of brain, body, and world (which includes social and institutional "scaffolding"), and points out that "the traditional divisions among perceptions, cognition, and action look increasingly unhelpful. ... [R]eal world actions often play precisely the kinds of functional roles more usually associated with internal processes of cognition and computation" (Clark 1997: 221). The human skills required in an organizational context, including those of bodily actions, may not, therefore, be entirely invariable (portable), apart from the specific context of associational cognition, but may be conditional on the ways in which individuals relate to each other in that context.[17]

This leads to the second reason why I dare to use the unconventional term "cognitive assets" instead of the customary "human capital." While the notion of the human capital usually (albeit not necessarily) refers to skills invested by individuals and portable through the labor market, I focus below on the quasi-collective nature of the respective skills of the management and the workers in the context of particular modes of associational cognition. Human cognitive skills are certainly embodied in individuals, but their characteristics and values are fully determined only in that context. The source of the so-called firm-specificity of human assets may be traced perhaps to their cognitive relationships with each other in a particular architecture and I want to make this point more explicit.

Further, the attributes and values of management's and workers' cognitive assets may not be determined solely by their mutual cognitive relationships. Corporate associational cognition uses a system of various non-human, physical assets as well, such as office buildings, computers, networks, machines, digitally-stored files, etc., as cognitive tools in common or individual uses. Then, it may be the three-way relations among those three types of assets that specify the varied modes of the organizational architecture of associational cognition. In order to make this point clear, let me adopt the classical distinction of three kinds of rights related to non-human physical assets: rights to decide on their supply as well as their withdrawal (ownership rights); rights to derive returns from the deployment and use of the assets (income rights); and rights to decide on how to use them in a specific way in associational cognition (use-control rights). I refer to the integrative holders of the first and second rights as the *investors*. The third type of right may be integrated with the first and second rights in some cases (as in the case of owner-managed firms), but they can be separated from the latter and entrusted to another agent (say to the management, but in some cases partly to the workers as well). Ownership and income rights are certainly important for defining the basic attributes of any form of corporate governance. However, as I am about to show, ways defining to whom the use-control rights are de facto accrued become highly relevant to the nature of associational cognition within business corporations and thus to productivity, incentive, and the bargaining power of the holders of cognitive assets (the management and the workers) vis-à-vis the owners of physical assets. Somewhat surprisingly, a single concept—to be introduced below—can lead us closer to the reality in this regard. What can such concept be?

2.3.3 *Essentiality of cognitive assets*

In the literature, the firm-specificity of workers' human assets is often referred to as a key notion for specifying the nature of organizational architecture (OA) and/or corporate governance (CG). For example, "the board-as-the-trustee-of-stakeholders" view by Blair and Stout (1999), as well as an earlier work of my own (Aoki 1984), highlights such a notion. Some writers refer to a complementary relationship between management's human assets and workers' human assets as an important defining factor of the OA–CG linkage mode. For example, Zingales (2000) points to its growing importance by rejecting the primacy of property rights over physical assets (residual rights of control) as the determinant of CG structure.[18] Although these concepts have merits for understanding some aspects of diversity in CG–OA linkage, they may well be considered to be widespread phenomena of modern business corporations that cross architectural differences. Firm-specificity of workers' human assets in general, as well as complementarities between management and workers' human assets, can only make associations between them relational, which would in turn make the economic outcomes of their joint efforts subject to individual or collective bargaining between them. But I argue that these aspects of human assets alone are not sufficient for differentiating some important modes of the OA–CG linkage. As is most dramatically exemplified by the clustering of entrepreneurial firms in Silicon Valley and the eventual acquisition of successful ones by established corporations, the firm-specificity of human assets cannot capture one of the important species of OA–CG linkage.

Instead, as a key variable differentiating discrete modes of OA–CG linkage, I adopt the following notion of cognitive assets, essentiality defined in terms of a three-way relationship among management's cognitive assets (MCA), workers' cognitive assets (WCA), and non-human, physical assets (PHA). (Below, the acronyms MCA, WCA, and PHA are used to refer to the respective assets as well as their personification, i.e. the management, the workers and the investors respectively, depending on context.) First, recall the Edgeworth notion of the complementarity between either of MCA or WCA on one hand and the use-control rights over PHA on the other (not between MCA and WCA as usually discussed in the theory of the firm). That is, if the marginal product of either MCA or WCA is increased by the assignment of use-control rights over PHA to it, then PHA is said to be complementary to MCA or WCA respectively. However, I ask a further specific question in the context of associational cognition as follows: Can it still be so for either or both of MCA and WCA, even if they are separated from mutual associational cognition? If not for WCA, then the departing partner (i.e. MCA) proves to be indispensable for associational cognition and we say MCA is *essential* to it. The symmetrical definition applies to WCA. To repeat more formally, XCA ($X = M$ or W) is essential, if its cooperation in associational cognition is indispensable in order for YCA ($Y \neq X$) and the use-control rights over PHA to be complementary. This concept of human assets essentiality is originally due to Hart (1995: 45). Hart primarily applied this concept to the human assets held by division managers as the determinant of the boundary of the firm. I apply this concept to understanding the roles and positions of MCA/WCA in associational cognition.

According to this definition, either, neither, or both forms of cognitive assets can be essential. Intuitively, MCA may appear to always be essential in any OA, as the workers are not likely to increase their marginal products merely by controlling the use of PHA with no management strategy or direction. But, as will be seen below, the degree to which MCA is essential may vary depending on the mode of OA, and if it is rather weak vis-à-vis that of WCA in the terms specified below, I will refer to such MCA as quasi-essential. On the other hand, WCA may, or may not, be essential (or quasi-essential in a similar sense as mentioned above, but to be specified further below depending on context). Thus there can be cases where MCA and WCA are both essential.

The extents to which MCA and WCA are essential can condition their relative bargaining power over the distribution of organizational gains, and accordingly their incentives to invest in their own cognitive assets. If only one of them is essential, then the holder of those assets can gain bargaining power by acquiring the use-control rights over PHA, because by the definition of essentiality she can be in a stronger position even without the cooperation of the other party (i.e. the so-called threat point in the theory of bargaining is improved on her behalf). If this arrangement of use-rights is indeed made, then her incentives to invest in her cognitive assets would be enhanced, and as a result the absolute size of organizational gains, not only her relative share in them, would be increased.[19] This is good news for the other party as well who participates in the sharing of them, even though his relative share becomes smaller (otherwise, he can withdraw cooperation). It is therefore likely that competition (and a fairness factor to be discussed later) leads to the integration of use-control rights over PHA with essential cognitive assets. However, if both cognitive assets are bilaterally essential, then the assignment of the use-control rights over PHA to either party would cease to be a defining factor for the distribution of relative bargaining power between the parties and thus for their incentives. I will discuss the potential causes and significant implications of these possibilities to emergent organizational architecture.

2.4 Five generic modes of corporate cognition and their implications for governance

I now set to construct miniature architectural models of business corporations as embodying a two-tier hierarchy constituted of the management and multiple operational agents called the workers. I identify discrete modes of organizational architecture (OA) with a combination of a particular mode of *vertical* cognitive association between the management's cognitive assets (MCA) and the workers' cognitive assets (WCA), as well as a particular mode of *horizontal* cognitive association among the workers' cognitive assets (WCA), as basic building blocks. A vertical mode is either hierarchical (H) or assimilative (S), while a horizontal mode is either assimilative (S) or encapsulated (E). Possible discrete combinations among them can identify different modes of OA. In this setting, possible roles of physical assets (PHA) are not yet explicit. However, as I will discuss subsequently, they are latent in the essentiality attributes of MCA and WCA in each mode of OA.

It is not only that MCA, WCA, and PHA play respective roles as cognitive assets in each mode of OA, but also that the holders of these assets are all interest-driven agents who try to derive the highest possible returns from their own assets through their corporate association (recall that, by those acronyms we refer to the corresponding assets as well as their holders). Their interests can be partly common and partly in conflict. For simplicity's sake, it may be presumed that the bargaining power of PHA vis-à-vis MCA and WCA is essentially determined by the demand and supply conditions of financial markets (and, as I gradually discuss, by other institutional factors surrounding markets). One of the fundamental bases of their bargaining power manifests itself in their willingness and ability to withdraw their own assets from the corporate association for outside opportunities, when beneficial. If MCA and/or WCA are essential in a particular mode of OA, investment in these assets by the respective holders empowers their bargaining positions, as well as being contributory to the overall efficiency of associational cognition.[20]

The web of these relationships in the OA would make inevitable a call for prior "agreements" among all the corporate participants about the conditions and ways that their assets are supplied, used, withdrawn, or discharged. The basic mechanism to control such processes can be conditional on the positions and relative bargaining powers of the assets holders in each OA mode. This OA-specific mechanism may be understood as the essence of the (generic) corporate governance (CG) structure. CG stabilizes and facilitates the corresponding mode of OA to sustain itself. A mode of strategic interactions and their stable governance outcome (i.e. CG), on one hand, and a mode of cognitive-technological associations among various assets (i.e. OA), on the other, thus become mutually reinforcing. Such a coherent linkage becomes a viable mode for business corporations. However, the coherent and viable linkage may not be unique.

Below I will describe five generic modes of OA–CG linkage. Each of them is distinguished by a unique pair of entries representing a mode of OA, the first denoting a vertical mode of associational cognition and the second a horizontal mode across various WCA. For each of the forms of OA thus defined, corresponding essential attributes of MCA and WCA are described, which in turn suggests a mode of CG that fits for that particular mode of OA. It may appear then that there is a rigid one-to-one correspondence between the mode of OA, on one hand, and the essential attribute of MCA and WCA, on the other. But, as discussed in Section 2.5, they actually co-evolve over time. The discussion of this section may be interpreted as capturing snap-shot pictures of possible evolutionary equilibria.

The five generic modes of OA captured in this way are previewed in Figure 2.1 in terms of the distribution of essentiality properties between MCA and WCA as coordinates. They are yet logical constructs, thus lacking immediate counterparts in reality. However, these generic modes may be thought of as capturing some basic aspects of variations of existing corporate structures in a stylized manner. For example, of the five modes discussed below the first three may be considered somewhat reminiscent of the simple stylization of the 'traditional' American (in the case of the H-mode), German (in the case of the G-mode), and Japanese (in the case of the S-mode) corporations in the past and the type of clustering of entrepreneurial firms seen in Silicon Valley (in the case of the SV-mode), respectively. However, some of those corporations in real life have been evolving features that may not be appropriately described by the respective stereotypes any more, but instead are suggestive of the fifth, cognition-rich mode incorporating reciprocal essentialities of MCA and WCA (the RE-mode). Whether this phenomenon indicates a trend toward further diversity in the corporate landscape, its convergence, or the emergence of a hybrid is an issue that I would like to explore throughout the book. But instead of speculating on this issue at this early stage, for now I will establish a simple classificatory framework as a benchmark for subsequent discussions.

Table 2.2. Five generic modes of organizational architecture

MCA	WCA		
	Essential	Quasi-essential	Non-essential
Essential	RE:(H-S/E)	H: (H-E)	H: (H-E)
Quasi-essential	SV: (S-E)	G:(S-E/S), S:(S-S)	—

Note: The first and second entries in parentheses in each cell denote the mode of vertical cognitive association and that of horizontal cognitive association, respectively. H, S, E denote "hierarchical specialization", "assimilated (shared) cognition", and "encapsulated cognition" respectively.

2.4.1 H-mode (H-E): The unilateral essentiality of MCA and private-contract-based governance

This architectural mode is characterized by the associational cognition in which the management is cognitively connected with the workers through hierarchical specialization. Namely, the cognition of the world surrounding the corporate organization and decision-making on the overall organizational action orientation are the exclusive responsibility of the management. Cognitive tasks at the operational level are divided into mutually independent modules and each module is cognitively connected only with its immediate supervisor through the latter's hierarchically specialized cognition. Thus, cognitions of operational modules are encapsulated from each other. This mode of OA appears in situations where management takes the leadership in strategic decision-making for the corporation as a whole, while workers equipped with specialized, marketable skills operate machines and tools of standard technology to implement the strategy. This architectural mode corresponds to a conventional economists' hierarchy model based on the specialized division of physical tasks and thus, may be referred to as the *H*-mode. Even if the workers share information regarding their common environments through management-designed tools (such as computer networks), cognitive actions at the operational level can be standardized, and the use-control rights over tools are firmly grasped by management. In terms of essential cognitive assets, this type of OA may be characterized as follows:

- MCA is *essential* in that the marginal product of WCA cannot be enhanced without the input of MCA.
- WCA is *not essential* in that MCA can enhance its own marginal product by the use-control rights over PHA even with WCA recruited from the external labor market.

The first condition of MCA's essentiality captures the core feature of this architectural mode in which WCA can be productively used only within the context and limits specified by MCA under management's prerogative. The second condition is prominent in the property-rights approach of Hart (1995).[21] Note that these conditions of the *unilateral* essentiality of MCA do not preclude complementarities stemming from cooperation between MCA and WCA and/or the firm-specificity of WCA in a normal state of operation, because the second condition only refers to the contribution of

MCA's control over PHA to its own marginal product in the hypothetical absence of the cooperation of WCA. If these two conditions hold, they would imply that the integration of management and use-control rights over PHA is known to be the (second) best solution for governance (when MCA cannot specify the level of effort of WCA).[22] It enables the management to improve on its bargaining position over the distribution of a firm-specific surplus vis-à-vis the workers by means of investment in its own cognitive assets. It results in higher over-all cognitive efficiency, while WCA may also benefit from it by sharing the increased joint product. If the ownership of PHA and its use-control rights are integrated and held by MCA, this investor-cum-manager corresponds to the classical notion of the entrepreneur.

The bifurcation of the owner-management integration can evolve, historically and/or logically, in either of the following two ways. The owner of PHA (the investor) lacks MCA (in the sense of cognitive assets) or the potential owners of PHA are dispersed so that the use-control rights over PHA are contractually entrusted to MCA through an employment contract. Alternatively, MCA (in the sense of human agent) lacks sufficient resources to own the PHA so they obtain use-control rights over PHA from the investors through equity contracts. In both cases, the investors (the joint owners of PHA) may be identified as the shareholders. As has been noted, in the orthodox theory of governance, the supremacy of the shareholders over MCA in this architectural mode is taken for granted and the latter is regarded as nothing more than the agent of the former. The so-called agency problem of this perspective, that is, the abuse and waste of PHA by MCA to their own advantage and to the detriment of overall corporate efficiency, must be controlled and, for that purpose, various legal means are devised such as stock-option contracts, monitoring through the corporate board, and the ultimate threat of the withdrawal of the PHA (sales of shares that may lead to takeover raids by an outsider OA–CG). This mode of linkage is thus customarily referred to as the shareholder-oriented model, and considered as representing the miniature model of the "Anglo-American model" in comparative perspective.

However, in practice as well as in theory, shareholder control of this mode of OA may not necessarily be taken for granted. First of all, in order for the shareholder-oriented model to be reasonable with shareholders' position as the residual claimants, the shareholders (or the board as their trustee) needs to be able to foresee competitive contribution of MCA to associational cognition and write accordingly an employment contact for MCA's appropriate rewards. This may or may not be possible.

Theoretically, as managerialist scholars and others argue, the essential role of management may be to cognize unique, but uncertain technological and commercial opportunities and reify them as organizational activities (e.g. Penrose 1959; Marris 1964; Williamson 1964; Chandler 1977). If it is indeed so, it may be hard to discern what the market rate for such MCA is, because its value may involve unique essentiality. On the other hand, there may be cases where the management does not offer any valuable MCA and yet is somehow entrenched in a secure position. Which is the case with respect to a particular corporation is an empirical question. But in either case, the distribution of a surplus after the contractual payments to WCA may involve elements of bargaining between the management and the shareholders.

A detailed study by Becht and Mayer (2001) of the specific variation in regulations across a number of countries found that many devices in the USA ensure management control by defending them from takeovers, while that is not necessarily the case in the UK. Thus, they concluded that the USA is "management-controlled" and the UK more "market-controlled." Also, a recent, data-rich study by Armour *et al.* (2009*a*) revealed that the legal protection of the shareholders against the boards was weaker in the USA until the passing of the Sarbanes–Oxley Act in 2002, suggesting possible collusion between the corporate management and the board.

Furthermore, as mentioned above, the non-essentiality of WCA may not necessarily preclude the firm-specificity of WCA. This is the case when MCA cannot immediately substitute new recruits from the labor market for the incumbent WCA, although the incumbent WCA cannot completely deny the productivity of MCA holding the use-control rights of PHA by withdrawal of its cooperation. Then, WCA can also hold a bargaining position over the distribution of value created by corporate associational cognition and may obtain corporate-specific premiums through individual or collective contracting with MCA. Again, whether such a bargaining position of WCA is due to their intrinsic asset value or the monopsonic position of their collective organization is an empirical issue. If the former is the case, then the OA mode based on the unilateral essentiality of MCA may gradually evolve into the reciprocal essentialities of MCA and WCA (the *RE*-mode), which I discuss more below and in Chapter 5, Section 5.2. If such is a possibility, we may refer to the WCA somewhat loosely as quasi-essential and the *H*-mode as being on the High Road. If the monopoly/monopsonic positions of inessential MCA or WCA are entrenched and lead to poor corporate performance, such *H*-mode may be said to be on the Low Road.

In sum, characterizing and/or legitimizing the nature of CG associated with the hierarchical mode of OA solely as "shareholder-oriented" appears to be rather misleading, theoretically and/or as a matter of fact, even though the claim to that effect is often made. In any case, in this mode of OA the distribution of corporate values among various assets holders, cognitive and physical/financial, reflects their relative bargaining powers, which manifest themselves in a web of firm-specific bargaining agreements and market-conditioned contracts. Thus, for now, we may broadly refer to the nature of CG over this generic *H*-mode of architecture as *private-contract-based*, although market-determined contracts and organization-specific agreements are supported and complemented by social conventions and legal rules (discussed in Chapter 3, Section 3.3.4).

At one extreme, there can be the case of the authoritarian, owner-managed firm where the workers do not have any bargaining power beyond market-determined employment conditions. There can be also cases where either the management or the shareholders acquire the whole corporate surplus beyond market-determined payments to the other. The pure shareholder-oriented model and the pure managerialist model may be considered to focus on either of such cases.

2.4.2 G-mode (S-E/S): The embedded, bilateral quasi-essentialities of MCA and WCA and their co-governance

Let us just imagine a situation where, prior to entry to a particular firm, the workers have formed "portable occupational skills" (WCA) related to the use-control of specific PHA (e.g. tools, machines). Within the same class of WCA, there is solidarity among the workers and they are willing to offer their services to any employer under the same rate and the same employment conditions. In practice, such a situation may be thought of as having historically evolved out of the legacy of artisanship and being sustained by a system of public training programs, occupation qualification certificates, industrial unions based on occupational categories and so on, as was the case in Germany (e.g. Streeck 1992; Jackson 2001; Thelen 2004). The individual management of the firm then confronts the following conditions in designing its OA.:

- Investment in occupation-specific WCA enhances individual workers' marginal satisfaction and/or productivity through participation in the (partial) control over the use of PHA even without any relational association with a particular MCA because of the potential portability of their WCA across corporations.

- The benefit management derive from retaining (at least partial) use control over PHA is invariant under the turnover of WCA with occupational qualifications, although this benefit is restricted by the need for further in-plant training of new workers.

If we literally apply the theoretical definition of essentiality to the above statements, the first statement implies that "individual" MCA is not essential for workers' associational cognitions. The second statement implies that "individual" WCA is not essential, although it may become "quasi-essential" because of the additional investment made in it within the plant. From the industrial perspective, however, neither the management nor the workers, as collective entities, can gain by mere accessibility to the (partial) use-control rights over PHA without the other party's cooperation. That is to say, they are both essential at the industrial level. Therefore, it may be said that MCA and WCA are both quasi-essential by being embedded in the industrial frame of bilateral essentialities. Then what do the management and the workers do at the individual corporate level? The "non-essentialities" of individual MCA and WCA at the corporate level imply that the allocation of use-control rights over PHA can affect the bargaining positions of both parties (technically this is a case of the endogenous threat point in bargaining theory[23]). Therefore, it becomes part of the subject of bilateral bargaining at that level and, given symmetric positions for both parties, its sharing can be a logical outcome.[24] The sharing of use-control rights over PHA and the associated cognitive-sharing between MCA and WCA provide the glue to cement them. It may be organizationally implemented through workers' participation in the formal corporate governance structure, for example in the participatory board. Then the assimilated cognition between MCA and WCA based on their embedded essentialities is secured under the formal co-governance structure.

Let us now make the possibility of separation of the ownership of PHA from MCA explicit. Then, logically or historically, the commitment of the MCA to the sharing of use-rights control over PHA with WCA can be transplanted to this evolutive situation. There must be three-way governance relationships in which WCA may be in direct relationship with the investor, not via MCA as in the *H*-mode, in order to secure their participation in the partial use-control rights over PHA. It may be institutionalized, for example, in the form of traditional German *codetermination* (thus, we may refer to this mode of OA–CG linkage as the *G*-mode for the sake of referential convenience). If the investors are interested in keeping their dominant ownership position, as well as restraining management's rent seeking and excessive risk-taking behavior, they would prefer additional financing to be in the form of long-term lending rather than disperse equity financing. In this way their interests become congruent with those of the workers.[25] These observations are consistent with other well-known, stylized features of traditional German practices, such as the historical role of banks in perpetuating a concentration ownership through inter-corporate shareholding and long-term lending, as well as associated conflicts of interests with market-oriented minority shareholders.[26] However, these traditional German features have undergone substantial modifications in the last two decades, to be discussed in Chapter 5, Section 5.3.

2.4.3 S-mode (S-S): The symmetric quasi-essentialities of MCA and WCA and relational contingent governance

The architectural mode of this model is such that cognitions between the management and the workers, as well as those among the workers, are assimilated to a great extent through informal, de facto cognition-sharing. In terms of cognitive assets essentiality, it may be characterized as:

- The cognitive contributions of MCA and WCA to the organizational goal are inseparable because of cognitive assimilation in that their marginal products are not individually distinguishable and thus remain ambiguous.
- Both MCA and WCA are symmetrically quasi-essential to each other in that their (unobservable) marginal products cannot be enhanced by unilateral control by either party of use-control rights over PHA without mutual cooperation.

The first condition corresponds to the "team" property of OA originally conceptualized by Alchian and Demsetz (1972) and elaborated later by Holmström (1979). The second condition implies that even if the external supply of PHA is necessary for the operation of this type of OA, PHA and either of the individual cognitive assets (CA) in isolation cannot be in complementary relationships. Then, both MCA and WCA may be considered as symmetrically essential (thus this mode of OA may be referred to as the S-mode in reference to both cognitive-sharing and symmetric essentialities). But, as their individual contributions are not separable, we may say that the essentiality of both cognitive assets is ambiguous: thus symmetrically quasi-essential. For this OA, it can be shown that the following type of CG is the second-best governance arrangement (Aoki 1994*b*, 2001: 291–305).

The investors who are unable to form a coalition with either MCA or WCA individually delegate the monitoring of their joint use-control of PHA to a relational monitor in exchange for some rents. If the collective performance of the team is expected to exceed a certain threshold point, the relational monitor allows the team of MCA and WCA to be residual claimants after contractual payments to PHA; and MCA and WCA divide the residual between them through internal bargaining, organizational rules, or conventions (such as seniority rules). When the collective performance of the team falls below the critical point, however, the delegated monitor is expected to bail out the team if the continuation value of the team is judged to be worth preserving, or withdraw PHA from the team and punish the team by dissolving it if not. On the one hand, the threat of a withdrawal of PHA exercises discipline on the members of the team as a whole, while the expectation of a bailing-out option can help preserve the value of the cognitive assets of the team in the event of a relatively minor problem, perhaps caused by temporal external shocks for which the team is not responsible. Since the use-control rights and residual claimant status shift, and ownership rights over PHA are exercised, contingent on the value state of the corporation, this governance structure may be called relational contingent governance. Contractual distribution between the insiders and the outside investors is *ex ante* determined by their relative bargaining power conditioned by the potential value of the insider's cognitive assets and market power of the investors. The relational monitor obtains fees from the services to the investors in the normal state. However, it becomes a residual claimant (actually loss-bearing) in the event of the bailing-out or liquidation of the team, which provides an incentive for earnest monitoring by the relational monitor.[27]

This model is reminiscent of some stylized features of traditional Japanese corporations before the 1990s (see Aoki 1988, 1990, 2001; Nonaka and Takeuchi 1995). The effectiveness of this type of CG for inducing the efficient cooperation of MCA and WCA can be enhanced under a number of conditions. First, MCA and WCA may be induced to be more cooperative, the lower the individual value of outside opportunity is for each of them. This would be the case when other corporate organizations in the economy are likewise organized with the cognition-sharing teams of long-term association, so that the reemploying individual MCA and WCA discharged from a failed corporation becomes harder without a substantial loss of value of their cognitive assets. Thus the convention of long-term employment may be considered as institutionally complementary to the linkage of relational contingent governance and cognition-sharing OA.

Second, speaking more concretely, the role of a relational monitor may be considered to be approximated by the so-called main bank that has relational associations with client corporations (e.g. Aoki 1994a). Thus, the institutionalization of the main bank system also constitutes an element of complementary institutional cluster surrounding this linkage. If the demands for external capital decline or the main bank becomes less effective in monitoring, the incentives of MCA and WCA may be lessened due to the lack of external discipline and their moral hazard behavior may become less easy to control. Chapter 5, Section 5.2 presents evidence of substantial change in this mode of OA–CG linkage and its departure from the S-mode in the core part of the Japanese corporate economy and discusses its causes, nature, and implications.

Although the resemblance of this mode to the traditional Japanese corporate structure in its heyday is easier to grasp, there is a rather unexpected example of this model—the individual entrepreneurial firm under the control of venture capital. While organization of the development effort within the entrepreneurial firm has a team aspect, the so-called step financing by the venture capitalist (VC), contingent on development progress, has an aspect of "relational contingent governance" (Kaplan and Strömberg 2003). That is, the venture capitalist (more precisely, the so-called angel who acts as the financier cum mentor at the initial stage) initially provides only a limited amount of seed money to fund start-up firms. Afterwards it (or more precisely, a VC specialized in the mezzanine stage) decides whether to provide further funding, restructure the organizations and salvage the potential values of their cognitive assets, or terminate the start-up firm completely, depending on the progress of the development effort. For a successful entrepreneurial firm, the relationship will end by its Initial Public Offering (IPO) arranged by the VC (or, precisely speaking, the VC specialized in the final stage) or by its acquisition by an established corporation within a niche market (Aoki 2001, ch. 11). However, the uniqueness of these relationships are manifest more clearly in the context of a clustering of entrepreneurial firms, which lead us to the next mode.

2.4.4 SV-mode (S-E): Tournament-like governance of the potential essentialities of WCA

Some aspects of the landscape of the American corporate economy have been dramatically transformed since the time when Chandler wrote about it in his 1977 book, and there is no doubt that one of the important impetuses for the change was the emergence of the clusters of small entrepreneurial firms, as typically observed in Silicon Valley, and the growth of some of them into most competitive corporations in niche markets. A book by Baldwin and Clark (2000) vividly depicts the process by which the seed of the emergence was sown in the traditional organizational architecture of IBM itself, once highly representative of the classical H-mode, and how this eventually force IBM's modification as well. In an attempt to design the large scale, all-purpose computer system, IBM/360, a small group of brilliant engineers laid out the decomposition of the whole system into modular design units, connected only via open interface rules: a quintessential example of the H-mode architecture! However, once the whole design is complete, modules can be improved independently, as long as they are compatible with the interface rule. Thus, the engineers from IBM started to leave in order to start their own firms specializing in the design of modular products, or in order to mediate and help such firms to be formed as venture capitalists, consultants and so on. It is therefore more appropriate to compare a cluster of entrepreneurial start-up firms (ES firms) as a whole, but not a single ES firm, with traditional giant corporations such as IBM. Indeed, the number of engineers in Silicon Valley as a whole has never exceeded those working for IBM in its heyday.

Therefore, let me treat the cluster of ES firms as a kind of virtual corporate architecture referred to as the SV-mode, with individual ES firms incorporating WCA necessary for actual innovative activities. Strategy-making in the sense of perceiving the potential direction of innovation-system development and reifying it by funding ES firms is spread and shared throughout the cluster as a whole, with VC firms, university professors, consultants, etc. acting as information-brokers and investors (Saxenian 1994; Podolny 2001; Burt 2005). In the case of an innovation network in the biotechnology industry, public research institutions, elite hospitals, and universities also play important nodal roles. Also the roles of strategy-making, information brokerage, and innovative activities may sometimes be inseparably integrated within dedicated biotechnology firms that have grown from ES firms (e.g. Owen-Smith and Powell 2004; Powell et al. 2005).

The cognitive actions involved in actual development efforts are encapsulated in individual ES firms in the case of information and communication technology (ICT) industry, because each of them is specialized, and they compete with each other, in the development of a particular module of a potentially large, innovative product-system. The design of such an over-all system is not *ex ante* decomposed into modular designs by the centralized planning of management as in the case of the development of IBM/360, but it evolves through *ex post* combinations of the modular designs of successful ES firms (Baldwin and Clark 2000; Aoki 2001: ch. 11). In order for such a mechanism to be workable, simplified interface rules among the modular products are to be made public *ex ante* or *ad interim* through communications, mediated by the various actors mentioned above. Modularization implies that technological and attribute complementarities between products are reduced so that the cognitions involved in the design effort can be encapsulated without hierarchical ordering (see Section 2.2.1 above).

Although information brokerage by VC firms results in cognition-sharing about the potential direction of industrial development, their cognitive assets are at most quasi-essential, because any of those cognitive assets is not individually indispensable to the actual development processes within ES firms. On the other hand, although financial assets are provided by the VC, they cannot be productive, unless they are used by ES firms. Thus the cognitive assets of ES firms may be considered potentially essential at the start-up stage, and its potentiality can gradually and selectively be actualized through the step-financing of VC firms as described above. At the end of the start-up phase, i.e. at the time of the IPO or acquisition, the potential essentiality of ES firm's cognitive assets would be *ex post* realized through the capital gains endowed to them through stock options and so on. IPO or acquisition by an established corporation would not necessarily lead to the traditional *H*-model, however, but rather to a new structure reminiscent of the *RE*-mode to be introduced next. As VC firms initially provide seed money to multiple ES firms proposing similar development projects but become increasingly selective in later-stage financing, the role of the VC firms is akin to that of a referee governing a tournament game played among ES firms rather than managing them with its own essential cognitive assets. Thus we may summarize as follows.

- Potentially essential cognitive assets may be encapsulated in entrepreneurial start-up firms (ES firms) but their potential may be realized *ex post* only if they have proved themselves to be winners in a VC-governed, tournament-like competition.

Under the high degree of uncertainty involved in the development of modular design and system integration, the tournament-like governance of the *SV*-mode is known to have two important performance characteristics: (1) it can create option values by running parallel development efforts (experiments) among multiple ES firms (Baldwin and Clark 2000), and (2) it can provide greater incentives for ES firms to invest in their own potential cognitive assets than under an integrated mode of architecture (Aoki and Takizawa 2002). These two attributes make the *SV*-mode particularly appropriate to the development of a large innovative product-system to be formed by *ex post* combinations of modularized parts. This is particularly the case in the ICT industry where the nature of digital technology makes the commercialization of design implementable on various material devices and media (e.g. wireless, fiber optics, copper cables, discs, etc.) so that design and manufacturing can be completely separable.[28]

2.4.5 RE-mode (H-S/E): The reciprocal essentialities of MCA and WCA and its external monitoring

The cognitive tasks of the management and the workers in corporate associational cognition are, in general, mutually complementary and there must be some degree of information assimilation between the two in any architecture. Yet, a situation may arise such that both the overall environment of the corporate organization facing the management (e.g. general market conditions, technological trends, political situations, social atmospheres and so on) and the local environments facing each of the operational tasks (e.g. task-specific technology, specific market conditions, and so on) become so complex that scarce cognitive assets, both MCA and WCA, are to be used in a focused, innovative manner. Then the vertical associative mode between MCA and WCA becomes more like hierarchical-specialization. However, suppose that the complexity of the cognitive tasks at the operational level requires high-level cognitive assets that cannot be substituted by MCA's use-rights control over PHA. This situation may be characterized as follows.

- Both MCA and WCA cannot increase their respective marginal products merely by controlling the use-rights to PHA in the absence of the other's cooperation. Namely, in order for them to use PHA productively, the management needs to be associated with WCA that are particularly fit for the implementation of its unique strategy, while the workers need MCA's strategy to be fit for the productive use of their WCA regardless of whether they can (partially) control the use of PHA. Then MCA and WCA become reciprocally essential.

As both MCA and WCA may be highly specialized in their respective cognitive actions, the holder of each cannot dispense with the other. Reciprocally indispensable human relationships become primary, while control over PHA becomes secondary. This is the essential difference of this mode (referred to as the *RE*-mode abbreviating the reciprocal essentialities of MCA and WCA) from the *H*-mode, although both may be characterized by the vertical *H*-mode. How, then, can this kind of relationship be governed?

From the purely theoretical point of view, Hart argued that the reciprocal essentialities of human assets implies that "the ownership structure does not matter since neither party's investment [in its own human assets] will not pay off in the absence of agreement with the other" (Hart 1995: 48). By the phrase "the ownership structure" Hart is referring to the assignment of the residual rights of control (i.e. ownership control) over PHA between the division managers of an organization, while I am dealing with the assignment of use-control rights over PHA between MCA and WCA. But essentially Hart's argument also applies here: ways in which the use of PHA can be controlled are theoretically "irrelevant" under the reciprocal essentialities of MCA and WCA, because they would not directly affect either parties' bargaining powers and thus their incentives for investment in cognitive assets without mutual cooperation. The manager cannot take advantage by controlling the use of PHA as is the case in *H*-mode. Various factors can be involved in this situation, including the nature of technology, types of cognitive assets to be deployed, and so on. In extreme cases where the contributions of cognitive assets are so important to the organizational goal (where knowledge creation is crucial), the issue of how PHA are to be provided and controlled may become less and less relevant to the design of the organizational architecture. So, one implication of reciprocal essentiality can be a diversity of OA mode within this class as well as that of the associated CG. In particular, at the operational level, the horizontal mode of associational cognition may be characterized either as cognition-sharing or cognition-encapsulation depending on the nature of the technology and the product's market.

Secondly, the irrelevance of the allocation of use-control rights to PHA implies that there may not be particular reason for productive gains to arise from possible collusion, or a need for the integration, of PHA with either MCA or WCA. Then, the direct role of the investors in CG becomes more modest than under the *H*-mode in the normal state of affairs. However, saying so does not necessarily imply that the share market does not play any role even in this case. It would perform the even more important information function of autonomously evaluating the effectiveness of a reciprocally essential relationship between MCA and WCA. If the share market is informative, the share price may be formed as a summary statistic of diverse opinions regarding the future values of the internal relationship between MCA and WCA. If the board of directors is entrusted to effectively replace or appoint top management contingent on the (expected) long-term share value prospect, the management can be disciplined to create and sustain the valuable internal relationship with the workers, while the workers are motivated to invest in their specific WCA. On the other hand, the shareholders themselves may be motivated to do a better monitoring job if they can benefit from making good judgments in selecting their own portfolios. Therefore, complementarities may arise between the creation and sustenance of reciprocally essential internal relationship, on one hand, and the efficient share market evaluation of its value, on the other. In such a model, the board of directors ought to act not as the agent of the value-maximizing shareholders but as the "trustees" for the stakeholders (Dodd 1932; Aoki 1984; Blair and Strout 1999), including MCA and WCA who are the source of value creation of the corporation as an associational cognitive system. The board should not force the management to increase the share value at the expense of the workers and/or through a collusive arrangement with the management, because it would be likely to destroy the valuable internal relationship of the MCA and the WCA.

Obvious examples of reciprocal essentialities may be found in knowledge-intensive, professional organizations, such as law firms, consulting companies, and so on, as well as in teams of creative talents directed by heavyweight leaders in the fields of arts, sports, researches, etc. However, I will submit some empirical evidence in the last chapter that reciprocal essentialities of MCA and WCA are also evolving as conspicuous features of some well-run business corporations in various routes of path-dependent transition from other traditional modes: the *H*-mode, *G*-mode, *S*-mode, and the *SV*-mode.

2.5 Frames of organizational games at societal, organizational, and individual levels

I noted above that the orthodox principal–agency theory is premised on the idea of human beings having pre-fixed tastes and beliefs prior to social interactions; every being encapsulating cognition inside their own skull and skin; disclosing their own states and information only to the extent compatible with their own material incentives in business organizations; and making decisions in a self-regarding manner.[29] Therefore the primary concern of principal–agency theory is to design contacts/mechanisms that are compatible with the incentives of people as derived from such a presumption. At the beginning of this chapter I challenged this premise by suggesting that cognitions can be distributed among the members of corporate organizations and that they may act as team players in an associational cognition. However, saying so does not imply that individual motivational factors are not important for the institutional arrangements of organizations and beyond. Having identified discrete generic modes of associational cognition and its governance, I will now try to elaborate further how those modes can constitute frames of organizational games at three levels: society, between individual organizations, and within individual organization. Instead of viewing the exigency of incentives as preceding and defining the problem of organizational design, I submit that motivational problems of organizational relevance arise, and are dealt with, in conjunction with the design of the organizational architecture. I will discuss this at the above-mentioned three levels.

First, I argue that at the societal level, the strategies of individuals and organizations together shape the process of co-evolution, in which individual cognitive orientations of organizational relevance, on one hand, and a broad societal frame for organizational architecture, on the other, co-evolve. Second, given an evolutionary outcome at this societal level, the general rules of the organizational game may be thought of as being selected as a kind of "agreement" among agents of the relevant asset holders, both physical and cognitive, which leads to the concept of the "organizational field" where corporate organizations of a similar mode cluster and compete. Of course, such an agreement is nothing but a theoretical construct for understanding the self-governing nature of business corporations. The point is that the general rules are specific to an architectural mode evolutionarily selected at the first level. With such rules as a basic referential frame, individuals then form their own cognitive frames of organizational games that they actually play. Within a particular organization, these individual frames meet together, generating the common frame for team-play as hinted in Section 2.2 above (and elaborated further in Chapter 4). But at the same time, individual cognitive frames are differentiated from one another in specific detail. Because of these differences needs for motivational alignment through concrete organizational and contractual design would arise at the individual corporate level.

2.5.1 *At societal level*

Let me start with the societal level. In the previous section, I discussed some possible variations of essentiality attributes of manager's and workers' cognitive assets (MCA and WCA) and their implications for organizational architecture (OA). However, those essentiality attributes are defined only in terms of their mutual relationships via the intra-organizational allocation of use-control rights of non-human, physical assets (PHA). It has not been explicitly specified what kind of inherent characteristics of cognitive assets can be particularly effective and relevant in each of those architectural modes but are not equally so in others. There is circumstantial evidence to suggest that there must be effective architecture-specific properties of cognitive assets. Thus, a mode of the OA may not be chosen independently of the availability of fit kinds of cognitive assets.

As a starting point let us note the rather obvious observations that each of the five described modes of OA can be regarded as having unique comparative advantages in particular markets and technology respectively, but not be fit for all possible environments. For example, the *H*-mode can have a comparative advantage in markets for standard products made by a simple or complex system of PHA, the creation of new markets by agile management strategy, etc., whereas the *S*-mode may have a comparative advantage in responding to markets of diverse product specifications serviced by continual fine-tuning of work-level coordination. A moment's reflection on the implications of Table 2.1 may suggest such reasoning (see Aoki 1986, 2001 for a further theoretical justification). The *G*-mode corporations may enjoy a reputation for reliable product quality as a result of its national and in-plant vocational training system (e.g. Thelen 2004) and tradition of a craftsman-like work-ethic. The *SV*-mode has an obvious comparative advantage in the rapid creation of an innovative product system through decentralized, competitive modular design (Baldwin and Clark 2000; Aoki and Takizawa 2002). The *RE*-mode is appropriate for an effective corporate response to fierce global competition where the combination of an innovative business strategy and a highly knowledgeable/ trained work force is imperative.[30]

If there are such differences in comparative performance among these modes of OA, then why does each economy not realize a diversified portfolio of varied OA modes in order to better serve a variety of markets? Why does a certain pattern of OA tend to appear as a national/regional convention and persist even in markets for which it appears to be inappropriate? Why did clustering of entrepreneurial startup firms emerge in Silicon Valley on the periphery of the American corporate economy, but not in the midst its traditional industrial centers (Saxenian 1994), while it was not successfully emulated in other economies despite government assistance? In spite of observed inertia in the past, will the pressure of market globalization drive the corporate landscape to become more uniform and flatter everywhere? If so, will it converge to something like the shareholder-oriented H-mode, as some people predicted so forcefully from the 1990s onwards? Alternatively, will a diversity of OA eventually evolve to some yet unrealized diversity on a global scale?

I have argued in the past, and still do in essence, that the key to answering these questions lies in recognizing that different types of human cognitive assets of organizational relevance may co-evolve with corresponding organizational architectural modes. With the help of an evolutionary game model (Aoki 1998), I have shown that the organizational convention of the H-mode and the S-mode could co-evolve with the societal accumulation of fitted types of human assets that I called the "individuated human assets" and the "context-oriented human assets" respectively.[31] If, say, the H-mode becomes the dominant mode of organizational architecture, the next generation of managers and workers tends to invest in the type of human assets, i.e. the individuated ones, that match the H-mode better, which in turn enables H-mode firms to recruit suitable human assets more easily, train them further, and so on. Eventually, the H-mode would become the established convention across all the industries in some economies, even if it lacks comparative advantage relative to the S-mode in some industries. A parallel argument holds for the S-mode as well with respect to context-oriented human assets. Then organizational conventions dominated by H-mode or S-mode architecture may evolve as a cluster, even though each of them may not be optimal for some industries. One cannot exclude the possibility that in this evolutionary model a mixture of the two architectural modes would evolve as an outcome of international trade, labor mobility, foreign direct investment, a critical mass of emulative experiments, and so on. Yet, even these strategies may not necessarily achieve global optimum because of the constraints of demographic distribution across economies and so on.[32] Another possibility that I did not discuss in the frame of the 1998 model, but may potentially be important, is that of a hybrid of the H-mode and S-mode (a variant of the RE-mode may be regarded as such and is discussed in Chapter 5).

Although I still continue to subscribe to the described evolutionary logic in essence, I now admit that the denomination of the types of human assets referred to above as "individuated" vs. "context-oriented" might have been somewhat unfortunate. As I emphasized at the beginning, human cognition can take place as a group-level system in the context of corporate organization. In that sense, aspects of human cognitive assets mobilized in an organizational context may be said to all be context-oriented. An organization cannot just be the collection of cognitions taking place inside the skull and skin of individuals, even in the apparently individualistic *H*-mode architecture. In any organization, information is collected jointly or in a specialized, but mutually complementary manner, and shared informally and formally; decisions are made collectively or individually but on the basis of inferring what other members would expect and do, and so on. However, there can still be subtle differences in the effective cognitive orientation of the agents involved, depending on the types of organizational architecture. In *H*-mode OA involving hierarchical specialization and encapsulation in cognition, members who play individually distinct roles in specific segments of associational cognition would be regarded as contributing relatively more to the organizational goals and receive higher esteem and respect (as well as awe, jealousy, and so forth) from peer members. In *S*-mode OA which involves cognition-sharing both vertically and horizontally in associational cognition, members who play contributory roles in terms of information sharing, cooperate in collaborative action, display a less explicit assertion of the "I" attitude, and so on would be highly regarded. These two types are characteristics of advantageous cognitive assets shared by both management and workers in respective organizational conventions. There is ample anecdotal evidence, which need not be repeated here, indicating such architectural-mode-specific differences in the prevailing mode of cognitions, emotions, and behaviors.[33]

Indeed, there have been scientific, experimental results suggesting culture-specific differences in cognitive orientation and behavior in cultural psychology,[34] sociological psychology,[35] and neuroscience.[36] But, how to interpret cultural differences remains controversial. Differences in cognitive orientations may be said to be cultural in that they are formed over time and shared by people in society or in a group. However, such differences should not be taken to be neither "fixed" by nationality (e.g. being Caucasian-American or native Japanese) (e.g. Oyserman *et al.* 2002; Chiao *et al.* 2009) nor across domains of cognition (e.g. families, friends, markets, or organizations). For example, Yamagishi's experimental results indicate that people's cognitive and behavioral orientation may be context-dependent. He designed experiments and derived interesting results showing that subjects exhibit "cultural" orientations in cognition and decision-making as default strategies only in situations where a negative evaluation by relevant others is to be avoided, but they exhibit different cognitive and decision priorities in other contexts where individual pay-offs and choices are closely linked (Yamagishi *et al.* 2008). This may suggest the possibility that people's behavioral and cognitive orientations may be nuanced depending on either being in organizational or market domains. In other words, we face games of various kinds in our daily lives, for each of which we may use different frames (subjective perceptions of games), and that we tend to use team-oriented frames for organizational games.[37]

Following these casual observations, experimental evidence, and scientific reasoning, I submit a hypothesis specific and relevant to our current concern: agents use similar, although individuated in detail, cognitive frames that are suited to a prevailing convention of organizational architecture. They are likely to co-evolve with an organizational convention as a result of individual strategies rather than being "culture-rooted," fixed preferences. Orientations of education within the family, at school, in the community, as well as conditions in the market for new job recruits, obviously all play an important role in determining individual strategies of investment in cognitive assets. Then, the organization-relevant cognitive orientations available in society may not be easily malleable but only slowly change. Any architectural mode prevailing in a cluster of business corporations, therefore, may be considerably conventionalized and may not be flexible enough to adapt to emergent technological and market exigencies in a short period of time. Of course, they are not entirely fixed either, as individual and corporate strategies are not completely dictated by conventions alone. Individual experiments, deviances, and so on, which may be suboptimal under a normal situation, may provide a new set of cognitive assets for organizational experiments with a non-conventional architectural design. However, I reserve discussions on such processes to Chapter 4 and assume for now a situation where some organizational architectural mode tends to be conventionalized.

2.5.2 On the organizational field

Borrowing the terminology of organizational sociologists, let us refer to the clustering of business corporations embodying a similar architectural convention as the "organization field" (DiMaggio and Powell 1983). Scott succinctly characterized the notion of organization field as connoting "the existence of a community of organizations that partakes of a common meaning system and whose participants interact more frequently and fatefully with one another than with actors outside of the field" (Scott 1994:

207–8). Hoffman defined it as "centers of debates in which competing interests negotiate over the interpretation of key issues" (Hoffman 2001: 351). What can it be in our model that may be taken as analogous to the sociologist's notions of the shared "meaning" and the negotiated "interpretations"? What are likely outcomes of "negotiations" among asset holders, cognitive and physical/financial, in the corporate organizational field?

Suppose that a certain type of organization-relevant cognitive assets have been accumulating and that, together with the potential supply of fitted cognitive tools, they are ready to be organized into a suitable mode of corporate architecture. However, that alone would not automatically assure the orderly organization of associational cognition. There must be some shared understanding and assurance for everyone about the fundamental rules for such matters, for example: how those assets are to be deployed, combined, or withdrawn at the individual corporate level; who controls the use of tools; who is to be made responsible for possible organizational failure and in what way; how is each to be rewarded, etc. It is such general understanding, or the general rules of the organizational game, that essentially makes business corporations self-governing with no external centralized control, while competing, co-existing, and co-evolving with each other. The provision of such self-governing rules is what underlies the basis of the corporate governance (CG) structure, even though at a practical level corporate governance rules are often formulated as formal statutes and enforced by a third party. Unless they are essentially self-governable, however, business corporations would not evolve as a viable element of the overall institutional arrangements in the economy. How and in what form can the governance rules evolve as a general understanding?

I posit that the fundamental rules of governance that underlie all the organizational games of a particular architectural mode can be theoretically understood as a general "agreement" among asset holders, cognitive and physical, in the organization field. Namely they must represent some essential properties of stable outcomes of hypothetical negotiation among these players. At the present level of theoretical abstraction, we do not need to assume that bargaining equilibrium is struck through formal collective bargaining among incumbent asset holders endowed with specific kinds and levels of assets, or designed by foresighted institutional designers. Theoretically, however, a liberal reinterpretation of the Nash axioms for a bargaining solution may help to clarify the basic nature of stable governance rules as a general "agreement." They represent the set of requirements, such as a deep sense of fairness that can be shared among the asset holders (corresponding to the Nash axiom of "symmetry"), stability that can withstand mutual competitive pressure in the organization field (corresponding to the Nash axiom of "Pareto efficiency" equilibrium), and cognitive economy (corresponding to the Nash axiom of the "independence of irrelevant alternatives"). These fundamental requirements were implicit in each of the structures of corporate governance as discussed in the previous section. If organization games are played by asset holders at the individual corporate level concerning what kind of rights and obligations are to be given to whom, those corporations that adopt inefficient rules may gradually be eliminated through competitive selection within a particular organizational field. (However, note that the notion of "efficiency" here refers to "local" efficiency relative to a particular organizational field, and not to "global" efficiency).[38] Agents who feel that they are not treated fairly by corporations may leave them or those corporations may lose their reputation in the organization field. Rules that require irrelevant information for agreement may be impractical and sustainable. Thus, a possible agreement is likely to be a Nash bargaining solution that evolves through competition and experience over time to set the fundamental rules of governance, or a basic frame of organizational games in the organizational field.[39]

It is also to be noted that a Nash bargaining solution can be characterized as the maximization of the weighted sum of payoffs of asset holders, MCA, WCA, and PHA (Aoki 1984; Binmore 2005).[40] In other words, a Nash bargaining solution can dictate in principle the overall organizational objective to be maximized in corporate associational cognition. Tirole (2001) is skeptical about the implementability and efficiency of the so-called stakeholder-society view of corporate governance and one of the reasons he offers is that giving management the objective of maximizing multiple stakeholder values may be ill-defined. But at least, at the theoretical level, this is not a well-founded criticism.

2.5.3 *Within individual corporations*

Concrete forms of OA–CG linkage and associated rules are then specified at the individual corporate level with the general agreement set at the level of the organization field as a template, but also dependent on individual corporate history, the bargaining powers of participating asset holders, relevant technology, regulations, and so on. Then, under the rules thus specified, an intra-corporate organizational game is played: it is a game in the sense that combinations of all the members of associational cognitions and actions matter for their individual interests. Individual members may have their own cognitive frames of the organizational game that they play. These frames are individuated but also largely meet with each other's via the specified rules of the organizational game.[41] Their individual interests are partly conflicting and partly harmonizing. However, they are compelled to accept the reality that they together cannot do better than follow the organizational rules derived from the general agreement in the organization field. Thus there can be a reason for each agent to believe that other members also follow the rules of their organizational game. Sugden (2003) rightly stresses the importance of assurance so that each player believes that other players also follow the rules of team play and also believes that everyone else does so too. He listed three possible mechanisms for such assurance: rationality (e.g. Gilbert 1989), agreement, and experiences. Sugden opted for the last mechanism as the most likely. As I seek the source of the basic frame for organizational rules in a Nash bargaining solution cum evolutionary outcome, the three mechanisms he listed may not be mutually exclusive alternatives but complementary.[42] With such an assurance as a background, each member is likely to frame the organizational game as a team play and identify themselves as team players.

Yet, agreement is only about the general rules of the game as embedded in organizations, with some of them even being implicit. Within this framework, there would still be a risk of a breach of the rules, organizational misconduct, room for maneuver, shirking, negligence, misunderstanding, lack of motivation by individuals, as well as the danger of sub-group coalition against the overall organizational goal maximization, and so on: categories so familiar to economists. To cope with these possibilities through contractual design, together with making the organizational rules as the focal point for team play, is the essential tasks of corporate management as stressed already in the classical writing of Chester Barnard (1938). However, this task is actually placed within the frame of the general rules of governance set in society and the organizational field. Depending on whether management is under the *H*-mode of an OA–CG linkage or some other mode, appropriate contractual designs could well be different. However, on this subject there is already a rich literature and not much that I can add to it now.[43]

Notes

1. For a rigorous proof of this claim, see Arrow and Lind (1970).
2. Apart from the practical implications of the debate between two views, the so-called stakeholders' view may be theoretically regarded as more general in that striking a balance can take various forms: discretionary control by the board of directors acting as the trustee of all the stakeholders (the idea originating in Dodd (1932)); implicit or explicit agreements/contracts among them with a variable balance of power exercised by them, in which shareholder-oriented governance and managerialist control can arise as special cases (i.e. as corner solutions with all the weight given to the shareholders or the manager. See the bargaining game approach to business corporations by Aoki (1984)).
3. See for example, Fogassi *et al.* (2005), Iacoboni *et al.* (2005), Rizolatti and Sinigaglia (2008).
4. Sperber and Wilson (1986/1995).
5. This is a contention that was held for a while by the evolutionary psychologists who argued that human beings developed a brain module in the Paleolithic era that helps us to detect who should not be trusted; see Barkaw, Cosmides, and Tooby (1993), Cosmides and Tooby (2004) and particularly Cosmides and Tooby (1994). Recent experimental studies indicate however that people's minds are not completely adapted in that era but, like the immune system, are continually adapting, over both evolutionary time and individual lifetimes (see, for example, Buller (2006)). Experimental neuro-studies also examine people's ability to detect others' lying on the basis of non-verbal information such as expression, eye contact, posture, and so on. See for example Ohmoto *et al.* (2008).
6. For example, Fehr and Gachter (2000, 2002), Gintis *et al.* (2006).
7. Gilbert (1989), Bratman (1993), Hutchens (1996), Rilling *et al.* (2002), Meijers (2003), Tomasello *et al.* (2005), Hurley (2008). See also Bacharach (2006) for an argument in this direction from a game theoretic perspective.
8. For pioneering work on the social brain function, see Adolphs (2003). Neuro-economics has recently been making progress in describing the neural mechanisms of a single-individual decision-making process, but so far attention has not focused on the social contexts of decision-making to a comparable extent. See Fujii *et al.* (2007) for critical comments based on their pioneering experimental results on social brain functions. Recent experimental studies of social brain function also suggest that our brains do not exclusively modulate cognitive responses to economic events in terms of direct economic calculation but also to others' behaviors in a social-context-dependent manner, measuring cost–benefit tradeoffs or benefit linkages between the two by the use of "common neuro-currency" (Montague and Berns 2002, Fehr and Camerer 2007, Izuma *et al.* 2008). I will discuss an implication of such interactions to the theory of institution in Chapter 3, Sections 3.4.1 and 3.4.2.

9. A similar claim is made by Hodgson (2004), albeit from a slightly different perspective.

10. Team theory, as developed by Jacob Marschak and Roy Radner (1972), was concerned with the design of the organization as a communications system by assuming away possible incentive issues. However, they developed this theory at a time when communications technology was comparatively under-developed so that the transmission of data relevant to the organizational objective was limited. It is discussed later (notes 13, 40) that the notion of the team is not necessarily incompatible with situations in which the agents have different payoff functions. For a different game-theoretic approach to teams, see Bacharach (2006).

11. Gavetti and Rivkin (2007) recognize that business strategy exists "in the minds of managers—in the theories about the world and their company's place in it," as well as being embodied in a company's activities. They developed a framework for dealing with the interactions of the two aspects, managerial cognition and organizational activities.

12. It is worth mentioning that Hayek's famous treatment of the dispersion of information in society is related to his original, pioneering work on human cognition (Hayek 1952). Many of his conjectures and inferences in the book are said to be being validated by recent developments in the cognitive and neural sciences.

13. The formulation is standard in the theory of team that assumes a common goal among the members, but different information and disperse decision-making among them (Marschak and Radner 1972; Aoki 1986; Cremer 1990). From game-theoretic perspective, a team is a Bayesian identical interest game where both players have an identical payoff function. Section 2.5 tries to explore conditions by which such assumption can become reasonable for organizations in which individual members have actually different utility functions. Properties derived for the two-agent case in the text can be generalized to multimember cases; see Pratt (1996).

14. Precisely speaking, the cognitive skill of each agent is measured by the inverse of the standard deviation of his/her observation error relative to that of the observed parameter.

15. The role of physical assets as cognitive tools in architectural design is explicitly dealt with in next section.

16. In orthodox mechanism design theory, the tradeoffs between the better use of dispersed information vs. coordination is discussed in terms of decentralization vs. centralization (e.g. Aoki 1986; Hart and Moore 2005). Alonso et al. (2008) introduced the possibility of incentive biased misrepresentations by agents into this framework. They conceptualize a decentralization model as "cheap communications" among the agents without a third party. In that sense it may be considered to be closer to the idea of "cognitive sharing" rather than dispersed information. They show that if the agents' incentives are sufficiently

aligned, this type of "decentralization" performs better than the centralization of information by the incentive-neutral manager, because in the latter the agents' incentives to misrepresent their information are enhanced.

17. Clark refers to the "core, basic, *portable* cognitive resources [which] may incorporate bodily actions as integral parts of some cognitive processes" (1997: 216; italics added) in the context of a partial concession to a criticism to his extended brain–body–world systems as integrated processes, but he immediately made the point that he does not "think that the portability consideration can ultimately bear sufficient conceptual weight."

18. Zingales (2000) argues that complementarities may be created by the entrepreneur as an instrument for controlling the workers.

19. To clearly expose the logic involved, a simple adaptation of a model of Hart (1995) is helpful to the current setting. Let $F(M, W, P: R_m, R_w)$ be the production function of the corporate organization where M, W, and P denote the input level of MCA, WCA, and PHA respectively; and R_m or $R_w = 1$, if the use-control rights are allocated to MCA or WCA respectively, and R_m or $R_w = 0$, if not. Let $u(M, R_m)$ and $v(W, R_w)$ be the payoffs of MCA and WCA respectively in the possible event that they have to rely on outside opportunities in the absence of mutual cognitive cooperation.

The joint net surplus to be created by the corporation is $F(M, W, P: R_m, R_w) - u(M, R_m) - v(W, R_w) - \pi$, where π is the required rate of return to PHA taken to be exogenously given. Then, assuming that the remaining surplus is divided between MCA and WCA equally as a Nash bargaining solution, their respective net benefits would be

$$^1/_2[F - u(M, R_m) - v(W, R_w) - \pi] + u(M, R_m) - c(M)$$

and

$$^1/_2[F - u(M, R_m) - v(W, R_w) - \pi] + v(W, R_w) - d(W),$$

where $c(M)$ and $d(W)$ are the costs of investment in M and W (consult Aoki (1984) for a more comprehensive application of a Nash bargaining approach to the theory of the firm). Then, the maximization of each with respect to M and W requires that

$$^1/_2[F_m + u_m(M, R_m)] = c'(M)$$

and

$$^1/_2[F_w + v_w(W, R_w)] = d'(W),$$

where subscripts indicate the (partial) derivatives with respect to indicated variables. Suppose that $u_m(M, 1) > u_m(M, 0)$ and $v_w(W, 1) = v_w(W, 0)$, then MCA is unilaterally essential and WCA is not essential. Since $u(M, R_m)$ represents the disagreement point of a Nash bargaining game for MCA, the endowment of use-control rights over PHA to MCA (i.e. $R_m = 1$) will increase MCA's bargaining power as well as incentives for investment in management's own cognitive

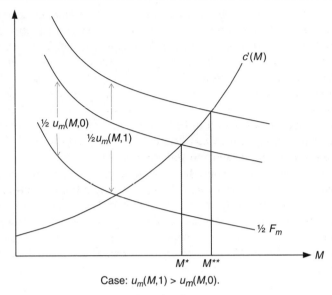

Case: $u_m(M,1) > u_m(M,0)$.

Figure 2.1. The case of non-essentiality of WCA

assets [as from M^* to M^{**} in Figure 2.1]. A parallel argument applies with respect to WCA. If $u_m(M, 1) = u_m(M, 0)$ and $v_w(W, 1) = v_w(W, 0)$, then MCA and WCA are reciprocally essential and the assignment of use-control rights would not affect either party's bargaining power, although it may have impacts on the value of F.

20. See note 19 for a simple proof.
21. Precisely speaking Hart considers the location of residual rights of control over PHA, while I am concerned with the location of use-control rights as I focus on ways in which PHAs are used as tools in associational cognition.
22. In the world of asymmetric information the first-best solution cannot be implemented. If there were a unique implementable first-best solution, then comparative institutional analysis would lose a meaningful subject of study.
23. In terms of terminology introduced in note 19, the threat points of Nash bargaining for both parties, $u_m(M, R_m)$ and $v_w(W,R_w)$, become endogenous variables depending on values of R_m and R_w. Thus the bargaining is required regarding their values and the sharing of use-control rights is a likely outcome in Nash bargaining (that is, $1 > R_m$, $R_w > 0$ with $R_m + R_w = 1$).
24. Although associational cognition in this mode is characterized with vertical cognitive-assimilation, its horizontal mode may be characterized at the beginning more by cognitive-encapsulation because of occupational qualification architecture based on specific public/industrial training programs for WCA.

However, it has recently become more flexible in practice in Germany and the horizontal mode is increasingly being characterized by elements of cognitive-assimilation in the form of skills-overlap, broader job descriptions, "group works," in-house training, the rising importance of including the views of a works council, etc. (e.g. Streeck 1992, 1995; Thelen 2007).

25. See von Thadden (1995); Aoki (2001: 287–91). According to OECD (2004), the portfolio composition of institutional investors in Germany is still predominantly in the form of loans and bonds rather than equity (i.e. the share of equity holding is 24% in Germany compared to 65% in the UK).

26. See, e.g. Franks and Mayer (2001), Franks *et al.* (2005).

27. There still remains the problem of *ex post* shirking of the relational monitor so as not to bail out the team at their own costs in the event in which it is supposed to do so. This problem can be partly resolved by the political-economy framework as is to be discussed in Chapter 3, Section 3.3.4.

28. In the case of an innovation network in the biotech industry, actual innovation efforts may be made by the alliance of multiple firms, including established firms. In fact, in this industry where scientific progress is fast and highly uncertain, the diversity of inter-firm connections appears to constitute an important feature of the competitiveness of individual firms. See Powell *et al.* (2005). More on this in Chapter 4, Section 4.3.2.

29. However, these presumptions are not necessarily consistent with the conditions for a Nash equilibrium to exist, because a Nash equilibrium in behavioral beliefs requires common knowledge (Aumann and Brandenburger 1995). I discuss this issue and its implications for the theory of institutions in Chapter 4, Section 4.2.

30. One further avenue of exploration for my approach may be thinking how it relates to the business strategy literature on competitive advantage. This perspective would suggest that different linkages between CG and OA will produce different sets of competitive advantage. The *H*-mode of managerial unilateral essentiality may be related to Porter's (1985) industry view of comparative advantage, which is essentially based on managerial expertise in understanding market opportunities. Meanwhile the *S*-mode may be seen as relating to the resource-based theory of the firm wherein competitive advantage is grounded in the long-term organizational capacities of workers, etc. in the sense of Penrose (1959), Nelson and Winter (1982), Nonaka (1991) and others. Finally, the *SV*-mode may relate to an understanding of competitive advantage emerging in economic sociology, where competitive advantage is based on VC's position within social networks that allows for access and the "brokering" of innovative combinations of entrepreneurial activities (Burt 2005), as well as in the business literature which points to the comparative advantage of modular architecture in highly uncertain development efforts (Baldwin and Clark 2000; Podolny 2001).

31. See also Boyd and Richerson (1985) for a similar evolutionary model, although they deal with gene-culture co-evolution with a longer time span that is not directly and exclusively relevant to organizational building.

32. Belloc and Bowles (2009) analyze an evolutionary-game model in a similar spirit to Aoki (1998). They examine implications of the co-evolution of patterns of "social preferences, such as reciprocity, truth telling, and the work ethic" (instead of "cognitive assets") on one hand, and institutions of employment contracts (instead of OA) on the other in the context of international trade. However, in their one-sector model, a diversity of cultural-institutional equilibrium can evolve only across countries, but not internally to each economy. Aoki (1998) discusses a possibility of diversity internalized in each economy, using a two-sector model with asymmetric industrial-market characteristics. If the impacts of globalization through the factors mentioned in the text become strong enough to overcome the constraints of domestic historical paths, domestic diversities may emerge on the global scale. I discuss a possible application of such a theoretical result in interpreting some aspects of the emergent global corporate landscape in the final chapter.

33. As a person who has worked in, or closely worked with, various academic, administrative, and business organizations both in the USA and Japan, I can supply plenty of anecdotal evidence on organization-culture specific cognitions and behaviors.

34. E.g. Markus and Kitayama (1991), Kim and Markus (1999), Kitayama and Markus (1994), Kitayame et al. (1997), Fiske et al. (1998), Oyserman et al. (2002).

35. E.g. Yamagishi et al. (1998), Yamagishi et al. (2008).

36. Using a cross-cultural neuro-imaging method, Chiao et al. (2009) show that there is a significant positive correlation between the index of "self-construal style (SCS)" (that is, a self-constructed notion of the collectivist-self vs. individualist-self) and neural responses to contextual self-description vs. general self-description. I would take this finding not so much as evidence of causation from the former to the latter, as the authors do, but rather as an identification of the two types of self-cognition based on different neuro-mechanisms. They show that SCS is not necessarily determined by nationality, however, and suggest the importance of further studies to explore how "other group traits that vary across cultures such as social hierarchy and communalism affect neural processing during social cognition" (op cit. p.7).

37. An implication is that agents may use different kinds of frames for games in domains other than organizations (e.g. social exchanges in the narrow sense, political exchange, markets, commons, and so on), although their choices based on those frames may be related to each other. I will discuss this matter in the following chapters.

38. The characterizations of the equilibrium part are given as sub-game perfect for the H-mode and G-mode (Aoki 2001: 287–91), equilibrium of a super-modular

game for the *S*-mode (Aoki 1994*b* 2001: 291–8), second-best efficient contract for the *SV*-mode (Aoki 2001: 349–71; Aoki and Takizawa 2002).

39. In a more general context Binmore (1994, 1998, 2005) expounded the idea that the fundamental nature of "social contracts" can be understood as an agreement reached by the agents placed under the veil of ignorance, i.e. in the fictitious situation where the agents do not yet know their social positions. Further he argued that such agreement can be characterized as a Nash bargaining solution (Nash 1953. More on this later in Chapter 4, Section 4.1). For an application of the idea to corporate governance, see Sacconi (2010). For earlier works on the application of a Nash bargaining solution to the theory of the firm, see Aoki (1980, 1984), McDonald and Solow (1981), Svejnar (1982).

40. A two-person Nash bargaining solution can be characterized by the maximization of the weighted sum of the players, with the weight for each of them being determined by the so-called boldness of each defined as the ratio of the value of his/her Neumann utility to that of its marginal utility measured at a Nash solution (Aoki 1984). Thus, once the basic governance rules are laid out according to the Nash axiom, then the weighted function becomes a potential function defined on the players' action space with the property that the change in any player's payoff from switching between any of his or her actions (holding other players' actions fixed) is equal to the changes in the potential functions (Monderer and Shapley 1996). The game with a potential function is called a Bayesian potential game. In potential game, the set of Nash equilibrium is the same as that of the solutions of an identical interest game (see note 13 above), that is the team (Ui 2009).

41. I will discuss in Chapter 4, Section 4.2 the idea that the commonality of individual frames (the "meet" of individual information sets in a technical sense) forms the societal/organizational frame as an institution.

42. In fact, a Nash bargaining solution can also obtain as an evolutionary equilibrium (Young 1991) as well as a sub-game perfect equilibrium (Rubinstein 1982) or Nash equilbrium of a potentil game (cf. note 40).

43. For *H*-mode, see for example, Milgrom and Roberts (1992), Roberts (2004) and for *S*-mode Aoki (1988, ch. 2).

3

Political and Social Games
Corporations Play

3.1 Beyond economics

Chapter 1 discussed the aspect of business corporations as a system of associational cognition and its governance. Five generic modes of their relationship were derived. Conceptually, one or a mixture of those modes may autonomously evolve in an economy and provide a basic frame for the internal workings of business corporations. The theoretical construct in the chapter suggests that the basic nature of business corporations is as a "rule-based, self-governing organization"(pages 9–12 above). At the generic level, business corporations are not to be regarded as creatures of formal statute, even though this may sometimes appear to be the case, both historically and in practice. Unless they were able to generate and sustain rules for their own internal architecture and governance, business corporations would not be viable, over time, as an essential element of a market economy. Having said this, however, we should also note that business corporations are embedded in various domains of societal exchanges that are much broader than the organizational field and economic markets. In those domains there are also formal and informal rules, for example political governance, statutory rules generated by politics (including corporate codes), social norms, stigma, deontic values, and so on. Even mighty business corporations cannot possibly ignore all these. How do the internal rules of business corporations become consistent with these societal rules? Do business corporations behave passively, taking those societal rules as constraints? Or, are they actively involved in making some of those societal rules to fit their interests? These are questions that are dealt with in this chapter. In order to motivate the inquiries further, let me mention two specific current issues.

First, there is a recent debate on the possible determinants of corporate governance and their implications.[1] Shleifer and his associates argued that for strong securities markets to develop and to realize better corporate performance, corporate law matters (the so-called legal origin theory). Specifically, common law systems are argued to be better adept than the civil law system at protecting the interests of minority shareholders, restraining any dynastic control of corporations and thereby deepening securities markets (La Porta *et al.*, 1998, 1999; Shleifer and Vishny (1997). Others, for example Roe (2003, 2006) and Rajan and Zingales (2003), argued that more basic institutions than corporate law matter and that, once basic institutions such as property rights protection are in place, a nation's politics would become decisive in shaping securities markets and corporate governance. They claim that the legal origin therefore does not matter as it cannot have a lasting impact on the evolution of corporate governance. In either case, statutory law is the product of politics, while business corporations are important actors in politics, engaged in lobbying and sometimes bribing, backing political campaigns, participating in political decisions through public discourse, corporate publicity, and so on. So, is it right that the causal relationship is only from politics (statutory laws) to business corporations (and securities markets)? Is there no essential correspondence between institutional modes of corporate governance on the one hand, and those of political governance on the other?

Second, we observe that business corporations are also active in social activities and are concerned with their social reputations. In particular, they are increasingly active in corporate social responsibility programs in this era of rising social concerns with the potential impacts of corporate activities on natural environments. But if it were the case that this problem is just a classic example of externalities, could it not be taken care of by appropriate legal provisions and regulatory instruments (e.g. markets for emission rights, pollutant taxes)? Is it correct that corporations are engaged in various non-economic activities to meet societal demands that are beyond their legal obligations? In other words why do they "over-comply" (Heal 2005, 2009)? Milton Friedman (1970) once forcefully argued that, as the basic aim of business corporations is to create and deliver wealth for shareholders, corporate social giving is not the right thing for them to do. However, there appears to be a paradox as some evidence, albeit not conclusive, suggests that corporate social giving is positively evaluated in share markets. Why is this? What are the relationships between corporate market activities and social ones? Are there any social activities that can be done by corporations but not by individuals for social welfare?

Needless to say, business corporations are above all economic entities engaged in various economic transaction games as strategic players (e.g. in oligopoly games, market-reputation games, buy-or-make games, bargaining games, etc.), on which the literature is bountiful, refined, and wide-ranging.[2] However, the above-mentioned issues and others suggest that business corporations are political and social entities as well, which compels us to deal with them in a trans-disciplinary manner beyond purely economic terms. Political and social factors seem to matter in shaping the structure and behavior of business corporations, while the latter may exercise equally important impacts on societal orders and national politics. The institutional scholar Douglass North argues for the necessity of a trans-disciplinary approach (inclusive of cognitive science) to institutions as follows:

This human environment is divided by social scientists into discreet disciplines—economics, political science, sociology—but the constructions of the human mind that we require to make sense out of the human environment do not coincide with these artificial categories. Our analytical frameworks must integrate insights derived from these artificially separate disciplines if we are to understand the process of [institutional] change. Moreover we must understand what is the underlying force driving the constructs that the mind makes. Why do rules, norms, conventions, and ways of doing things exist? What induces the mind to structure human interaction in this way? (North 2005: 11)

How should we make a trans-disciplinary approach to institutions? As I mentioned in the introduction, traditionally economics, political science, and sociology start out with completely different premises regarding how the societal order is to be understood: the orthodox neoclassical economic approach is built on methodological individualism, political science is concerned with power, and sociology regards social categories such as norms, values, and meanings as primary. Their division may not be "artificial" and their reconciliation and integration may not seem to be trivial. In this and the next chapters, I dare to explore a unified and integrative framework for dealing with organizational, economic, social, and political institutions in general, and the role of business corporations in their linkages in particular. I do so by relying on game-theoretic frame and language.[3] One might immediately react to this suggestion with skepticism: is this not a disguised attempt to resurrect the so-called economic imperialism? Is it not that game theory is a construct of methodological individualism par excellence?

However, I submit that we need not confine the meaning of games to a strictly classical, individualistic sense. I hope that discussions in the previous chapter on organizational frames of corporate cognitive-governance have already suggested an alternative possibility. In keeping with the emergent view on human cognition, I argued that the members of business corporations might rely on the evolving organizational frame as the rules of games, and comply with them in a manner that is not entirely self-regarding. When individual agents, including business corporations, interact with others in political and social domains, their motives and modes of behavior may not be identical with those in the economic domain where the self-regarding exchange of goods between agents may lead them to mutually beneficial positions. Emotional, non-material factors, as well as public-mindedness, sympathy and so on, may play certain roles. Business corporations certainly need to allow for these into their calculations. Needless to say, the non-economic domains are distinct in their means of interaction in terms of social symbols, formal language, coercions, and so on. However, those interactions could still be viewed as games in that others' actions matter for one's interests and vice versa so that all of us have to try to achieve something by inferring how others behave and how they react to our own behavior. Business corporations are not exceptions in this regard. Thus, many authors since Plato have drawn analogies between social order and the rule-based game playing. The historian Huizinga, who presented such a view systematically based on extensive knowledge of comparative history and culture, noted that "it is very curious how the words 'prize', 'price' and 'praise' all derived more or less directly from the Latin *pretium* but developed in different directions" (1938/1950: 51).[4] It may not be far-fetched to view these words as capturing some essential aspects of payoffs in the game playing in the political, economic, and social domains respectively.

Below, I will try to go beyond a mere analogy and homology, however. Instead of viewing the division of the subject matter and the methodology of economics, sociology, and political science as being arbitrarily drawn, I would rather attempt to formulate games in organizational, economic, social, and political domains made disinct by discrete sets of players, their interactive instruments and physical/psychological consequences of interactions. However, these games may not be isolated and independent of each other in society but in fact be interrelated, and the orders generated by the playing of these games may be linked or mutually reinforcing. This is why political and social games are not irrelevant, but are crucial for understanding what business corporations do and what the implications of their activities are. In order to explore such interrelationships, game-theoretic language will prove to be quite useful. I summarily refer to games played recursively within a population as "societal" games (reserving the terms "social game" or "social-exchange game" in a more specific sense as a subclass of the societal games).

We may identify the rules of the societal games, or the orders created by them, as institutions. However, scholars are still not in complete agreement as regards what can be viewed as institutions, where they come from, how they should be theoretically approached, and so on.[5] These issues may at first sight appear merely scholastic. However, they are of enormous practical significance in understanding how corporations can evolve, whether law or politics can fundamentally change their behavior and structure, what impacts corporations exert on the social order, and so on. In any case, for any rules to be effective in society, they must be cognized by all the players and observed by them to be operating effectively (enforceable) in the recursive play of games. Therefore, for this chapter, I simply posit that the rules of societal games, or institutions, are represented by the salient patterns of the recursive states of play (the existing societal order, so to speak). It amounts to identifying the rules of societal games with an equilibrium summary representation of play. In the next chapter I provide a game-theoretic foundation for such a view to be reasonable and discuss the cognitive conditions required for institutions to evolve as such. For now, by taking the equilibrium view of institutions for granted, I immediately proceed to discuss simple models of rule-generating, political and social games and try to identify possible multiple equilibria that may arise in them as varied forms of institutions.

3.2 Heuristic characterizations of the societal rules

Needless to say, the order of society is never in equilibrium in strict sense. It is always subject to endogenous movements and experiments, external shocks, evolutionary adaptations and selection, etc. On the other hand, society is not in complete chaos or even in a highly unstable state except for occasional critical moments. Under normal circumstances people share some general ideas regarding the ways in which society is organized, even though many of them may not be happy about some aspects. My starting point is to capture such stable properties of society as equilibrium phenomena. In short, I conceptualize institutions as the effective (self-enforcing) rules of societal games as follows:

Institutions are commonly-cognized patterns by which the societal games are being recursively played and are expected to be played.

I will provide a rigorous game-theoretic, knowledge-theoretic justification for this conceptualization in the next chapter. Here I am content to heuristically point out a few important properties of institutions that are implicit in this conceptualization. Let us consider Figure 3.1 in which left- and right-hand boxes represent the dimensions of individual players and their interactions. i.e., the domain of the game, respectively, whereas upper and lower boxes represent the behavioral and cognitive dimensions respectively. We start at the lower-left corner. Any individual player of the societal game cannot play effectively to achieve his or her own goal of action (payoff, whatever it may be) without having some belief about others' possible choices as well as about others' possible reactions to his or her own choice. How can they form such beliefs? It is to be noted at the outset that I use the word "belief" here and throughout the remaining part of the book in the sense of "behavioral belief" in game theory unless otherwise specified, i.e., expectations about others' actions and expectations, or more generally expectations about state of play of the societal game, but not in the sense of normative beliefs or "values"—what people feel is legitimate behavior or what people believe should happen. I will briefly touch on possible relations between the two concepts of beliefs in the next chapter.[6]

How can such behavioral beliefs be formed endogenously? This question immediately invokes the famous infinite regress problem first noted by David Lewis (1969). For a player to choose her action, she has to infer what other players would do, but others' actions would depend on what

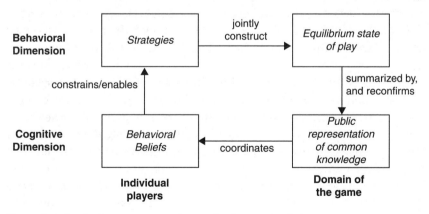

Figure 3.1. Institutions as commonly cognized patterns of play

they expect her to do, which would depend on what they expect she expects they expect and so on ad infinitum. However, let us leave aside for now the problem of how this dilemma can be resolved in practice (to be discussed Chapter 4, Section 4.2), and assume that each player somehow forms his or her own beliefs and acts accordingly (the move from the lower-left box to the upper-left box).

The players in society together generate a "state of play", defined as a profile of action choices by them (the move from the upper-left box to the upper-right box). However, it does not mean that every player can be aware of, or is even interested in, what the actual state is in detail. One's cognitive competence is incomplete so that one cannot distinguish some of the choices of other players from some others, or such distinctions may be irrelevant in some cases for one's own objective and so on. However, suppose that the salient features of evolving states of play are summarized and represented by some public indicators (e.g. public events, social symbols, formal agreements, written rules, established organizations with specific public functions, and so on) in a manner relevant and accessible to every player (the move from the upper-right box to the lower-right box). Suppose the players derive their individual behavioral beliefs from these social categories and their own cognitions (the move from the lower-right to the lower-right box).

Imagine that this circular process somehow comes to be stabilized and that stable public representations summarizing the salient features of moving states of play emerge. They represent common knowledge about the states of play in that every player knows them and every player knows that the others know them. If they reason symmetrically based on the common knowledge, they will come to share beliefs regarding the salient ways of the societal game to be played, although their beliefs differ in details. The formation of such shared beliefs in turn will contribute to the reproduction of the same salient features of the evolving state of play and so on. Beliefs that become shared in this way are robust with respect to fluctuations of individual choices within a limited range, because it is nothing more than a summary representation of possibly moving states of play. I pinpoint the stable combination of *common knowledge/beliefs via public representations* as the essence of self-enforcing rules of the societal game, or simply as the *institutions*.

The rules of societal games, or institutions, are thus *endogenously* constructed and become self-enforcing because of the equilibrium property. Formal rules consciously designed externally to a domain of a game, such as statutory law intended to regulate economic transactions, may play a mediating role for generating shared beliefs among players. But they may not necessarily generate the state of play intended by the legislature unless the designed statutes are confirmed endogenously by actual states of play generated via players' cognitions, beliefs, and incentives. Although endogenously constructed, self-enforcing societal rules would appear as *exogenous* entities to each individual player beyond their direct individual control.[7] As such, those rules may be conceived as *constraining* by individual players, because ignoring them will not be beneficial to them. However, they are actually *enabling* at the same time, for the players who have only bounded cognitive capacities those rules can aid their knowledge of how others are likely to play, helping them to play effectively. Institutions thus provide frames for individual players to know about the basic workings of society. Substantial problem-solving work can be off-loaded to such frames. Individuals as well as corporations can ease the cognitive burdens necessary for making action choices consistent and compatible with others' behavior. In that sense the *positive* (experience-induced) rules of the societal game can serve as a *normative* guide, as they provide prescriptions for effective action choices. Having stated briefly the basic nature of institutions as equilibrium phenomena, I apply the idea to the political and social aspect/roles of business corporations in the rest of this chapter. I begin with the polity.

3.3 Institutional complementarities of political and corporate governance

3.3.1 *Law, politics, or neither?*

What is the nature of the relationships between politics, laws, and corporate governance? As already mentioned in the introductory part of this chapter, one of the most celebrated theories in recent corporate governance literature is the so-called legal origin theory advanced by Shleifer and his associates in a series of papers (e.g. La Porta *et al.* 1998, 1999, 2008). The essence of their arguments is that the legal provisions of various countries concerning corporate governance and security regulations can be roughly classified into two groups based on their legal origin: the civil law tradition of Continental European origin (more precisely, French, German, and Scandinavian origins) and the common law tradition of English origin and that the difference has autonomous and enduring consequences via current laws on the performance of each corporate economy, such as the degree of financial deepening through the provisions of protection of (minority) shareholders' rights vis-à-vis dynastic or collusive block-holding, and thus economic development in general.

Many counter arguments have been presented, however. Franks *et al.* (2005) argue that British capitalism for a long time was typical of family capitalism and similar to the Continental tradition, contrary to what legal origin theory implied. The empirical methods employed by Shleifer *et al.* have also been questioned, for example, whether a single large economy like the USA and small economies like Nigeria, Sri Lanka, and Ecuador can be treated as generating qualitatively and quantitatively comparable indices. They classified the second and third largest (corporate) economies, Japan and China, as having a German origin, but their corporate governance rules have been changed considerably through various political events and the development of their economies. Now Japanese legal provisions in terms of shareholders' rights are much more akin to those of English origin, while corporate governance practice is noticeably different from those in both England and Germany. A recent shift from fairly dense cross corporate ownerships to highly dispersed ownership in Japan,[8] which I will discuss in more detail in the final chapter, mostly occurred in the 1990s under essentially the same corporate laws that had been in place in the preceding years, and it was corporate law that responded to the change rather than vice versa.[9]

In a series of articles Deakin and his associates critically examine technical aspects of the index construction based on cross-sectional data and used for the common law/civil law divide by the legal origin theory. By constructing their own longitudinal data sets covering the period 1995–2005 for major economies, they derived many different observations and implications than the legal origin theory. For example, they found, among other things, that shareholder protection measures were even higher for the developed civil-law systems than they were in the USA, until the latter caught up by passing the so-called Sox regulations in response to the Enron–World.com scandals (Armour *et al.* 2009*b*). Through such dynamic analysis, they argue that the content and implications of the distinctive "legal cultures" of the two legal traditions are not properly captured by the indices constructed by Shleifer and his associates (e.g. Ahlering and Deakin 2007). All these suggest that legal origin may have some impact on evolving legal rules in a path-dependent manner, but it may not be the only, or even the most important variable, to explain current legal rules and their economic consequences. As economies grow, formal rules may be endogenously changed, and in this process other factors—political and social—may exert significant interactive impacts.[10] But how can we understand the nature and workings of such processes?

In a series of Clarendon Lectures, Mark Roe advanced a systematic argument to cast doubt on the legal origin theory of corporate governance from a political science perspective. He argued that it is politics that should be taken as a major determinant of corporate governance and ownership structure.

By determining one of three basic pieces [that is, ownership, management, and employment] politics can thereby often determine the others as well, because the pieces fit together—like pieces of a jigsaw puzzle—as complements. That is, some politically required employment pieces fit well with only a few types of management pieces. Hence politics could, say, determine a particular labor structure, which might call forth only one type of ownership or management structure. (Roe 2003: 5)

Specifically Roe argued that in countries where social democratic political regimes prevail which "emphasize distributional considerations, and favor employees over capital owners when the two conflict," owners are bound to react by concentrating ownership in order to contain the agency costs of management. He made the general claim "much of the firm's structure is affected, sometimes determined, by its political environment." As one of those who introduced the concept of institutional complementarities, I like in principle this three-way "jigsaw puzzle" analogy. But I wonder if it is really the visible hand of the politician that completes the puzzle. Causation may run the reverse way as well, that is from the corporate economy to polity. For example, the concentration of ownership in the capital market may urge employees to call for protection from politics and the state reacts to this demand for societal stability. To be fair, Roe considered this kind of reverse possibility as well, but treated them only as a "backlash" toward a given structure of political institution. In vulgar public debates it is even heard, although Roe is certainly not responsible for it, that politicians are to be blamed for bad corporate governance. But the problem may not be merely with the politicians' moral attitude, competence, and so on.

Intuitively it may not be hard to sense that, if there can be multiple modes of corporate governance, each mode may only fit with a particular mode of political governance and vice versa. But it is desirable to have a sound logic of two-way relationships between them. However, if we try to see possible fitness on a one-by-one basis, basic logic may be obscured and explanations may appear to be rather ad hoc or even post hoc.

Therefore, I will first construct a generic model of political exchange between the government and private agents free from specific context as a sort of rule-making, constitutional game. There is no specific characterization of the private agent; nor is there for the nature of the government. They are to be specified endogenously in the model. I conceptualize the multiple equilibria of this generic game as capturing some essential elements of discrete, generic forms of the political "state" as I did regarding varied modes of organizational architecture and governance. It may be remembered that the English word *state* derives from the Latin *status*. *Status* applies to something that is established, recognized as fixed or permanent in a particular position, as do its derivative English words static and stable.[11] As such the political "state" may be thought of as being amenable to "equilibrium" analysis, possibly yielding many varieties.

By establishing one form of the political state as an equilibrium state, the government and private agents settle on a certain order among them. Thus a state is not merely a government organization or the rules that it makes (which could be broken or ignored), but an order that the government itself is subjected to. It comprises stable common beliefs held by private agents, as well as by the government, regarding possible outcomes of their (deviant) behavior, under which a predictable pattern of behavior is to be sustained. In this sense, the state may be said to have an aspect of endogenous normative order.

After identifying possible generic forms of the political state in this way, I proceed to substitute various, more colorful entities as private agents in those forms: voters-cum-taxpayers, two political parties, the industrial union and the business association, interest groups such as banks and non-financial corporations, industrialists and the peasant class, business corporations and non-governmental organizations (NGOs). This would allow us to identify a number of varieties of the political state, in each of which corporations are positioned in a specific way.

Then I examine the fit of each form of the political state with a particular mode of corporate governance, this time as a sort of equilibrium relationship across the domains of organizations and polity. Namely, out of the possible multiple equilibria, in both the organizational and political domains, particular pairs, one from each domain, are seen to fit together and be mutually reinforcing. It is not the polity, as Roe claimed, that decides on which combination is to be selected. Nor is it the legal system as a consequence of the polity, as the legal origin theory claimed. A choice is made as the outcome of mutual interdependence between the political game and the organization field. This is an instance of what I call institutional complementarities: the concept solidly based on game-theoretic tools as defined below. The logic may appear rather abstract, or intuitively obvious after it has been described. But some subtleties are involved in the concept and its analytical power is beyond that of an intuitive and ad hoc notion of institutional complementarities as sometimes found in the literature.

3.3.2 A generic model of the comparative political state

Let us now begin by formulating a simple model of a political-exchange game as a three-person game à la Weingast (1997), with the government and two private agents as players.[12] As mentioned above, the latter are to be specified later as more concrete entities, depending on context. However, in order to conceptualize the generic forms of the political state as multiple equilibrium states, let us leave it anonymous for now. Yet, in order to discern its discrete forms, it is essential to have more than one private agent and examine the possible consequences of various types of collusions (side-payments) among the players: between the government and either of private agents, between the private agents against the government, as well as a three-party coalition.

Imagine that the government is assumed to supply public goods (including the protection of property rights and human rights, social and national securities) by using resources unilaterally extracted from the private agents in various forms: taxation, inflation, conscription, etc. The fact that the government can have such unilateral power of extraction implies that the government may also potentially have the power to transgress one or both private agents' property and other rights for its own private benefits in the form of consumption, wealth accumulation, monument building, and so on. This possibility is referred to as the "fundamental political dilemma of an economic system" (Weingast 1997). Whether or not the private agents are able to deal with the problem, and how, is of fundamental importance to distinguishing various forms of the political state.

Imagine the base-line state of play in which the government provides the standard public goods and finances them by resources extracted symmetrically from the two agents with no surplus for its own personal benefit. The options for government action in each period are simply composed of the following moves: "stick to the base-line" or "transgress" the private rights of one or both private agents by charging extra levies beyond the base-line. The private agents "approve," "resist," or "yield" to government's choice of action. Suppose that the government can acquire (the maximum) rents,

G, by an extra levy on either party. To resist the government's transgression incurs a cost, c, for each private agent who chooses to do so. However, we assume that only if both private agents cooperate against the government's transgression, could the large cost, C $(> G)$, be inflicted on the government (e.g. loss of power). Isolated resistance by a single private agent is not able to prevent the government from successfully levying extra obligations on private agent(s). In this case, further efficiency losses, $2L$, are imposed on the private sector, as the government uses acquired rents in an unproductive way for its own private advantage. These costs are equally born by both private agents.

Choosing an action in response to the government's action, private agents may not necessarily assess their preferences in an exclusively self-regarding manner. Letting the government infringe on the other's rights and doing nothing against it may impose some private external costs on the non-victimized as well. For example, non-cooperation may give rise to conflict with the victimized in the private sector. Or, he or she may not like to see the other agent's rights being infringed by the government because of its own views on public interest, social justice, empathy, and so on. Let P denote the political payoff-loss of each private agent incurred by those private external costs when the other agent becomes victimized but she/he does not cooperate with the victimized in resistance. By taking the state of play represented by {stick to the base line, approve, approve} as a reference point, we can simply represent the game structure in the following decision payoff matrix when the government chooses to levy extra obligations on private rights.[13] The rows distinguish the choices of the agent who becomes the target of a government transgression and the columns those of the agent who escapes the target of government's transgression. Each cell indicates the corresponding payoffs for the government, the targeted, and the non-targeted in that order.

Table 3.1. Political payoff matrix in the event of government transgression

The targeted	The non-targeted	
	Disapprove	Approve
Resist	$-C, -c, -c$	$G, -G-c-L, -L-P$
Submit	——	$G, -G-L, -L$

Under this simple framework, what kind of equilibrium is likely to evolve? Although the setup is extremely simple, somewhat surprisingly we can derive a variety of equilibria characterized by the self-sustaining common beliefs held by the government and the private agents, depending on the relative values of the parameters, time discount factors for the private agents, historical conditions for forming a possible coalitional structure, and so on.

First, consider the most obvious case in which the costs of resistance are too high for both private agents to avoid direct and indirect damages from the government transgression (i.e. the case in which $c > G + L$): in other words the case in which the government's power is high enough so that steady transgression by the government on both private agents can result as a static Nash equilibrium of a one-shot game. If the game is repeatedly played, one-shot equilibrium can become equilibrium of repeated games with high social costs $2L$ per period (in this case the government infringes the rights of both private agents so that $P = 0$). If $G + L > c > L + P$, then the government can victimize either private agent without worrying about the cooperative resistance of the other agent in each period and gain payoff G. This can be made more likely, if the level of public spirits of private agents is low (i.e. $P \doteq 0$). Let us call these two equilibrium states of play the *absolute predatory state* and the *arbitrary predatory state*, respectively.

Suppose next that $L + P > c$: the case where the consequence of government's transgression on a private agent can incur high efficiency and private external costs on the non-targeted private agent so that there is a risk of opposition from the non-targeted as well. However, if $G > L + P$, that is, if government's potential gains from transgression on a private agent is high enough relative to the efficiency and external costs of the non-victimized, the government can make a promise of a side payment at least equal to the amount $(L + P) - c$ to quell any possible protest from the non-victimized. Then the transferee would lose the incentive to cooperate with the victimized. The state of play characterized by the triple {Infringe and make side-payment, Submit, Accept side-payment and approve} can become a static Nash equilibrium of a one-shot game and thus the equilibrium of repeated games as well, provided it is commonly believed that one of the private agents has been, and is expected to be, always the target of an extra levy. We refer to this self-enforcing state as the *collusive state*, which entails social costs of $2L + P$ in each period.[14] The maximum amount that the government can offer to the non-transgressed is bounded by G. If $(L + P) - c$ becomes greater than this amount, then the non-transgressed would drop out of the coalition with the government and the collusive state is not viable. That is, this state is possible only when the government is strong enough to extract G from one agent that is large enough relative to efficiency loss L and the level of private external cost P of the non-transgressed agent.

Another possible state is for the government to secure a steady stream of rents from either one of the private agents alternately over time with no side payments to the other. Suppose that each agent becomes the target of government's extra levy every other period so that its expected burden-bearing per period is $\frac{1}{2}(G + 2L + P)$. If $\frac{1}{2}(2L + P) < c$, then the government can levy the amount $G < 2c - (2L + P)$ from one agent alternately without worrying about possible coordinated resistance from the other, provided that private agents are myopic. Then the actual political payoff configurations would become on average $\{G, -\frac{1}{2}G - L, -\frac{1}{2}G - L\}$ as the private agents mutually expect that they are alternately becoming the target of the government levy so that $P = 0$. In this state, the government obtains a sort of consent from both private agents that levies are imposed on them over time alternately, but the room for such a device would get smaller, as conflict cost c gets smaller. I refer to this state tentatively as the *correlated state*, as this stable state can be characterized as the so-called correlated equilibrium of the game (Aumann 1987). One way of interpreting this state at the generic level is that the private agents agree to alternate the burden-sharing contingent on some probable events and the government extracts rents as a return for mediating such an arrangement. I will give a more concrete example of this interpretation later.

The most interesting possibility is the case of expected coordinated resistance by both private agents against any government transgression.[15] What can make such cooperation by private agents self-enforcing? Imagine a situation in which the government is expected to somehow randomly aim at levying either of the private agents as in the previous case. Then, if one party becomes an actual prey of the government today, there is no reason for the other private agent to be sure that it may not become the prey in the future. Under this circumstance, it becomes mutually beneficial for both private agents to coordinate their resistance to prevent the government from engaging in any transgression, if they are sufficiently farsighted. Then the government would refrain from transgression on private rights because of the fear of a big conflict cost, C (e.g. the loss of power).

Consider the following strategy profiles of repeated games: (1) the government always infringes on one private agent randomly, if and only if either private agent has never resisted its transgression in the past. Otherwise it honors the rights of both agents and sticks to the base-line. (2) When the government tries to impose an extra levy, private agents submit, if and only if either of them has ever done so in the past. Otherwise, they always cooperate to resist the government's transgression. When does such a threat by the private agents become credible so that the prescribed strategy profile becomes the common belief of the players? In other words, when can the benefit of coordinated resistance become greater than its cost c for each agent?

If the private agents do not resist government transgression, then the expected loss of each agent in the future periods will be $\frac{1}{2}(G + 2L + P)$ as in the correlated state. The present value sum of future losses is this amount times $1/(1 - \delta)$, where δ is the private agent's time discount factor. If this amount is greater than the current net cost of coordinated resistance, $c - (L + P)$, the threat of coordinated resistance can become credible. Then, it is certainly in the government's self-interest to limit itself to behave decently, entailing the political payoff profiles characterized by {0, 0, 0}. This condition is likely to hold, if the private agents are far-sighted (δ is large), even if the level of P is relatively low, that is, even if each agent is only self-regarding. We may refer to this equilibrium outcome as the *democratic state*.[16] In this state, the commitment of the government to limited power is credible, since the common belief is that any transgression by the government is punished by the withdrawal of the support of private agents, incurring large costs to the government. The democratic control here means more than just majority rule.[17] The latter can become a "tyranny of the majority" (a form of "collusive state"), if the private agents are not far-sighted. Also, the democratic state does not necessarily hinge on agents' empathy with others, although it can be helpful.

If the resistance cost, c, is sufficiently low relative to the efficiency losses, L, and/or private external cost, P, there can be multiple equilibria of repeated games. The democratic state, as well as the collusive and correlated states, can become self-enforcing states, once either of them is established. However, these states have different implications for the payoffs of private agents as well as to the compatibility with institutions in other domains. For parameter values compatible with all three modes of states, the private agents are better off under the democratic state than under the collusive and correlated state. However, it is to be noted that although factors like resistance cost (alternatively, government power), public-spirits, and so on are treated above as parameters, their values would be to a great extent co-determined with a particular institutional setup of the state. For example, a high level of public-spirits or empathy that may be represented by a high level of P may make the democratic state more viable, but the latter would also nurture public-spirits or empathy among coming generations, which may not be easy within the framework of the predatory state. Thus, those parameters may be better characterized as the "quasi-parameters" (Greif 2006). The above exercise should be regarded, therefore, only as an attempt to examine what ranges of parametric values can be compatible with a particular institutional setup of the political state. In the following sub-sections, I will identify discrete, substantive forms of the collusive, correlated, and democratic states and suggest a few possible examples of evolution from one form of a state to another that may be driven by the mutually reinforcing mechanism with the game on the corporate domain.

3.3.3 *A strategy-based conceptualization of institutional complementarities*

Business corporations and their members—the investors, the management, and the workers—are all important players in the political-exchange game, individually or collectively, contributing to the shaping of the political state. Conversely, the institutional form of the political state and consequences of its behavior, such as statutory laws, regulations, policy, etc., impact on corporate structure and behavior via incentives placed on their individual members. The relationships between the two can be reciprocal, generating diverse forms of mutually reinforcing combinations of political and corporate governance. Thus, the concept of institutional complementarities has become a much talked-about theme in political economy in the last decade or so. But there are two different approaches to this concept. One is based on the game-theoretic language that I presented earlier (Aoki 1994b, 2001) and followed below. The other is presented by the so-called "varieties of capitalism" school in their comparative studies on the liberal capitalism of the Anglo-American type vs. the coordinated capitalism of the German type (e.g. Hall and Soskice 2001; Amable 2003; Crouch *et al.* 2005). They list observed institutional features in different domains, say the state, corporate governance, employment relations, and so on, in each economy and refer to the presumed mutual functional supports among them for economic performance as institutional complementarities. Thus their concept is built on a post hoc justification of "functional complementarity" (Streeck 2009: 18).

However, I submit that from such a functionalist perspective, it is hard to explain how these complementarities evolve in decentralized market economies where agents of different positions and orientations in terms of wealth, organization, politics, and so on interact with each other.[18] For example, was it not possible that at least some German businessmen, in principle, preferred management prerogatives to codetermination even in the heyday of the German model? If so, why did they not earnestly pursue a route toward it much earlier than the 1990s? What was the nature of their agreement with the industrial unions then? It is certainly not the case that German institutional arrangements were designed by some hegemonic institutional designer and imposed on people. Furthermore, are there only two varieties? Do we not observe in some economies that institutional arrangements evidently function poorly but still survive through some mechanism of mutual reinforcement? Hall and Soskice argue, "institutional complementarities generate disincentives to radical change" (2001: 64). In that case, can an institutional change occur only through a Big Bang caused by external shocks?

In spite of these difficulties of the "varieties of capitalism" version of institutional complementarities, I would argue that the concept itself remains an important one in understanding the role of institutions. We only need to ground this concept on a solid logical basis that is useful for analysis rather than employed merely as post hoc explanatory tools applied to observed specific cases. I succinctly re-state below the essence of the analytical concept of institutional complementarities and its important implications. It is based on the idea of mutually reinforcing behavioral equilibria arising as a result of the strategic play of games across domains (Aoki 1994b), but not that of isomorphism latent in different institutional elements existing, say, for the sake of functional efficiency. Then, I discuss its applications to much broader possibilities of complementarities between political and corporate governance and their historical evolution. One of the clear advantages of the game-theoretic approach is that it is able to track analytically how institutional complementarities become either stagnant due to strategic conflict among the players, modified, or evolve endogenously without invoking ad hoc notions such as inertia, functional isomorphism, external shocks and so on.

When agents are confronted with a strategic choice in one domain, they may regard institutions in other related domains as externally fixed constraints on their choices, even though they are actually endogenous outcomes of their own play in those domains. As a result, institutions viable in each of these domains may become interdependent and mutually reinforcing. This intuition can be game-theoretically formulated as follows. Suppose simply that x' and x'' are two possible equilibrium states of play in domain X, while z' and z'' are two possible states of play in domain Z (note that x and z are vectors composed of the strategic choices of all the players).

The players in domain Z are partly or totally overlapped with those in domain X. Suppose that the payoff difference $U(x', z) - U(x'', z)$ increases for all the players in domain X, when z', rather than z'', prevails in domain Z (they do not need to have the same payoff functions). By the same token, suppose that the payoff difference $U(x, z') - U(x, z'')$ increases for all the players in domain Z, when x', rather than x'', prevails in X. Then the games in X and Z are said to be super-modular, and x' and z' (alternatively, x'' and z'') are said to complement each other.[19] If the super-modular condition holds, then an equilibrium combination, and thus a viable overall institutional arrangement, can be either (x', z') or (x'', z'').

An important implication of this logic is first that those two clusters may not be Pareto-rankable (i.e. some players prefer one combination, while the rest prefer the other, yet either combination may become equilibrium). Or, it can happen even that although one of them is Pareto-inferior to the other (i.e. every player is worse-off under one arrangement vis-à-vis the other), it can still prevail as equilibrium, once it is achieved. Namely, a cluster of institutions that is clearly inferior from everybody's point of view can still prevail (Aoki 2001: 225–9). This provides a powerful and useful analytical basis for institutional analysis. It explains why there can be a variety of overall institutional arrangements across economies, even if economies face the same domain characteristics (e.g. the same technologies, common markets, etc.), as well as why a sub-optimal overall institutional arrangement can persist in some economies while a better institutional arrangement is viable in others. Institutional pieces cannot be altered independently from each other (the analogy with a puzzle is valid in this sense).

Secondly, institutional complementarities are not necessarily conditional on consensus among the players in domain X regarding the absolute ranking of x' versus x'' (i.e. it is not required that $U(x',z) - U(x'',z) > 0$ for all z) or those in domain Z regarding the absolute ranking of z' versus z''. Institutional complementarities can hold if only a weaker agreement occurs in the direction of an incremental change in their payoffs associated with a parametric change in z or x. For example, the investor may absolutely prefer x' to x'', while the workers may absolutely prefer x'' to x'. But if the latter's disfavor of x' becomes somewhat mitigated by the presence of z' rather than z'', then the workers may strategically choose x' (actually a component of x' corresponding to his or her choice) rather than that of x'' that would result in a Pareto-inferior mixture of x' and x'' for z'. Then the overall institutional arrangement (x', z') may emerge as a behavioral equilibrium and become sustainable even if there is a conflict of interests among the players in their institutional preference and even if there is no conscious social-engineering design for the sake of functional efficiency. It can evolve even as "unintended consequences" of strategic choices of individual players in disparate domains under certain historical conditions.[20] These attributes of institutional complementarities may not necessarily be made clear by its post hoc conceptualization in which a preference for institutional choice is dealt with in collective, functionalist terms. Also, as we will see in the next chapter, a behavioral equilibrium approach can be easily amenable to evolutionary discussion.

3.3.4 Institutional complementarities in democratic states

Table 3.2 exhibits discrete forms of institutional complementarities between political governance and corporate governance. The first entry is self-explanatory without the help of the analytical apparatus introduced above. As for the second entry, recall that the previous section argued that one possible condition for the democratic state to become self-enforcing could be randomness in the government's selection of the potential target of its transgression. Purely imaginatively, such could be the case when all the private agents are small and anonymous from the viewpoint of the government. It is not surprising that the advocates of the libertarian state—the state whose role is supposedly limited to the protection of private property rights and other minimal base-line tasks of the government—are at the same time naive believers in the atomistic market competition in which all the traders are small and anonymous. Although this combination

Table 3.2. Institutional complementarities between political and corporate governance

Political governance	Corporate governance
Predatory state	Discretionary government control
Democratic state	
Libertarian state	Atomistic entrepreneurial control
Competitive electoral-representation state	Private-contract-based
Corporatist state	Co-determination
Collusive state	
Social democratic state	Dominant stockholder's control
Developmental state	Contingent government control
Degenerate developmental state	Authoritarian ownership control
Correlated state	
Bureaucracy-mediated, pluralistic bargain state	Contingent relational governance by main banks
Private activist politics	Negotiation with NGO, self-regulation

appears to be logically consistent, it requires a sense of humor to appreciate its reality. Needless to say, modern business corporations arise as visible systems of associative actions, cognitive and physical, that cannot be reduced to anonymous atoms.

For the rest of the entries, the logic of institutional complementarities expounded above is useful. First, by taking the mechanism of wage determination, either corporate- or industrial-level, as a parameter, institutional complementarities between two forms of the democratic state on one hand and those of the corporate architecture-governance linkage, H-mode and G-mode, on the other are endogenously derived. For simplicity's sake, assume the situation where the role of the investor (capitalist) and that of the manager are integrated in the classical entrepreneur so that the game in the corporate domain is played between the entrepreneurs and the workers. Suppose that the entrepreneurs prefer, if possible, not to give the workers both a wage premium over the externally determined rate (either by market or supra-corporate collective agreement) and partial use-control rights over physical assets (PHA) for the sake of their own material interests and managerial prerogatives. But they may actually need to grant the workers one or the other in order to motivate the workers to invest in "quasi-essential" cognitive assets (WCA). If there are no external constraints over wage determination, then the entrepreneurs may prefer to retain use-control rights to enhance their bargaining power vis-à-vis the workers (see Chapter 2, Section 2.4.1) and provide a firm-specific wage premium to the workers. Also, the workers may prefer developing specialized skills to gain a wage premium rather than participating in the use-control of physical assets. Then the liberal wage contract regime complements the hierarchical control of associational cognition (the H-mode). By applying the reasoning developed in Section 2.4.1, private contract-based corporate governance would evolve to form a coherent arrangement in the corporate domain, when the dual entrepreneurial functions of managing and financing need to become separated.

Conversely, assume that the entrepreneurs and the workers deal with each other by private contract at the corporate level. They do not have direct access to the political process as collective entities other than in their individual capacity as voters. Then, a competitive electoral representation system of political governance may evolve under which one party represents the interests of investors and corporate managers relatively more favorably, while the other is more responsive to the interests of the workers, with the support of the rest, say, individual proprietors, professionals, farmers, and so on, being distributed between the two parties depending on various issues.

Suppose that two parties have been competing for governmental control through a general election and are expected to remain competitive in the future with unpredictable electoral outcomes. Then, the basic logic of the previous section applies and it may become a stable common-belief equilibrium that both parties are to be reasonably restrained in representing the interests of their own and constituencies when they are in power from the fear that they may otherwise be punished in succeeding elections by voters. Then the outcome of the game may be characterized as the majority-representative, democratic state in which the party in power is committed to behave relatively decently under the expectation of unpredictable electoral choice. The government is constrained not to intervene discretionarily in the private affairs of business corporations or in favor of any particular interests. Both parties may consent to act mutually within the limits of agreeable rules when they are in power.

In particular, the government in this form of the state does not intervene in matters related to management actions that are not outright illegal (the so-called "business judgment rules" for the court), or private disputes between management vs. the workers unless it affects the stability of society. It may facilitate contract-based corporate governance by formalizing evolving practices into general rules for private contracting. As the ruling party changes as the political atmosphere fluctuates in a cyclical manner, the policy orientation may fluctuate accordingly. However, the essential attribute of the "liberal state" in the European sense would hold in that the government does not interfere with labor markets and private contracting except for according to agreed laws.[21] Thus, via decentralized wage setting, the rule of law by the competitive electoral-representation state on one hand and private contract-based corporate governance on the other become mutually complementary.[22]

As an alternative, consider the situation in which the industrial wage rate is negotiated between the business association and the industrial union above the individual corporate level and the agreement is enforced by the state. Then the entrepreneurs do not find any room for motivating workers' investment in cognitive assets by using workers' compensations as a major instrument, and need to opt for sharing the use-control rights over physical assets to motivate the workers' accumulation of quasi-essential assets. For the workers as well, the only option is to also demand participation in use-control rights.[23] Thus the G-mode architecture and associated governance by co-determination becomes a solution (cf. Section 2.4.2).

Conversely, if such a governance arrangement prevails at the corporate level, then the investors, the managers, and the workers may all be better off letting the government remain in a passive role, only to enable industrial-level agreements enforceable so that any potential government transgression can be controlled: the state analogous to what Streeck (1997) once called an "enabling state" or Katzenstein (1985) a "semi-sovereign" state in characterizing the German corporatism state in its heyday.[24] Thus via the industrial level wage bargaining, the codetermination and the corporatist state become mutually complementary. This also suggests that the gradual demise of industrial-level bargaining strategically motivated by the managers and workers of some corporations may trigger a co-evolutionary modification of such institutional arrangement (to be discussed later in Chapter 5, Section 5.2).

I assume above that the workers possess bargaining power vis-à-vis the entrepreneurs (the investors cum the managers) based on "quasi-essential" cognitive assets. Alternatively, suppose that there is a historical tradition of concentration of corporate ownership that is not matched with the bargaining power of the workers, both collectively and individually. Then the mode of architecture–governance combination would be like a variant of the *H*-mode with strong ownership control. But suppose that the government administration is architected in a similar, hierarchical fashion as business corporations in the sense that strong administrative power is built in. Then, the government administration and the workers may find it mutually beneficial to collude against the dominant owners. The government may become active in the protection of workers' class-interests by regulating the minimum wage rate, setting standard working conditions, etc. for the sake of social stability, distributional considerations, and most importantly for the assertion of its own power. The nature of such a "social-democratic" state may be then thought of as a variant of the collusive state to the extent that government power manifests itself in restraining the potentially strong power of the dominant owners.

For the owners, exclusion from the collusion is not beneficial, which is, however, less intolerable if they have a strong corporate governing position (a super-modular condition!). Conversely, once such a political state is in place, the owners with dynastic backgrounds would try to exercise countervailing power against the government–labor collusion by retaining block-holdings of corporate shares. This latter aspect is the one emphasized by Roe (2003) with respect to the French case, but the concentration of ownership may be the cause as well as the consequence of this state. Thus, the social-democratic state and the (dynastic) owner control of corporate governance are institutionally complementary. However, they are so within the national framework of institutional arrangements.

If some of the national institutional constraints are lessened, for example by a change in corporate ownership due to the globalization of financial markets, then a movement to change such arrangements is bound to be set in by the strategic play of the players of all kinds including the government (to be discussed in Chapter 5, Section 5.2).

3.3.5 Evolutionary bifurcation of the developmental state

Another case of institutional complementarities may be illustrated by a parable motivated by the observations of developmental experiences in East Asia including Japan, Korea, Taiwan, Indonesia, and China. Although concrete patterns of institutional evolution differ markedly across these economies, they have one common, generic feature in their initial conditions for the development process: a dominant rural economy populated by small-scale peasants (e.g. tenants, small landholding cultivators, etc.). This is one major generic difference from Latin American economies where large landholdings and employed agrarian workers are prevalent as well as from sub-Saharan economies where landholding and cultivation are relatively unsettled.[25] The parable constructed below may suggest ways in which the patterns of institutional development starting from such initial conditions could bifurcate and evolve further through the force of institutional complementarities.

Let us imagine the generic model of the developmental state as a form of the collusive state: the strong government levies heavy taxes on the class of peasants and transfers a part of the rents thus acquired to the industrial sector for economic development. Such a governmental form may have originated in a political takeover by lower-ranking bureaucrats in a preceding state (as is the case with the Meiji Restoration in Japan), military clan (as is the case with South Korea and Taiwan), revolutionary party (as is the case of the Chinese Revolution), or something similar through a drastic political event. Instead of engaging in industrial management themselves, however, the government selects a few collusive partners from a pool of potential industrialists (e.g. the traditional merchant houses, rural entrepreneurs, members of the ruling clan, party, or dynasty) and transfers a part of the acquired rents to them in the form of industrial subsidies. However, such a transfer is contingent on their continuing to contribute to the country's industrial development that is considered to enhance national prestige and thus that of the government. Suppose that the prevailing beliefs are such that, if any of the industrialists fails to lead industrial development, they will be punished by the termination of the subsidy and they will be replaced by other potential industrialists (or, as in Korea and Taiwan in the 1970s, the punishment may be even more harsh). With such a carrot and stick approach to the contingent subsidy, the developmental state may become conducive to fast economic development.[26]

Economic development under such a developmental-state-cum-contingent-government-subsidy may eventually bifurcate into one of the following institutional paths. First, it may evolve into a degenerate collusive state. This is the state where the industrialists nurtured under contingent subsidies grow too big to be punished and hence the threat of being replaced in the event of a failure to sustain growth is no longer credible. Then the incentive discipline of the contingent subsidy ceases to operate with the consequence that industrial development becomes stagnant with heavy efficiency loss. Collusion between the government and the incumbent industrialists becomes inertial and corrupt (as in the case once dubbed "crony capitalism"). As outsiders of the collusive structure (e.g. the industrial urban workers with rural backgrounds) start to resist the behavior of the collusive elites, the political stability of this state may be threatened. If the government tries to ease the tension by expanding public expenditure beyond its taxing capacity (e.g. by foreign borrowing), the economy becomes destabilized as well (e.g. 1997 Asian currency crisis).

An alternative evolutionary path could be initiated when the government becomes aware of the (potentially) rising discontent of the disadvantaged groups (the industrial workers, the peasants, and so on). As suggested by the generic model of a comparative political state in the previous subsection, if the potential "cost of resistance" of the disadvantaged declines, and/or if the industrialists become aware of the costs of inefficiency and possible public consequences of government intervention, the nature of the state is bound to be modified. To stay in power, the government finds it necessary to depart from exclusive collusion with the business group and starts to act as a mediator between the interests of the advantaged and disadvantaged sectors in order to retain legitimacy and continue to collect rents, although these may be declining. By then, the form of the government may have been gradually transformed from an exclusive club of political elites into a partly-merit-based, permanent bureaucracy. The nature of such a bureaucracy-mediated state can be considered as an instance of the "correlated state."[27]

If an evolutionary path is to take place into the latter case, it would become every party's preferred way to decentralize corporate governance from direct contingent government control. The government may not be able to keep direct control, but wish to retain an overall grip via the control of financial intermediaries, say, the banks. The industrialists would prefer to self-govern by themselves as much as circumstances allow, but they still need government assistance in the event of business difficulties. The workers recruited by them from the rural sector and elsewhere prefer some assurance of their employment status in the absence of mature labor markets. One possible evolving outcome could then be relational contingent governance by the main bank as described in the previous chapter.

For example, Japan evolved along such a path, facilitated by unique historical and political conditions including workers' family backgrounds from the egalitarian, autonomous rural community of peasants; the political removal of dynastic control of business corporations by the Occupation Army after the Second World War, as well as War-time government control over financial allocation. Gradually, the S-mode form of organizational architecture and corporate governance as described in Chapter 2, Section 2.4.3 evolved as an "unintended outcome" of these factors and events (Aoki 2001: ch. 10). The emergent corporate governance structure shared a contingent aspect with that of the developmental state after transition from it, but it was more decentralized. Major commercial banks played the role of relational monitors vis-à-vis non-financial business corporations. In good times the business corporations paid premium to the main bank, while the latter was committed to assisting and bailing out the former at its own cost in their bad times. If such an arrangement becomes common knowledge, its generic nature can be characterized as a correlated equilibrium as in the case of the correlated state. The permanent bureaucracy is expected to enforce such arrangements in exchange for the levy of rents on both of them, as discussed in Chapter 5, Section 5.2. Thus the bureaucracy-mediated bargain state and the relational contingent governance complement each other.

This institutional arrangement started to crumble in the 1990s, just as in the case of the corporatist state in Germany. The present day institutional arrangements in Japan and Germany, although still fluid, are already substantially different from the ones described above. But, as I intend to discuss this in the next chapter, such changes have never been designed, intended, and initiated in polity. The presence of institutional complementarities certainly means that it is difficult to change only one piece of a coherent arrangement. But, if shifts in some quasi-parameters surrounding it become significant enough to cause substantial strategic adaptations by the agents in some domain, then overall institutional arrangements may become subject to a test because of complementary relationships across the domains. Institutional complementarities thus never imply that existing institutional arrangements are frozen nor remain inertial. It implies, however, that the process of change, if it occurs, is initially conditioned by existing complementary relationships and cannot be arbitrarily designed and enforced by law. The process itself would not be straightforward either, if initial changes in quasi-parameters have different implications to the political payoffs and behavioral beliefs of agents of different types. Such is certainly the case to be discussed in the final chapter, in which some domestic complementary constraints are lessened through the globalization of markets, human and organizational mobility, information and so on.

3.3.6 *Private politics and corporate self-regulation*

Finally, as a way to build a bridge to the next section of social-exchanges, one important emerging phenomenon in the political process may be mentioned. It is concerned with the potential for direct political interactions between agents in the private domain, bypassing the government. For example, some private agents may find it costly or ineffective to rely on a government-mediated process to control public goods, because the running costs incurred by the government are too high, or the government is in collusion with a particular interest group and its action is believed to be biased. Further, the transnational activities of business corporations may make it difficult for them to be regulated only through the apparatus of nation states. Then groups of private agents may choose to negotiate with target agents directly through actions affecting the latter's economic interests or social reputation.

Such can become the case when activist NGOs directly negotiate with business corporations for the purpose of achieving certain social and political causes. Strategically they may choose certain demands (e.g. demands for environmentally friendly actions) vis-à-vis targeted business corporations in exchange for rewards (e.g. endorsement, certification) if accepted, or by the threat of inflicting damage (e.g. product boycott, publicity to hurt a corporate reputation) if not. Business corporations may strategically choose whether or not to yield their demands, if targeted, as well as whether or not to take precautions by self-regulating their own actions. Such strategic exchanges can yield various outcomes, depending on the parameters of the game (Baron and Diermeier 2007). They are different from market exchanges in that Pareto-improving outcomes from the status quo will not necessarily be assured. Although these political exchanges may be regarded as "private" (Baron and Diermeier 2007), the government may not be completely out of the domain of strategic interplay, however, because it may find it strategically desirable to emulate and/or enforce certain outcomes of private negotiations through subsequent legislation or in an attempt to salvage a Pareto-worsening outcome by mediating conflicts.

The next two sections deal with corporate social reputations in a broader context.

3.4 Social exchanges that corporations are embedded in

3.4.1 *A third way to social norms*

Traditionally there have been two major social-scientific approaches to social constructs such as social norms in relation to economic analysis. The first approach, which may be referred to as dichotomous, is to treat social norms simply as irrelevant, or at most as exogenous, to economic analysis. In a seminal book published in 1947 which laid down a conceptual and analytical framework of neoclassical economics for a few decades to follow, Paul Samuelson haughtily claimed that "many economists would separate economics from sociology upon the basis of rational or irrational behavior" (1947: 90), implying that economics has nothing to do with such things as social norms. However, since North (1990) emphasized the importance and relevance of social norms in a seminal treatise on New Institutional Economics as one of the important determinants of economic performance, economists became increasingly interested in integrating this notion into economic analysis. For example, Ostrom (2005) argues that the so-called "social dilemma," equivalent to the tragedy of the commons as defined by Harding (1968), was resolvable by individual internalization of the norm. Yet the norm mostly remained as given for economic analysis. For example, it was treated as an exogenous parameter of a preference function and its origin was regarded as explained outside economics (possibly in sociology).[28]

Oddly, however, it was not only in neo-classical economics but even in some once-influential sociological theories such as the Parsonian paradigm, that social values were treated as a quasi-exogenous entity waiting to be individually internalized through socialization processes such as family rearing, formal education, religious teaching, etc. (Parsons 1951). But a deeper and more meaningful approach could be to view social norms/ customs as endogenously generated and sustained through the social interactions of people and to make this process a focus of analysis (e.g. in the manner of the phenomenological approach of Berger and Luckmann (1966); New Institutional Sociology by DiMaggio and Powell (1983, 1991); the game-theoretic approach of Ullman-Margalit (1977), Bicchieri (2006), and others). Such an approach, which may be called the endogenous perspective, has an immediate analogue in economics as well.

Kandori (1992) and others characterized the social norm as an equilibrium outcome of a bundle of trading games played by an arbitrary number of traders. Members of a community are sequentially matched pair-wise to play a trading game of a two-person prisoners' dilemma type, but they are somehow informed of at least partial records of previous plays of successively-encountered trade partners.[29] A social norm is identified with collectively shared (equilibrium) beliefs regarding the possible outcome (punishment) of "cheating" as well as not punishing cheaters (the so-called "meta-norm" (Axelrod 1986)), which would deter cheating on the actual path of play. Note however that in this approach the "social" norm is constructed within the domain of an economic trading game itself. Namely, punishment is the rejection of trading with the past cheater. As a result it could happen that the mechanism even leads to the extinction of trading unless a possible contagion of cheating-punishment can be controlled by a certain degree of forgiveness. One important insight derived from this kind of approach is, therefore, that not all norms are Pareto-improving. Some norms may make everybody worse off.

Greif's celebrated model (1994, 2006) on cultural belief as regulating possible dishonesty in long-distance trading among the Maghreb traders is constructed in the same spirit. But there is one important innovation in his work. Based on documentary analysis, he argued that shared beliefs off the-path-of-play sub-game (i.e. expectations of punishments of cheating by ostracism from the merchant community) were made credible because of traders' dense social structure and shared historical legacy (accordingly, "cultural" beliefs). Social categories play an important role to sustain the norm as an equilibrium.

These rationalist constructions of norms as equilibrium shared-beliefs are full of meaningful implications and I will essentially follow this course of discussion.[30] However, norms that are endogenously generated only within economic-transaction domains may not be the only ones that are relevant to economic analysis. For example, if players are not technologically excludable from a relevant domain as in the case of commons, is it the case that a social norm cannot evolve to deal with its possible "tragedy" *à la* Harding (i.e. over-exploitation)? Then, could a legal regulation or the establishment of property rights be the only solution? These questions are not irrelevant to the corporate sector either. For example, corporations are significant beneficiaries of global commons, that is, atmospheric, aquatic, and other natural environments, in their production activities, while the consumption of their products has significant impacts on these environments regardless of consumers' awareness. Is it only public regulations that can control corporate behavior to be consistent with public interests in natural environments? Are the increasing interests of corporations in the so-called social responsibility (CSR) programs just a kind of charity, a smoke screen for making profits, a device to evade possible criticism against environmentally unfriendly actions, or over-compliance against the interests of shareholders? Alternatively, can there be any productive, or socially beneficial, social-exchanges between business corporations and other social entities?

In order to deal with these and other possible social issues, I adopt a third way, which is to consider explicitly both the domain of the economic-transaction game and the domain of the social-exchange game, and then to link the two. It is, so to speak, to de-couple the social and economic aspects of exchanges and then re-couple them from a new perspective. It assumes that the group of players repeatedly play both the economic-transaction game and the social-exchange game, with different instruments (action choices) and different types of payoff consequences in the respective domains, but each player reasons the possible reactions of others to its own actions in both domains and coordinates its own strategies across the two domains to balance hedonic (materialistic) and emotional (social) payoffs. In this way, the economic and social-exchange games are strategically linked and some choices that are not strategically viable in an economic-transaction game in isolation may become viable with the support of a certain mode of social interactions.

Below, I start by conceptualizing the social-exchange game in the most generic form to establish how it can be made fundamentally distinct from conventional economic-transaction games. As mentioned, the two forms differ in terms of players' intentions (i.e. the nature of their payoffs), the technical rules of the game, and the instruments of play. I also distinguish between the concept of social capital accumulated by individual agents for future benefits, on one hand, and societal-level equilibrium outcomes generated by the individual accumulation of social capital, such as social norms, stigma, social status, and so on, on the other. These two concepts, closely interrelated but conceptually to be distinguished from each other, are often confused and sometimes incite debates in the literature regarding whether the concept of "social capital" is an appropriate one.[31]

The generic notion of a social-exchange game is then extended to the domain in which corporations play together with citizens in asymmetrical ways. In those games corporate social capital can be attributed to individual business corporations through their non-profitable social-exchange actions, such as corporate social responsibility programs (CSR). It may or may not be reflected in share prices; this is an empirical question. But I will argue, with some factual background, that, although corporate social capital can be made conceptually distinct from market-specific reputation capital, it may have significant theoretical and empirical implications for corporate incentives and mode of corporate behavior.

3.4.2 The social-exchange game and social capital

Suppose there is a community (group) of agents who mutually interact with each other by means of symbolic messages (words, gestures, gifts, etc.), physical actions (helping, violence, etc.), the offer of non-marketable goods (valuable information, gossip, etc.) and so on to affect the emotional payoffs of others. We will call the set of such mutually interactive agents and the sets of their instruments the domain of social-exchanges and their interactions on the domain as the playing of the social-exchange game. It is one class of societal games played recursively in a population. A few words may be due here to distinguish this class from games in the economic domain.

First, although exchanges of symbolic messages (e.g. speech acts) may be involved in other types of domain as well, those in the social-exchange domain are distinguishable by the nature of the exchanges as well as the players' objectives. Any economic exchange is essentially a contract that cannot be implemented without a mutual agreement between two (or more) specific parties, although it may be unilaterally or bilaterally defaulted *ex post*. However, social exchanges can occur without explicit agreement but with "unspecified obligations of reciprocity" (e.g. gift-exchange, mutual help),[32] or multilaterally within a network of agents directly or indirectly connected with unspecified routing (e.g. helping any other member of a population as needed). Later I will discuss under what conditions the unspecified obligations of reciprocity can be believed to be fulfilled among the agents concerned. For now it may be noted that there is a good body of psychological and experimental studies to indicate that reciprocity is deeply embedded in many social interactions (e.g. Rabin 1998; Fehr and Gächter 2000, 2002; Gintis *et al.* 2006; Benabou and Tirole 2006). Second, the utterance of speech or the dispatch of other social symbols in social exchanges may well be generated by the sender's own direct interests/emotions (e.g. appreciation, empathy, envy, jealousy, anger, and so on), but their messages are necessarily intended to have an impact on the objects' emotional payoffs, either positively (e.g. pride, satisfaction, consolation, retribution, and so on) or negatively (e.g. shame, guilt, feeling of excluded, and so on): kinds of emotions which Elster (1998) characterizes as "social."[33] In that sense, they are distinct from mere speech acts, or the so-called "cheap talk" (information transmission without any direct effect on another's payoffs) in the signaling game in the economic domain. Also I assume that engagement in social exchanges may not necessarily be "cheap" for agents, because there may be a cost in terms of time, effort, the value of a gift, and so on.

Each agent can derive positive/negative payoffs from another's actions directed toward him or her. However, in order to be able to expect continual positive actions from others, he or she must reciprocate positive actions toward them. If somebody is mean to him/her, on the other hand, he or she may wish to revenge the opponent to stop further malicious action.[34] Thus, the expected emotional payoffs or equivalently social payoffs, of agents over time in the social-exchange domain will be conditional on others' actions that are expected in response to their own actions. Thus, an agent's social payoff from a social-exchange becomes, in reduced form, the function of his or her own action although implicitly via his or her own belief about the other's reaction. The social payoff of one's own action may be measured at margin by the marginal opportunity cost in terms of a hedonistic payoff sacrificed in the economic domain. It may be noted that the tradability between monetary rewards and emotional payoffs is experimentally confirmed by some recent neuro-science studies founded on the notion of "common neuro-currency" due to Montague and Berns (2002).[35] Let us refer to the present value sum of an agent's expected social payoffs over time as his or her *social capital*. This represents an agents' expected capacity to derive positive net social payoffs over time as well as to use it to derive benefits in other domains. Some scholars adopt the term "social capital," referring to intangible collective assets held by society as a whole (e.g. norms, networks, the educational level of the society) in a manner analogous to tangible collective assets (e.g. public goods, commons). But we conceptualize social capital as accruing to, and used, by individual agents (including individual corporations).[36] As will be discussed shortly, it is to be conceptually distinguished from social norms and other such social categories that evolve as the societal outcomes of playing the social-exchange games in which individual agents accumulate social capital to derive future social and other payoffs.[37]

An individual agent's social capital has double features. First, it is the object of individual investment.[38] It depreciates without effort. Thus, agents exchange social symbolic actions in such a way that they consider the most fit/desirable in order to increase, as well as to make the best use of, their own social capital. I will provide concrete examples later, but it may be commented at this point that the basic structure of social-exchanges as described indicates its strategic nature, even though it may not always be played in an exclusively self-regarding manner.[39] Social-exchanges based on reciprocity thus defined are different from altruism. Altruism is a form of unconditional kindness. It derives from the nature of agents' preferences and, as it is, it is not directly related to either strategic play or the endogenous rules of societal games.

Secondly, an individual agent's social capital actually depends not only on his or her own actions but also on his or her belief regarding others' actions, others' beliefs regarding the initiator's beliefs and so on. In this sense, the social-exchange game shares the same problem of infinite regress as the psychological games introduced by Geanakoplos, Pearce, and Stacchetti (1989) and applied by Rabin (1993). However, the concept of the social-exchange game as a class of societal game *recursively* played within a population suggests a reasonable solution to this problem. If agents are recursively engaged in social-exchanges within an informative, homogenous community, then their actions are more easily known and others' beliefs are more easily inferred. That is to say, in a small community, experiences, information and expectations may be shared. Then there may evolve some standard of social exchange—norms of reciprocity—through practices and customs (on this I will elaborate further in Chapter 4, Section 4.2). Such standards may be theoretically regarded as representing a Nash equilibrium of a psychological game *a la* Geanakoplos *et al.* (1989) in summary form. It would constitute shared beliefs about salient ways by which the social-exchange game is being recursively played and is to be played.[40]

These shared beliefs would serve as a guide for the agents to act properly when acting socially.[41] For, as a Nash equilibrium, it is not beneficial for agents not to follow them, once established. The failure of compliance with the implied norm would be believed to be punishable ("sanctioned" in the traditional sociological terminology) by the loss of social capital. Such a loss may not necessarily take the form of external sanctions by others—perhaps ostracism in the extreme case. If norms are internalized, they are followed even when violation would go unobserved by others, because not doing so may create a guilt-consciousness, shame, or some other negative emotional payoff. Such moral sense need not be considered to be derived from an abstract super-natural axiom or primarily imposed by an external authority like a school or church. But it can be regarded as originating in practices. Aristotle noted that "moral goodness (*etike*)...is the result of habit, from which it has actually got its name, being a slight modification of the word *ethos*" (Book II.i: 91). Arrow also noted "internalized feelings of guilt and right are essentially unconscious equivalents of agreement that represent social decisions" (1967: 79).[42]

3.4.3 *Linked games*

I have presented a simple argument that the genesis of norms may be regarded as endogenous outcomes in the social-exchange game. However, we do not necessarily need to regard them as exogenous constraints for instrumental choices in the economic domain. Economic and social exchanges may be linked and norms may evolve through interactions of the two. As an example to exhibit the basic logic in a simple way, let us consider the dilemma of the commons. That is, suppose that there is a commons that is economically and/or aesthetically valuable to the members of a community, but that in order for them to be valuable in a sustainable manner collective maintenance efforts are required. Efforts are costly to the members so that there is the potential risk of free-riding. Suppose that it is technologically not feasible to exclude any member from benefiting from the commons, however. For example, it is impossible to prevent an individual from breathing air. Similarly, it is difficult to hide a landscape; problematical to divert flowing water in order to block individual uses. Then, the usual reputation mechanism to control a member's moral hazard behavior in the collective maintenance effort may not be feasible. Also suppose that it is not possible, either politically or by other means, to solve the free-riding problem by establishing property rights on the commons or forcing the members to be engaged in the collective effort against their individual incentives and wills. Suppose, however, that the members of the community are mutually engaged in various social-exchanges which allow them to derive social (and practical) payoffs with some cost in terms of time, effort, resources, psychological burden, etc. The exclusion of any individual from the social exchanges implies the deprivation of his or her social capital.

97

Then, even though exclusion from the use of the commons is not technologically possible, shirking from the collective effort to develop and maintain the commons may be punishable by the exclusion of the shirker from the benefits of the social-exchange game, for example ostracism. Suppose that the members follow the following strategy combinations: (1) Play "shirk" in the commons game and "do not participate" in the community social-exchange game if one has ever played "shirk" in any previous commons game or has ever been ostracized in the community social-exchange game. Otherwise, "cooperate" in both the commons and community social-exchange games; and (2) "ostracize" any members, and only those members, in all future periods who have ever shirked in the commons game in the past. Suppose that the belief of each member is such that almost all other members have played and will play in the future the strategy combination just prescribed and that each knows that. Under the conditions that members' time horizons are reasonably far-sighted and that members do not feel any inconvenience by punishing deviants, then it can become beneficial for each member to follow the prescribed strategy and the implied beliefs become credible and shared. The common beliefs generate cooperative participation of the members both in the commons game and the social exchange game as their individual best choice. Namely, given the shared beliefs, the cooperative states of play in both games are sustained.[43] We can refer to such a standard of cooperative behavior, supported by the common beliefs, as a social norm.[44]

Once such norm is historically estabished, each member no longer needs to calculate prescribed strategies from scratch or be conscious of its rational property, collective or individual. The norm provides a cognitive frame for the members to which they can offload their cognitive burden. Members may sometimes be tempted to shirk, but be frightened at the thought of what might happen to them if they actually do so. As mentioned already, they may refrain shirking from a guilty conscience, even if others may not detect their shirking. Or, they may follow the standard of behavior simply out of habit or as a disposition. There is neither a reason nor benefit to act otherwise.

In this example, the social exchange game is "linked" to the commons game in such a way that the social capital of each agent created in the former game can be used as an incentive instrument for cooperative behavior in the latter game. In that sense, it may be regarded as a game-theoretic restatement of the notion of "social embeddedness" expounded in the seminal writing of the economic sociologist Granovetter (1985). However, my point is that social norms are not something given from outside economic domains to unilaterally embed and control economic practice in a unidirectional manner. Rather, the standard of economic practices, is maintained by the agents who coordinate their own strategies in the economic and social-exchange domains by attempting to derive economic benefits as well as accumulate their own social capital, taking the tradeoff between a material payoff and a social payoff into consideration.

3.4.4 *Social exchanges on work sites*

The parable in the previous sub-section is offered to clarify the logic for the case where N symmetric agents are involved in a social-exchange domain. However, there are cases in which differentiated social capital may be attributed to individual agents, leading to such social outcomes as status differentiation, stigma, and so on.[45] Let us consider examples drawn from the linkage of organizational and social exchanges. Imagine first the shop floor where information sharing is practiced and the demarcation of jobs among the workers is ambiguous (cf. the *S*-mode organizational architecture stylized in Section 2.4.4). For example, voluntary teaching of green recruits by veterans, sharing of tips for doing things not covered in the manuals, mutual help in solving emergent problems such as machine breakdowns and so on are practiced there. Workers assiduous in such group-oriented cognitions and actions can generate a substantial degree of externalities within the team. Although there may be practices of intended reciprocity, the disparity among the workers in terms of their ability to provide such externalities is inevitable, while their (marginal) contributions to collective outputs may not be precisely measurable and difficult to compensate immediately in pecuniary terms. Even if so, if the more able agent is partly compensated by the ascription of greater individual social capital in terms of high esteem and respect paid by fellow workers in the peer group, it may embed cognitive-sharing.

The rank hierarchy (*shokkaisei*) that was traditionally practiced (and still partly is practiced) in Japanese factories can be regarded as a formal representation of differentiated social capital allotments. This organizational scheme is often confused by Western scholars with the functional hierarchy in which each rank is associated with a particular job description. Thus they mistakenly regard that Japanese corporations are more minutely hierarchically-structured in terms of command–obey relationships. But what the ranking hierarchy specifies is basically a differentiation of status that is characterized by graded salary differentials. Therefore workers doing the same job may be spread across different ranks, while workers in the same rank may be responsible for different cognitive and physical tasks. Although the wage differential across ranks is rather compressed, it is apparent that the more able workers obtain a non-pecuniary satisfaction from the organizational recognition that is symbolized by faster promotion along the rank hierarchy. To what extent such a mechanism of status differentiation contributes as an incentive to the able, as well as a restraint on free-riding by the less able, may depend on the intensity of the social interactions among the workers on the shop floor. This implies that if a tendency toward individualistic values evolves in society at large, implicit tensions may be created in a work place based on team-oriented work.

In the previous chapter Section 2.4.4 also suggested that within the Silicon Valley clustering a fair amount of information-sharing takes place regarding general industrial strategy-making, while actual development efforts that would become potential elements of its implementation are firmly encapsulated within individual entrepreneurial start-up firms. These two aspects are complementary in generating innovation systems under conditions of high uncertainty. Information sharing in the clustering at large is mediated, or brokered, by venture capitalists, university professors, consultants, angels, etc. and so on in a manner somewhat reminiscent of academic exchanges. To promote useful information exchanges, reciprocity and mutual trust are important to restrain selfish, take-but-not-give attitudes, while informative brokers and helpful mentors are held in high esteem and accumulate a good reputation.[46] Thus, the dense social exchanges embed the SV-mode of organizational architecture as well, and the agents who invest in social capital in this network can expect future economic and social returns in terms of business opportunities and social status.

A norm is important even under a competitive frame of organizational architecture in which workers' jobs are standardized, mutually isolated, and paid for by individual piece rate; so Burawoy (1979) told us in his fascinating field study at a Chicago factory. If the piece rate system stands alone, it could generate a "rat race" (Akerlof 1976) among the workers, triggering rate-cut ratchet effects. However, Burawoy depicted that the workers normally aimed to achieve a certain individual target rate—known as "making out" in the workers' slang. Some were satisfied with 125 percent, while others would aim for a higher rate. But there could be a ceiling (say, 140 percent) imposed and well recognized by all members. If someone tried to achieve more than the ceiling, he would be socially ostracized (although he may not mind being ostracized) or even beaten up by fellow workers, while anyone who could not attain 100 percent was scorned. The author argued that "making out" could not be understood simply in terms of achieving greater individual earnings; its rewards included relieving boredom and obtaining social relations and psychological rewards, while it restrained over-competition. The culture of "making out" was generated by the workers themselves, but once established it was experienced as a set of externally imposed shop floor norms. In contrast, in some other circumstances the culture of competition may be nurtured at the workplace in such a way as to induce individuals to compete to excel. Such competition may contribute to higher organizational achievements for a certain period of time, but may generate a momentum for instability at the same time. The spectacular failures of some financial service houses that triggered the 2008 crisis may be regarded as a typical case of this, an idea to which I will return in later chapters.

3.4.5 Does the share market internalize corporate social capital?

The above examples of social embeddedness are drawn from the simple, more or less symmetric N-person games, although a differentiated distribution of social capital may result from play. Sociologists look at more complex social networks unevenly connected to each other with strong and/or weak ties (e.g. Granovetter 1985), big and/or small holes across closures (e.g. Burt 2005), closed conduits vs. diffused channels (Owen-Smith and Powell 2004; Powell *et al.* 2005) and so on. However, I will take up next another simple social-exchange game situation in which agents are divided into two subgroups using different types of instruments. For example, the giving of knowledge, helping, positive or negative goods, etc. by the members of one group are reciprocated by emotional appraisals, such as praise, appreciation, criticism, etc. by the other group. The latter affects the differential levels of social capital attributable to each member of the former. This situation has been traditionally analyzed as externalities in economics, but not as a kind of exchange, unless an explicit bargaining situation is created between the two *à la* Coase (1960). If the number of agents belonging to the latter side is relatively numerous, however, it may be hard to implement effective bargaining. But the spontaneous attribution of social capital to the former that is contingent on their actions may play an important role in the domain of social exchanges itself, but also may have further impacts beyond that domain. Indeed, such a situation can be quite relevant to the contemporary corporate world. This section discusses situations in which corporations are embedded in a social-exchange domain and can invest in their own corporate social capital for possible future economic gain.

A question has already been raised regarding whether business corporations should be considered as nothing more than entities solely engaged (or ought to be engaged) in economic transactions in product and factor markets. A negative answer was given by citing their roles in shaping the mode of political institution together with other social players. Now we ask if there is any point in regarding them as engaged (and ought to be engaged for unique societal benefits) in exchanges with the society of citizens at large beyond their own markets. In posing questions in this way I set aside from my immediate concern with such matters as corporate brand names embodying an accumulated reputation in particular markets (in terms of consumers' expectations regarding product quality, after-purchase service, delivery times, etc.). Costly signaling (such as advertising) that would not directly affect the utility of the buyers is also left outside the scope of our discussion for a while (although advertising may promote so-called conspicuous consumption). The distinction between a market-specific reputation and social capital is sometimes subtle and ambiguous in practice, and even often complementary, as will be seen later. But I start by questioning whether or not business corporations accumulate (and ought to accumulate) social capital even outside their own product markets and, if they do, what are the potential implications for their market and non-market behavior.

Indeed, corporations and citizens of society at large may be viewed as directly and informally engaged in social exchanges. If a business corporation pollutes a natural environment and/or generates health hazards through its economic activities or products, it will be subjected to public reactions beyond own markets in terms of bad social reputation, public protest, product boycott, etc., even if those economic activities are not immediately illegal within existing statutory frameworks. On the other hand, some corporations voluntarily provide resources for social benefits such as environmental protection, poverty reduction, public health, education and scientific research and so on through so-called corporate social responsibility (CSR) programs. They can be considered as corporate provisions of public goods or voluntary reductions of external costs.[47] As such they may not immediately contribute to their profits or be required by law. In response to social contributions that are costly, however, citizens at large possibly ascribe social recognitions to provider corporations, which would contribute to the accumulation of their *corporate social capital*. To repeat, this could be distinguished from market-specific reputation capital. For example, a tobacco company may enjoy a high reputation among smokers, but its corporate social capital may be low due to its products causing a health hazard (although tobacco companies are known to be big spenders on CSR programs). But then why should business corporations be concerned with their social capital? As Friedman (1970) once forcefully argued, is it not individuals (e.g. individual shareholders in the capacity of citizens) who should contribute to the provision of social benefits and not business corporations whose objective should be maximizing shareholders' values? Who really benefits from CSR?

Those who are committed to the so-called stakeholder-society view of corporate governance may argue that the accumulation of corporate social capital can be regarded as an asset collectively beneficial to the stakeholders of the corporation; for example the employees who can take pride in working for an organization known to have a good social reputation; environmentally conscious citizens who derive satisfaction from owning "green" stocks in the corporation even if they have to give up some dividend income; the embedding community which can expect a sustained social contribution from the corporation; the social entrepreneur having a "warm glow preference" (Baron 2007) for creating a CSR firm even at a high financial cost and so on. Indeed, in this way corporate social capital may function to cement corporate assets: cognitive, financial and societal at large. Let us refer to the holders of the described orientations as the CSR stakeholders.

Although the above stakeholder-oriented view has some merits of its own, there is also a subtle aspect of corporate social capital that may not be completely offensive even to the shareholder-oriented view. If shareholders try to select their portfolios only from stocks of business corporations engaged in CSR, orthodox financial theory tells us that they must perform worse in terms of financial returns, because they restrict the universe from which stocks can be picked. But, interestingly enough, empirical evidence seems to suggest, if not conclusively, a possibility that expenditure on CSR and stock price performance may be correlated (e.g. Dowell, Hart, and Yeung 2000; King and Lennox 2001; Siegal and Vitaliano 2007; Heal 2009).[48] Why should this be? Two simple, but plausible, reasons could be that (1) profitable corporations may be more willing to contribute to costly CSR; and (2) CSR may be adopted as a strategy for enhancing profitability by attracting socially responsible consumers (Baron 2007; McWilliams and Siegal 2001; McWiliams, Siegal and Wright 2006). The first possibility may not be dismissed outright. For example, socially responsible investment (SRI), which now accounts for well over 10 percent of professional managed funds in the USA, are not performing any worse in comparison to other funds, but their portfolios are overweighted by the IT-related stocks which showed relatively better growth from the mid 1990s to the financial crisis of 2008. However, event studies by S. Dasgupta et al. (2001, 2004) found that capital markets reacted to recognition by the media or government of superior (or inferior) environmental performances of corporations in a positively (respectively, negatively) correlated manner, suggesting causation from environmental performance to stock prices. Also, Siegel and Vitaliano (2007) found that, when profits are treated as endogenous (i.e. controlling profits due to the "strategic" CSR), they appear to have no influence on the CSR adoption decision.

The logic of capital pricing involving CSR due to Graff Zivin and Small (2005) and Baron (2007) suggest the following interesting story. Suppose that a contribution of CSR is positively but partially (say, θ%) reflected in the stock value of a corporation. This implies that, for citizens-cum-investors who value the corporate giving more than that proportion, the stock price is virtually discounted. This is because they can contribute to a social cause at less cost to themselves (i.e. $100 - \theta$% less). Therefore, contrary to Friedman's assertion, they are better off by buying the stocks of a CSR firm than making a social contribution as individuals. Therefore, the presence of CSR corporations can increase aggregate social giving. Although the CSR entrepreneurs (and possibly other stakeholders) bear the remaining cost (i.e. $(100 - \theta)$% of corporate giving), they can derive social satisfaction not only from their own contribution but also by expanding the opportunity sets for CSR shareholders by providing an alternative to personal giving. But this does not complete the whole story yet.

Business corporations may also be engaged in the development and commercialization of environmentally-friendly technology that may be appreciated by citizens as a whole but also potentially contribute to its profits: the CSR which is characterized as "strategic."[49] The development can be costly, but its social value may not necessarily be fully appreciated by potential buyers of its products alone. For example, potential buyers of eco-friendly cars may be able to save expenditure on fuel after purchase but may not be willing to bear the full development costs charged in the form of a higher price for the car. Thus, the managerial calculus of market-specific reputation capital alone may not immediately warrant a business corporation pursuing costly technological development and its commercialization. However, as public concern with environmental degradation and the sustainability of energy supplies rises, failure to do so may be damaging to the accumulation of corporate social capital, while investment in environmentally-friendly technology may contribute to its accumulation beyond the immediate profits from car sales. The ascription of corporate social capital made possible by technological contributions to the cause of society would help the corporate organization to cohere and enhance its cognitive and financial abilities to develop further technology.

The attribution of corporate social capital may amplify the value of market-specific reputation, because it may enhance the beliefs of potential buyers of products regarding their user-cost-efficiency, durability, and so on, as well as its symbolic value to them (e.g. environmental "conspicuous" consumption). In other words, corporate social capital may serve as a positive signal (analogous to an advertisement) and contribute to the prospects for long-term profits net of the cost of CRS. Thus, corporate social capital can be complementary to market-specific reputation capital. When *de facto* property rights in global commons are shifting from the corporate sector to the public in general, it becomes even more essential for individual corporations to cope with this substantive institutional change through its own technological potential and social capital accumulation. In this situation, the CSR entrepreneur can be motivated to carry strategic CSR further, beyond the value-maximizing level (Baron 2007).

Corporate CSR activities, pure and strategic combined, can link economic, commons, and social-exchange games between business corporations (and their stakeholders such as CSR entrepreneurs and employees) and concerned citizens. Concerned citizens may be engaged in those games by attributing corporate social capital to CSR corporations, investing in CSR stocks, as well as being potential buyers of the products of CSR corporations. CSR stakeholders bear the costs of corporate social giving in exchange for their own social payoffs. CSR corporations are engaged in these games as social-givers as well

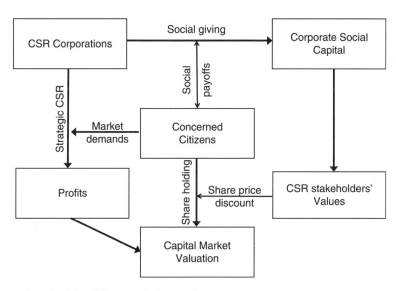

Figure 3.2. Social and business linkages of CSR

as potential developers of profit-making, environmentally friendly technology. For CSR corporations, these activities are complementary as described. As we discussed in Chapter 2, corporations can do more than a mere collection of individuals can do. This can be especially true with regard to the development of environmentally-friendly and renewable energy technology. It requires innovative entrepreneurial initiative, the organization of inter-disciplinary inputs of knowledge and effort, foresight and patience, etc., which may be effectively provided by CSR corporations, both small and large. Thus, if the linkages of games as depicted in Figure 3.2 can indeed evolve, strategies that have not been viable in terms of economic calculations alone may become supportable as societal equilibrium.

Notes

1. For a good overview of the debate, see Roe (2006).
2. For example, see Ghemawat (1989), Milgrom and Roberts (1992), McMillan (2002), Roberts (2004).
3. Although not focusing on business corporations, Gintis (2007, 2009) is engaged in a similar attempt to integrate various disciplines of the behavioral sciences through game theory.
4. Huizinga developed an elaborated argument that an essential property of the social order is nothing but the rules of the game that evolve through history. According to him, even the primitive rituals of savage society do not merely represent the mystical beliefs of the savage overwhelmed by the natural forces imposed on them. Rather they should be interpreted as outcomes of conscious play among the primitive people to create a social order. He argued that "in myth and ritual the great instinctive forces of civilized life have their origin: law and order, commerce and profit, craft and art, poetry, wisdom and science. All are rooted in the primitive soil of play" (Huizinga 1938/1950: 5).
5. See for example, North (1990, 1995), Hurwicz (1993, 1996, 2008), Ostrom and Walker (1994), Aoki (1996, 2001, 2007), Greif (1997, 2006), Williamson (2000), Ostrom (2005, 2007), Hodgson (2006), Greif and Kingston (2008).
6. I also exclude beliefs about what would happen in environments, like a kind of statistical prediction about states of nature.
7. This endogenous–exogenous, dual relationship may be considered as somewhat akin to the Marxian notion of "*Versachlichung* (reification)," literally "making [some idea] into a thing" (from Latin "*res*" meaning "thing"): the phenomenon under which human relationships appear as external material relationships (Marx 1844). In my case, the equilibrium outcome of players' interactions is recognized by them through objectified public representations. Also it is the way Durkheim (1893) explained "social facts" as being produced by

individual actions, but existing as an objective social reality outside the decision parameters of any particular individual action.

8. In terms of their measures of the dispersion of ownership in major corporations (top 20), Japan ranks highly and much closer to the USA and the UK than to Continental European countries (90% in Japan, cf. 80% in the USA, 100% in the UK, 50% in Germany) (La Porta *et al.* 1999, Table II, Panel A). However, It should be noted that, if measures of ownership dispersion were based on 10 smaller listed corporations with market capitalization of at least $500 million at the end of 1995, then Japan would rank somewhere between the UK and the USA on one hand and Continental European countries on the other.

9. There was a major change in the Commercial Code in 2002 only after well-run corporations had substantially transformed their organizational architecture. I discuss this in Section 5.2. See also Gilson and Milhaupt (2005).

10. It may be that this endogeneity (reverse causation) problem was recognized by Shleifer *et al.* and that this is why they introduced the legal origin as an "instrumental variable": the variable which only affects the explanatory variable (in their case, the current legal rules), but no other matters that may affect endogenous variable (in their case, various economic performance indicators). Recently, they admitted however that the use of the legal origin as an instrumental variable was not warranted, but still maintained that they can measure economic consequences of legal origin via various institutional routes besides legal rules (Boter *et al.* 2004; La Porta *et al.* 2008). There are of course such multi-path dependent effects of legal origin. But their estimates in (La Porta *et al.* 1998, 1999) cannot be interpreted as measuring the causal impacts of current legal systems on economic performance. This is particularly so when there are complementarities between legal systems and other institutional factors that are both influenced by legal origin.

11. Incidentally, it is interesting to note that the English word *institution* also originates in the verbal form of the same Latin word, *stature* meaning "establish" (Williams 1976/1983: 168).

12. The following model is a slight modification of the model that Weingast used to inquire into the nature of, and conditions for, democratic control of the government. I use it to identify discrete forms of the political state as multiple equilibria, including the democratic state but not limited to it.

13. The terminology "decision payoff" is due to Kahneman (1994). It is a numerical measure underlying a decision that may not be limited to the hedonistic experience associated with the consumption of a good but may also reflect other motives, say reciprocity, altruism, public mindness, and so on.

14. There may be a case where, through such transfer, the productivity of the transferee improves.

15. This is the case that Weingast (1997) dealt with.

16. This is an instance of subgame perfect equilibrium.

17. As Hayek said, "The ideal of democracy rests on belief that the view which will direct government emerges from an independent and spontaneous process.

It requires therefore the existence of a large sphere independent of majority control in which the opinions of the individuals are formed" (1960: 109).

18. The functionalist notion of institutional complementarities is also questioned by Ahlering and Deakin (2007).

19. Topkis (1978, 1998), Milgrom and Roberts (1990); Aoki (1994b, 2001: ch. 8).

20. I discussed this in Aoki (2001; ch. 13) the ways in which complementary institutional arrangements in post-World War II Japan, composed of the S-mode organizational architecture (cf. Section 2.4.3)), the main bank system, lifetime employment system and a form of correlated political state that I termed "bureau-pluralism" (or the "bureaucracy-mediated, pluralistic bargain state" in this book) evolved partly as a result of the "unintended consequences" of social engineering by the military government during the Second World War and the Occupation Force in the period after the War.

21. In the context of a theoretical and empirical comparison between the majority voting system and the proportional representation system, Pagano and Volpin (2005) submit that the most likely interest-group alignments in the former are those that favor a combination of financial market and labor market liberalization.

22. This combination may be considered as corresponding to what North, Wallis, and Weingast (2009) referred to as the "Open Access Orders:" the social orders characterized by open access to the competitive political process and third-party enforced corporate system. They argue that the transition from what they call the natural state to the modern social orders is essentially characterized as the establishment of this order. The authors (2009: 260–2) classify organizations into two classes: adherent and contractual. The former is said to be voluntarily supportable, while the latter utilizes third party enforcement. However, one may wonder whether the competitive political process and the third-party enforced corporate organizations represent only one viable combination in the modern society and whether the causation is from the polity to the corporate system as they suggest. I would rather aim to explain the essentially self-organizing and self-governing nature of modern business corporations first and then go on to consider how its particular species (the H-mode) and the competitive political process become mutually complementary among the possible many as discussed below.

23. In reality, industry-level bargaining outcome may be supplemented by the payment of a premium at the individual corporate level. It may be regarded as a part of a package of agreements on workers' in-house training, participation in the use-control rights over PHA and associated cognition-sharing between MCA and WCA and so on. Such was indeed the case in Germany in the past, but the percentage of firms doing so and the premium over the going rate have tended to decline since the latter half of the 1990s, while less competitive corporations began to drop out of the industry-level agreements (e.g. Thelen and Kume 2006; Streeck 2009). I will discuss the implications of this in the last chapter.

24. Of course, in reality many historical factors have been involved in the co-evolution of codetermination and corporatism in Germany, some even dating

back to the time of Bismarck's design of a compulsory public health insurance system and a social securities system with equal representation for workers and employers. The post-Second World War institutionalization of industrial bargaining in the coal and steel industries in the British occupied Ruhr region was one important factor. See a series of works by Streeck (1992, 1997, 2009), Lehmbruch (1999) and Jackson (2005) as well as Aoki (2001: 163–5) for historical discussion.

25. An excellent treatise on this is Teranishi (1997).

26. This model is analyzed in Aoki (2001: 187–91). It is meant to model some aspects of the development process observed in Korea and Taiwan in the 1970s and early 1980s. See also Bardhan (2005) chapter 1 for a discussion of the East Asian developmental state from the perspective of contingent transfer.

27. This kind of evolutionary reasoning may provide food for thought on the possible evolutionary path of the Chinese state. The political-economic pattern of China's development in the last three decades can be characterized as having features of the developmental state, although the government's assistance to industrial development was not limited to the traditional state-owned enterprise sector. A portion of development finance was sourced in the form of direct foreign investment, yet domestic resource transfer from the agriculture sector was crucial for industrial development, including the flourishing of self-financed township and village enterprises during the early transition phase (Wu 2005). However, there are increasing signs of a need for paradigm change in industrial and social development patterns as represented by growing public concern and dissatisfaction with income inequalities and environmental degradation. The government is gradually shifting its stance to respond to such needs, although keeping a firm authoritarian grip, which may result, as one possibility, in a gradual transition to a type of bureaucracy-mediated state under one-party rule. It appears to be rather simplistic to limit the possibility of political reform in China to an immediate and direct transition to the competitive electoral representative state of an American type.

28. There are exceptions to this. Ostrom (2005) came to endogenize norms as evolving as a response to the "lawless state of nature" reminiscent of the veil of ignorance à la Rawls. For other treatments along the same lines as this (e.g. Heath 2001, 2008; Binmore 2005), see the discussion in the introductory section of the next chapter.

29. Kandori (1992) posited that past cheaters carry visible signs on their foreheads when they enter new trades.

30. For a game-theoretic approach to social norms, see Ullmann-Margalit (1977), Bicchieri (2006). A novel game-theoretic approach to social norms is proposed by Gintis (2009) who identifies them with correlated equilibria. A correlated equilibrium specifies a single probability distribution over the states of play for which every player can maximize his or her own payoffs. Thus, if there is an external device to indicate what is to be a state, every player is better off by following that instruction, provided that they have reason to believe that

others also follow. He identifies a social norm with such a device and regards the equilibrium probability distribution to be provide by the culture-gene co-evolution process.

31. See for example Dasgupta and Serageldin (2000), particularly the concluding chapter by Dasgupta (2000).

32. The notion of "unspecified obligations of reciprocity" as a distinctive character-istic of social-exchanges was emphasized by Blau (1964/1986).

33. By emphasizing impacts on relational others, a speech act in the social-exchange domain may be considered as akin to the "perlocutionary act" conceptualized by the linguistic philosopher Austin (1962).

34. Rabin (1993) assumes that if an agent is treated by another unkindly and does not do anything in return, he leaves the situation bitter, but can mitigate the loss partly by taking revenge.

35. The possibility of building a bridge between measuring economic and social rewards is suggested by functional magnetic resonance imaging (fMRI) experi-ments by Izuma, Saito and Sadato (2008). They found that the acquisition of one's good reputation activates rewards-related brain areas, notably the stria-tum, and they partially overlapped with the areas related to monetary rewards. See Fehr and Camerer (2007) for a similar evidence.

36. Coleman (1988, 1990) is one of the first who developed the notion of social capital in the framework of rational choice sociology. Coleman's starting analogy of social capital with "credit slip" is close to what I conceptualized in the text (Coleman 1988: 20). He also repeatedly refers to social capital as "a particular kind of resource available to an actor" (1988: 16). Thus he appears to subscribe to an individual notion of social capital at the micro-level. However, by making "the micro-to-macro transitions," his examples and applications come to include such collective notions as "norms," "study circles" of student radicals, safety in urban dwelling environments, trust among merchants and so on.

37. There are diverse notions of social capital as well as criticisms of them in the literature (e.g. see Dasgupta and Serageldin (2000) for various conceptualiza-tions of social capital and the debates surrounding them). For example, Arrow "urged abandonment of the metaphor of the capital and the term 'social capi-tal'" (Arrow 2000: 3). While admitting the plausibility of the hypothesis that social network could affect economic performance, he pointed out that "the reward for social interactions is 'intrinsic' and lacked the important property of capital as saved for future benefit at deliberate sacrifice today" (*ibid.:* 4). Also Solow asks "Just what is social capital a stock of? . . . What are those past invest-ments in social capital?" Skeptical of any satisfactory answer forthcoming, he "doubts that 'social capital' is the right concept to use in discussing whatever it is we are discussing – the behavioral patterns I mentioned earlier, for instance" (Solow 1999: 7).

   One well-cited notion of social capital is due to Putnam (1993). In my view, it is a somewhat mystical entity that "comes into being not through individual intentional action, but is said to be 'inherited' with its origins hidden in the mist of the past." The existing stock cannot therefore be individually owned. A collectivist notion of social capital is articulated by Hayami (2006) as "the structure of informal social relationships conducive to developing cooperation among economic actors with the effects of increasing social product."

38. Glaeser, Laibson and Sacerdore (2002) adopted an individual approach to social capital, in which the interactive aspect of its accumulation among the agents is captured as complementarities between its individual stock on one hand and its aggregate per-capita stock on the other. They estimated impacts of individual characteristics, such as age, physical mobility, level of human capital, on the level of individual social capital.

39. Readers may recognize certain parallels between my concept of the domain of social-exchange game and Bourdieu's concept of "fields of social relations" in his reflexive sociology, as well as between my and his concepts of individual's social capital (1986). Bourdieu even alluded to the game nature of the fields (Bourdieu and Wacquant 1992: 98–101). However, Bourdieu's individual social capital is regarded as an instrument of dominance over others, while mine is not necessarily limited in this way.

40. In order for psychological equilibrium *à la* Geanakoplos *et al.* (1989) to exist, they recognized that all higher order beliefs must match actual behavior. To see how such conditions can be approximated, we need a more elaborate theoretical setting. I will discuss this in the next chapter.

41. Such belief systems as prescriptions for action choices may be considered as analogous to what some sociologists conceptualized as "socially-constructed-realities" (Berger and Luckmann 1966), "taken-for-grantedness" (Zucker 1977; DiMaggio and Powell 1983, 1991), "schemata" (Fiske and Pavelchak 1986), "scripts" (Schank and Abelson 1977) and so on.

42. There is now a debate among experimental economists about why experimental subjects often keep promises in trust games even though it is not individually rational in the traditional sense. Charness and Dufwenberg (2006) reported that their experimental results suggest guilt-aversion to be a primary motive, where-as Vanberg (2008) and others claim that their results demonstrate that people have a preference for promise keeping per se (the so-called commitment-based explanation). However, based on reasoning in the text, I suspect that it may be difficult to discriminate the two explanations in the context of one-shot games.

43. It is a correlated equilibrium in which the prescribed strategies are played with probability one. It also constitutes a sub-game perfect equilibrium of linked game under the said condition. See Aoki (2001: ch. 2.1) and note 30 above.

44. I derive the parable from historical experiences of a rural community of small landholding peasants during the Edo period in Japan where the collective management of the irrigation system contributed to the rise of agricultural productivity. The peasants in the community were collectively responsible for tax obligations to the Han government, but otherwise they were relatively

egalitarian, autonomous holders of paddies scattered along the collective irrigation system. Because of geographical constraint of water supply utilizing natural land slope and the structure of scattered landholdings, the exclusion of a particular peasant family from the use of the irrigation system was rather difficult and they relied on the practice of ostracizing deviants, known as *mura-hachibu* (exclusion from cooperative, mutual community exchanges except in cases of fire and death. See Aoki (2001: ch. 2.1)).

45. An inductive-game model due to Kaneko and Matsui (1999) derive such phenomena as stigma and social discrimination as endogenous outcomes of agents' inductive inferences from their own experiences (the playing of the game) rather than as consequences of distorted preferences.

46. Information brokerage in the network is the focus of social capital theory by Burt (2005). Also see Owen-Smith and Powell (2004) for evidence of punishment on firms' negative brokerage efforts.

47. CSR may include corporate actions aiming at avoiding distributional conflicts, but I limit my immediate concern to cases of public goods/external costs.

48. For a good survey on this and discussion of related subject see Heal (2005).

49. In my game-theoretic framework, all corporate activities including the accumulation of corporate social capital (the "pure CSR" as opposed to "strategic" CSR) are strategic.

4

The Evolution of the Rules of the Societal Games

4.1 Contested issues in institutional analysis

The last two chapters discussed the way that business corporations cognize, decide, and act as a team; interact with society at large beyond their own specific markets; and govern themselves as well as play politics within the embedding frame of public governance. The basic patterns of these interactions were captured as equilibrium states of play of societal games (Section 3.2). The equilibrium approach can shed light on the nature of some basic attributes of institutions such as diversity (multiplicity of equilibrium), endurance, mutual coherence (linked games and strategic complementarities), and so on. Chapter 2 discussed the fact that, once such patterns are established within the organizational field and a business corporation, its members can offload some of their individual cognitive burdens onto them. By taking them for granted and following them automatically as the rules of the organization game—or routines—they can use their scarce cognitive assets in a more focused way. In other words, those rules may be regarded as extended cognitive resources that the members of business corporations create together and share. Likewise, the various societal rules facing business corporations may also be regarded as extended cognitive resources of business corporations that they created together with other social entities. But, how can equilibrium arise in the societal games first of all?

A moment of reflection undoubtedly suggests, however, that the societal games that business corporations play are actually never in static equilibrium. They are in constant flux. Then, how much do individual agents, including business corporations, need to know to cognize a certain stable pattern of the moving states of play? Further, even the basic patterns of the states of play change over time. They may sometimes change drastically in a short period of time, but more often they evolve gradually. For example, we observed a few decades ago that there were more or less national properties of corporate governance (CG) that fit particular modes of organizational architecture (OA) as well as other national social and political institutions. However, as will be demonstrated in the next chapter, the landscape of corporate economy has been changing on a global scale over those decades under the pressure of global market integration and as a result of the accumulation of various cognitive assets. Almost certainly, it will change further, triggered by the pressure of the economic turmoil of the late 2000s, although the direction of future change is not yet known for sure.

How do the rules of societal games change? Is it that business corporations react individually to the emergent economic and technological exigencies and that the states of play accordingly evolve as the aggregation of their individual choices? Or does something more than that need to be involved? To what extent can the rules of societal games be designed and changed by statutory laws, international agreements and so on? Do informal social norms, meanings, and values precede and constrain the "rational" choice of corporate behavior?

The questions posed above have often incited opposing answers in the past, depending on the traditional divide of disciplines into economics, sociology, jurisprudence, and so on, as well as differences in methodological orientations between methodological individualism vs. holism, rational choice vs. evolutionary theory, etc. Recently some important progress has been made in respect of these questions, however, across such diverse fields as epistemic game theory, cognitive and neuro sciences, analytical and phenomenological philosophy, and so on. This recent progress suggests that the above mentioned disciplinary and methodological divides may not be productive for a basic understanding of the nature of the change in the rules of societal games or institutions. This chapter, therefore, begins with a succinct overview of contested issues in institutional theory, particularly the diverse meanings attached to institutions (and the rules of the game) by scholars, to see how we can learn, or derive an agenda for further inquiries from various theoretical approaches (Section 4.1). Section 4.2 discusses how the recent progress in cross-disciplinary study can suggest a coherent answer to these contested issues. Finally, based on these discussions, Section 4.3 presents a simple conceptual framework for institutional evolution, to be applied in the final chapter for an understanding of the ongoing evolution of the corporate landscape. This chapter may appear to deal with rather abstract, academic subject areas, but I submit that it has significant bearings on the development of the trans-disciplinary approach to institutions at the generic, comparative, and substantive levels, as well as being applicable to policy level issues (However, those readers who regard Section 4.2 too formal may wish to skip it. The essence of the argument was heuristically stated in Chapter 3, Section 3.2).

4.1.1 *Pre-play design vs. spontaneous order*

In a seminal book on New Institutional Economics, North (1990) identified institutions with formal rules (such as constitutions, property rights law, contracts, regulations, and the like) and informal rules (like social norms). North considers that "(while) the formal institutions may be altered by fiat, the informal institutions are not amenable to deliberate short-run change" (2005: 157). Likewise, in his early writing, the philosopher Rawls (1955) distinguished two concepts of rules: "the rules of a practice" defining "offices, moves and offenses" prior to any motion, on one hand, and maxims and "rules of thumb" on the other that are "summaries of experiences of generations." Rawls invoked an analogy of the former type of rule with the rules of baseball: if a batter in the box inquires of the umpire whether he is allowed to be at the bat even after three calls of strikes and if such a deal is negotiable, the game cannot be played fairly and with interest. This example makes the distinction between the two types of rules rather stark in terms of pre-play design against the spontaneous nature of informal rules. But are they really distinct species? If so, how are the formal rules designed and under what rules?

North (1990, 1995, 2005) argued that the formal rules of (economic) games are determined in political markets. The cumulative play of economic games, together with parametric changes in their environments (such as technology) represented by price changes, generate demands for a change in the rules of the economic games, to which political entrepreneurs (elites) will respond by creating new rules for the economic games. It is as simple as that, if it is only the formal rules for the economic-exchange domain that we are concerned with. But how about the rules for the rule-making mechanism in the political exchange domain? One obvious way to respond to this question may be to envision a hierarchy of rule-making mechanisms. For example, Ostrom (2005: 58–64) envisages that the "operational" situations of games are embedded in "collective-choice" situations; the latter in "constitutional" situations; the last in "meta-constitutional" situations as a nested structure. This approach appears to raise the dilemma of infinite regress, however: rule-making calls for rule-making for rule-making and so on ad infinitum. How can we sever such a potentially infinite sequence realistically at one point?

A theoretical solution to the infinite regress problem may be to inquire into the possibility of meta-rules satisfying some socially agreeable properties that can design the rules of societal games once and for all. As is well-known, it was Hurwicz who pioneered such an approach. He considered the possibility of designing the rules of the game ("mechanisms" in his terminology) as composed of rules for message-exchanges and decision-making among individual agents to achieve some socially given goals (e.g. a Pareto-efficient allocation). He considered it imperative that, in order to avoid the great sin of centralized planning under a dictatorship, mechanisms be designed in such a way that implied rules are not imposed on individual agents against their private motivations.[1] However, then, agents may be motivated to misrepresent their true preferences, intentions, and beliefs in designed mechanisms, if they expect to benefit themselves by doing so. Therefore, he inquired whether any mechanism can be designed to implement a socially desirable goal as a self-policing Nash equilibrium under the requirement of "privacy-preserving:" that is, the condition under which individual agents reveal their true intentions only when these are consistent with their hidden preferences (Hurwicz 1973, 2008; Hurwicz and Reiter 2006).[2] He considered that such a design possibility cannot be taken for granted. In fact, he surprised even the smartest contemporary economists by proving a theorem that even in a simple model of a two-person Walrasian price mechanism, it can always be possible for the selfish agents to misrepresent their preferences from own egoistic calculations, but as a result fail to achieve together a Pareto-efficient allocation (Hurwicz 1972).[3] This was an alarming warning about the difficulty of making social engineering compatible with efficiency, individual rationality, and privacy at the same time in situations where cognition is indeed completely individuated. Later the mechanism design theory found some conditions for social choice to make such compatibility possible.[4] It has found a useful application in solving specific design problems where the criteria for social choice are rather agreeable, such as in the domains of auctions and matching (e.g. between public schools and applicants; exchanges of donor-kidneys without payment to ensure donor–patient combinations are biologically compatible; the matching of residences for new doctors and hospitals).[5]

Notwithstanding of such progress, we may not take the implementation of designed rules for granted particularly when people's preferences diverge or are in conflict. If the rules of the game are understood as a prescribed set of "legal" strategies for players and its physical consequences, there can be the possibility for someone to undertake "illegal" strategies. Then, guardians for the prescribed rules are needed. But then there can be the possibility that the guardians themselves are not to be trusted. "But who will guard the guardians?", which was the theme of a Nobel Prize Lecture by Hurwicz (Hurwicz 2008). Although the question may appear to invoke another problem of infinite regress, Hurwicz seemed to be more optimistic at this stage of his life. For one thing, he invoked the idea of the "intervenors" which he introduced earlier in his relatively unknown paper (Hurwicz 1993: 63–4). He argued that these players are those who desire the prescribed rules to be implemented and at the same time have the assets to prevail in the game. They may be "an individual, an organization, a social class or even an unorganized human mass." Judges and other public officials could be first-level guardians. If the latter hold elective offices and if they do not properly perform their duties, citizens who are voters may function as top-level guardians who have an incentive and the power to "intervene" by throwing them out of office. This argument is reminiscent of the nature of the "democratic state" derived as one equilibrium of the generic model of the political exchange game discussed in Chapter 3, Section 3.3.2. We can interpret this as a case in which a democratic political institution itself can function as an ultimate enforcer of the rules applied in other domains.

This suggests more generally the need to inquire into strategic interactions across various domains, say between the political-exchange domain and the economic-exchange domain. For example, business corporations and their members may well be players in the political game who demand rule-changes that suit them. Then the rule-making mechanism in the political domain itself, that is, a political institution, not just its consequence (e.g. policy, statutory laws), may well be affected by ways in which business corporations form their own interests, exercise powers to affect government behaviors and beliefs, and so on. The causation may not run only from the polity to the economy, but may be reciprocal, in terms of institutional building. We have already discussed this possibility in Chapter 3, Section 3.3. North himself points out that "changing just one institution in an attempt to get the desired performance is always incomplete and sometimes a counter-productive activity" (2005: 157).

If such interactive processes across domains are the important driving forces of potential institutional evolution, the same may be said of between formal and informal rules. By using a sporting analogy, opposite to Rawls', McMillan made a good point for the evolutionary argument: he pointed out that folk football originally evolved in medieval European towns as rough games in which two separate groups tried to get the ball, a stuffed pig's bladder, to the opponents' end of the field. The numbers of players in each team were not rigorously specified and the rules evolved spontaneously and were followed, sometimes even without a formal referee. It was not unusual for the rules prevailing in one village to differ from those in neighboring villages. However, after a few hundred years of play, these folk rules were suddenly replaced by formal rules set by a top-down method. He commented: "A typical market is born and grows like football" (McMillan 2002: p.13). This analogy also suggests that, practically as well as theoretically, only one way of coping with the inevitable dilemma of infinite regress seems to regress into the historical past rather than onto a higher level of abstraction on the logical dimension (such as the device of the meta-game). From such a perspective the existing rules of the societal game may be regarded as evolving over time through the process of competition, emulation, selection, mutation and so on in various domains of societal games. Even the designed rules are based on experiences.[6] As is well known, such an evolutionary view of the rules of societal games can be traced back to Hume (1739/1992), who was followed by contemporary writers such as Sugden (1986), Young (1993, 1998), Binmore (1994, 1998, 2005), Thelen (1999, 2004), and Bowles (2005), among others.

4.1.2 Deontic constraints vs. rational choices

Recently the philosopher Searle (2005) argued in his essay on institutions directed to the economist audience that "deontic power" prescribing peoples' duties, rights, obligations, etc. must precede an individual's desire-oriented choices. Also Heath (2001, 2008), a philosopher with a game-theoretic background, argued that instrumental choices by self-regarding, consequence-oriented agents in an economic exchange game cannot yield a definite societal outcome and need to be exogenously constrained by deontic considerations. Such views are remindful of the famous Kantian dichotomy between categorical imperative and hypothetical imperative. The former prescribes what you ought to do regardless of what your personal objective may be, while the latter tells you what you should do if your objectives are given.[7] Kant imagined "an ideal legislator in the kingdom of ends" as a theoretical device for characterizing the nature of deontic values.

As discussed in Chapter 3, last Section 3.4, ever since North (1990) emphasized the importance and relevance of informal rules as one of the important determinants of economic performance, social scientists have been increasingly interested in integrating this notion into economic analysis. For example, Ostrom (2005) argued that the so-called "social dilemma" (equivalent to Harding's tragedy of the commons problem) is resolvable, among other ways, by an individual internalization of norms. In her theoretical setting, norms are treated as exogenous parameters of agents' preference functions, although they are assumed to be evolving as a response to the fictitious "state of nature" without formal law. Likewise, Heath (2001: 135–45) introduced the individual utility function composed of a desire-based ranking of actions and categorical preferences (normative reason) for actions. The latter are then explained as compromised solutions of non-strategic moral discourses among people in a manner reminiscent of the Kantian device. He goes on to suggest further that the essence of such compromises may be characterized as a Nash solution to the bargaining game in the domain of public discourse. Roughly speaking, this solution satisfies the requirement of fairness, efficiency, and stability so that it may become self-enforcing. However, the deontic values are still considered by him as constraints on instrumental choices.[8] There are neither feedbacks nor co-evolutionary links between the domain of rational choices and that of public-discourse. However, we discussed in the last chapter the possibility that social norms and economic choices may co-evolve closely.

In an attempt to endogenize deontic values, the game-theorist-cum-philosopher Binmore (1994, 1998, 2005) elaborated the idea of the original states that have popped up in the literature in various forms since Kant. He used it as a basis for synthesizing evolutionary and rationalist interpretations of the nature of "social contracts." He posits that the device of the original state by Rawls (1971) provides a hypothetical standpoint for considering the deep structure of human fairness norms. In this state, members of a society are placed under a veil of ignorance in which their positions in society are supposed to be unknown and to be determined by a lottery, yet they have to agree on social contracts prior to the assignments of particular social positions. He considers that this device conforms to the deep structure of fairness norms that people embody through the long history of gene-culture co-evolution and actually use every day. However, its specific form can vary, conditional on the culture as common knowledge.

Binmore posits that agents enter the original position with "empathetic preferences" that place weights on utility units of various positions in society and they are then engaged in hypothetical bargaining to reach social contracts. As everyone's allotment to a specific position is unknown at this point, a stable solution may only be obtained when individuals' empathetic preferences become identical with each other's. However, the symmetry of empathetic preferences does not imply that equal weights are given to all social positions and that weights are the same over time and across societies. They are determined by a historical, cultural process generating common knowledge. A fictitious Nash bargaining solution on the utility possibility set depicted by symmetric empathetic preferences is assumed to dictate social contracts that satisfy an agreeable sense of fairness.[9] Readers may recall that my approach to the organizational frame in Chapter 2, Section 2.5 adopts the use of Nash bargaining game theory as a way to synthesize deontic, rational, and historical factors in the making of corporate-organizational rules.

4.1.3 *Endogenous vs. exogenous views of the societal rules*

One possible way to theoretically resolve the infinite regress dilemma could be, albeit incompletely, to seek the origin of the rules of the game within the very same game. Namely, the rules of a game may be identified with salient properties of recursive states of play such that every player takes them for granted and believes it beneficial to adapt to them in his or her choice. The action choices of the agents based on these beliefs in turn confirm and reproduce them. The self-sustaining outcomes of the recursive process from actions to beliefs and from beliefs to actions (as depicted in Figure 3.1) can be regarded as an equilibrium state of play of the game. A heuristic conceptualization of the rules of societal games along this line was given, and some of its basic attributes mentioned, in Chapter 3, Section 3.2. In the last two decades or so various authors have explored this approach using varied concepts of equilibrium.[10] The endogenous view of the societal rules (institutions) may be contrasted with the concept of the rules of the game as externally-designed and exogenously given to the players discussed above, although we subsequently discuss possible relationships between the two.[11]

Of course even the equilibrium approach cannot resolve the dilemma completely, because in any modeling of a game it is inevitable that some human constructs will be included a priori (Field 1981). For example, the equilibrium approach to comparative organization in Chapter 2, Section 2.4 started with the premise that there can be such entities as corporations composed of investors, management and workers, and asked what institutional forms of associational cognition and its governance are possible for them. The equilibrium approach to the political state in Chapter 3, Section 3.3 assumed the existence of the government and examined what kinds of its relationships with private agents are stable and self-governing. Those analyses were not able, or intended, to explain endogenously why corporations are there (although this was partially discussed in chapter 1), why governments are there. They were given as primitive rules of the generic, rule-making games, albeit devoid of any concrete institutional forms prior to the analyses. Societal rules are then taken as endogenously generated and self-sustained in these games. Thus an equilibrium approach to societal rules may be characterized as the quasi-endogenous view of institutions. But, in spite of this limit (or, shall I say, because of it), there are some merits to this approach.

First, as seen in the last two chapters, for a model of reasonably limited specification there can be multiple equilibria. The existence of multiple equilibria was considered troublesome for classical game theorists, because it was interpreted as implying that the theory lacks predictive power. However, their research agenda, known as refinement, to specify the equilibrium concept further so as to narrow down all the possible equilibria to a unique one has now been considered futile. But the possibility of multiple equilibria is not troublesome for the quasi-endogenous view of institutions, as it implies the possibility of a variation of potential institutional arrangements, even inefficient ones. It only implies that the game-theoretic approach cannot be complete by itself, because selection from the possible many has to be explained by other reasoning, possibly historical (Greif 2006).

Second, the equilibrium approach can, as I showed in the last two chapters, allow us to deal analytically with possible interdependencies and mutual fit of the rules of games across different domains. Particular types of corporate cognitive-governance structure (OA–CG combination) are associated with appropriate social norms and political governance and vice versa. It anticipates, therefore, that there is no centralized mechanism of rule-setting: neither a theoretical meta-game nor a practical rule-setting game (such as political markets *à la* North). However, if everything depends on everything else, then there must be a way to escape from a circular argument. As suggested already, this must be sought in the historical past, that is, in the evolutionary process.

4.1.4 *Regularity of agents' actions vs. societal cognitive categories*

There are also some more subtle points to the equilibrium approach that have not been made explicit so far. In approaching institutional and/or social structures there have been two opposing viewpoints in the social sciences and the humanities: One is to regard them as systems of action regularity, while the other regards them in terms of shared cognitive categories. Traditional views of institutions in economics may be said to have leaned toward the former, including those who regarded customs simply as behavioral patterns. Transaction cost economics regards inter-agent transactions as the unit of institutional analysis (Williamson 1975, 1996). Even a pioneer of the equilibrium view of institutions, Schotter, defined institutions as "a regularity in social behavior that is agreed to by all members of societies, specifies behavior in specific recurrent situations, and is either self-policed or policed by some external authority" (1981: 11). In sociology as well, such formidable writers as Max Weber and Talcott Parsons may be thought of as basically subscribed to the action-oriented approach. Weber defined sociology as the discipline to understand the meanings deeply underlying people's actions, although it was not clear whether the word "meaning" refers to the scholars' objective interpretation of social actions or the actors' own subjective intentions (Seiyama 1995). Parsons posited that the unit of analysis of the social system ought to be actions.

In contrast to this action-oriented view, there are varieties of thought that place the primacy of the analysis of institutions, and accordingly that of their nature, on cognitive categories such as symbols, beliefs, or social meanings attached to certain systems of actions as rituals. Such an approach is typically found in anthropological, sociological, ethnomethodological, and phenomenological studies of social interactions. Weber may be included in this school of thought if the "meaning" in his word refers to collective one. In game theory too, the epistemic game theory interprets mixed strategy equilibrium as equilibrium systems of beliefs rather than that of randomly selected actions (Aumann and Brandenburger 1995). Greif in his comprehensive treatise on institutions gave a definition of institutions as "a system of rules, beliefs, norms, and organizations that together generate a regularity of (social) behavior" (2006: 30). Clearly the primacy of cognitive categories over actions is recognized.

Actually these seemingly contrasting views may not be opposing, but may be complementary. Certainly, the regularity of behavior, or the stable state of recursive play of the game, may be mediated by publicly cognized rules and norms, shared beliefs, and so on. But how are such cognitive categories created first of all and then sustained as credible, meaningful, and forceful over time? The regularity of behavior, or the stable state of recursive play of the game, must be generating and confirming the validity of the cognitive categories. For example, Chapter 3, Section 3.4 discussed a process by which social norms may be generated and supported by the regularity of the behavior of agents. Thus, an equilibrium pattern of players' actions is sustained by a corresponding belief of the players, while the former reproduces and reconfirms the latter in the societal games when played recursively. Accordingly, "institutions are simultaneously both objective structures 'out there' and subjective springs of human agency 'in the human head'" (Hodgson 2006: 8).

However, an important question remains: How is the circular process of actions–beliefs initiated to endogenously change the rules of societal games? Can institutional change be understood only as a quantum jump from one equilibrium to another? The next section begins to consider this question by first asking under what conditions of behavioral belief does stable equilibrium become possible and what does it look like. This consideration, although abstract and apparently devoid of immediate relevance to the theme of this book, hopefully provides a key to identify the basic factors that play major roles in the process of institutional evolution and, more specifically, the nature of the evolving corporate landscape.

4.1.5 Toward a three-level approach

As a way of concluding this simple overview of various approaches, let me summarize a few observations that have been made in order to clarify the methodological agenda facing us.

1. There is no way to escape from the dilemma of infinite regress in trying to locate the primary source of the rules of societal games. As the existence of the ultimate meta-game for rule-making is not possible, it appears to be reasonable to regress into history in search of the successive sources of the societal rules. In other words, it seems reasonable to assume that the rules of the societal games evolve historically. New rules evolve out of existing rules as common knowledge, which implies a path-dependent nature of institutional change.
2. The failure of the primary domain of rule-setting domain to exist also implies that the rules of societal games in various domains—organizational, economic, political, social, and others—are mutually interrelated and linked. There is no domain that can be singled out as primary.
3. In order to deal analytically with the self-enforcing property of the rules of games in various domains, as well as their interrelated properties, an equilibrium approach using generic, rule-making games may provide an insight. However, the existence of an equilibrium play of societal games appears to require certain conditions. What are they?

4. Thus, a *three-level* approach to institutions may be needed. At the basic, ontological level, the generic conditions that allow the equilibrium rules of societal games to exist are explored to clarify the role of history, the relationships between individual choices and social categories, and the relationships between physical behaviors and cognitions in institutional evolution (this agenda is to be followed in the next section). Then, at the intermediate (comparative and historical) level, substantive forms of the rules of societal games are to be identified as multiple equilibria of rule-generating games, and patterns of their interrelationships across domains are to be explored synchronically across countries, as well as diachronically over time (this was done to some extent in the previous two chapters). Finally, at the empirical and policy level, the concrete process of rule evolution will be analyzed using context-specific game models, or some formal rules may be designed and proposed with the aim of mediating a rule-change so that the societal game can be played in a manner acceptable to society. But this needs to be done with an understanding gained from analyses of the preceding two background levels.

4.2 The societal rules as shared cognitive frames

4.2.1 *Shared beliefs via institutions*

In Chapter 3, Section 3.2 I presented an informal, narrative description of the process by which the societal rules would emerge as common knowledge/beliefs. In this section I provide a more formal knowledge-theoretic definition of common knowledge/beliefs and some important theoretical conditions for them to arise in the context of the societal game. It may appear too abstract at first sight, but it turns out to be of great relevance to institutional analysis.

A foundational discussion of how equilibrium (coordination) could be possible was given in the seminal work of the philosopher David Lewis (1969). He made the point that, to play a game, each player needs to reason what the other players are likely to do, which depends on what others expect him or her to do, but others' expectations also depend on how they conjecture about what he or she would conjecture about them to do and so on ad infinitum. What Lewis himself was really concerned with was the problem of how this desideratum can be resolved in practice in society.[12] Likewise, our problem is: when individual agents do not know, cannot know, or even need not know others' every action in detail, but act on expectations, how much do agents need to know/expect in common and in what way? What is required for a societal order to arise as convergent expectations among the players and how is it recursively sustained? These are the issues that I would like to discuss in this Section in a manner relevant to institutional analysis.

Suppose that a profile of strategic choices by all the players in the societal game defines a state of play and that its objective consequences relevant to agents' payoffs are completely describable by it (in other words, the possible uncertain impacts of "natural" environments on consequences beyond the control of the players are assumed away). Yet, agents may not be able to cognize, or may not even be interested in knowing, every detail of the possible states of play. Agents' cognitive competence may be imperfect, so they may not be able to distinguish one state from some other states, or a distinction among certain states may be irrelevant to an agent to the extent that these consequences are not distinguishable from his or her own subjective point of evaluation. Then the extent to which each agent is interested in knowing and can know would vary from one agent to another.

So let us consider the set of all possible states of play (which are perfectly known only to outside observers) denoted by A and imagine that the knowledge potentials of each agent in the game can be represented by partitioning of the set A in the following way: if some state a in the set A occurs (or will occur with some choice of his/her own), then he or she only knows the state is in the subset $P(a)$ of A which is called his/her information set at a. Namely, he or she regards states belonging to this subset as if they are the same state. (However, we assume that each player can know his/her own choice precisely.) Suppose that any possible state of play is in some information set of each agent and there is no overlapping among his or her information sets. Thus, an agent's information sets partition the set of the states of play completely. If some agent's information sets are distinguished only by his or her actions, it means he or she cannot know anything about the state of play except for his or her own choice.

As said, there are differences among agents in society as regards how the set of possible states of play are partitioned. Over a certain range of states of play, partitions might be finer for some agents than others, while over other ranges they could be coarser. In other words, these agents are more informative for the former range of states, but less so for the latter. Such differentials could be due to differences in agents' cognitive capacity, relevancy of states to individual preferences, agents' cognitive environments, and so on.[13] Given cognitive differences, when a state of play a occurs, take the

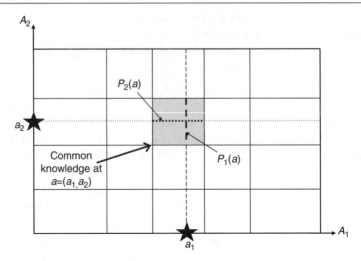

Figure 4.1. Common knowledge of the state of play *à la* Aumann

smallest set of states of play that includes the information sets of all the agents at *a*. This smallest set is technically called the meet of the information sets of all the players at *a*. This set (and any set that includes this set) constitutes common knowledge at *a* according to Aumann (1976).[14] It represents an event that every agent in the game, even the least informed, knows about it happening when the state of play is *a*.[15] However, how do other agents know that he knows it? How does he know that others also know this and so on? Somewhat surprisingly, Aumann's definition is claimed to be logically equivalent to the definition of common knowledge *à la* Lewis involving the infinite hierarchy of reasoning.[16]

Aumann's definition of common knowledge is certainly transparent and logically clear. But without a hidden assumption the meet of all the agents' information sets that contain the actual state of play by itself represents nothing more than the mutual knowledge that all the players know. But in order for every player to know that every other also knows it and so on, he or she must know how the others partition the set of states of play. Such an assumption may be innocuous, if possible states are only defined by physical, objective phenomena potentially accessible (with some public information) to every agent (thus there is no game!) or the game is played by a small number of agents who know each other well and mutually use a very limited number of publicly knowable choices.[17] If possible states are defined by the actions and/or the beliefs of agents, some of which can be more or less private or even only in their minds, then the assumption should be made explicit, and further it should be clarified why it is reasonable to make such an assumption or under what conditions it is likely to hold. Otherwise, Aumann's definition is on the same level of practical difficulty as the Lewisian infinite hierarchy of inferences. How can every agent in large societal game know others' informational partitions (knowledge potentials), even if incomplete?

A solution to the above question is to go back to the original, somewhat "overlooked" (Cubbit and Sugden 2003) reasoning of Lewis.[18] His analysis was actually about shared belief rather than common knowledge and his inquiry was intended to clarify the crucial roles of the common background information and inductive standards that the agents apply in reaching shared belief. His arguments can be summarized as follows. Suppose that:

1. there is some proposition P^* at some state of play a such that every agent in society has reason to believe that P^* holds;
2. P^* indicates to every agent that every other also has reason to believe that P^* holds;
3. every agent infers from P^* that societal states are in E.

Lewis claimed that if and only if such P^* holds, E is the common knowledge (actually shared beliefs) at a (1969: 56). Lewis called P^* the basis for common knowledge. What can it be? For example, he stated that "[c]oordination by means of an agreement is not, of course, an alternative to coordination by means of concordant mutual expectations. Rather, agreement is one means of producing those expectations [of several orders]" (1969: 34). "[Another] source of mutual expectations is precedent: acquaintance with past solved instance of their coordination problem" (1969: 36), leading to the phenomenon called *Conventions*, the title of his book.

There are two crucial elements that would build bridges between Lewis's construction and Aumann's: the base of common knowledge P^* and the ability of agents to reason symmetrically from P^* to E. The inference E in Lewis's scheme can be regarded as corresponding to the set which defines common knowledge *à la* Aumann. But they are induced via a proposition P^*, mutually accessible to all the agents. If P^* indicates E to every agent in the sense of (1) and (3), then, applying (2) recursively to it, every agent has reason to believe that every other agent also believes that E is the case and that every one knows that and so on.[19] Agents with such cognitive orientation may be referred to as "symmetric reasoners," following the terminology of Vanderschraaf and Sillari (2001/2007).

The above setting may be applied even to a one-shot game situation. But as Lewis's reference to conventions indicates, it can become more forceful and meaningful in the context of societal games played recurrently in society. In this context, P^* is something that would induce certain common beliefs among the agents regarding the salient feature E of recursive states of play, while reasons to believe it are provided by experiences of recurred states. Let us refer to such P^* as the (equilibrium) *public indicator*. Namely, P^* indicates to every player that the actual states of play are in E and that everyone knows it, which would recursively induce states of play included in E, which in turn confirms the validity of P^* and so on ad infinitum. Thus, P^* serves as a mediator for the rules of societal games to arise and be sustained: the societal rules in the sense of "*commonly-cognized patterns by which the societal games are being recursively played and expected to be played*" (cf. Section 3.2). P^* provides a cognitive frame for the players by summarily representing the states of recursive play. What can serve as such indicators? Laws, formal rules and agreements, norms, organizations of specific public functions, and so on can do so, if they can be regarded as representing something to be believed to prevail and to happen (and thus self-enforcing) from players' experiences. Even some linguistically represented "moral/normative beliefs" (as conceptually distinguished from individual behavioral beliefs) may serve, if they are accepted as taken for granted in the public domain. We may simply refer to those "stable," "self-sustaining" public indicators as *substantive forms of institutions*.[20]

As for the assumption of symmetric reasoning, admittedly it is strong and may often fail to apply, but I propose to keep this assumption as a reasonable reference point for further discussion. As stated, if the set E represents a set of recursive states of play, it may be considered as representing a pattern of play that is commonly perceived by all the agents. And pattern recognition is considered to be the basic operation of action-oriented internal representation (belief) according to the major schools of the cognitive sciences (e.g. the connectionists), and as such it is likely to be shared among people, even if it is incomplete.

4.2.2 *The limits of methodological individualism*

I have discussed how shared beliefs could arise in a way applicable to any situation (including nongame situations). Let us now deal more specifically with game-situations and consider under what conditions agents' beliefs about possible states of play can become equilibrium. As before, I assume that agents' individual cognitive capacities are limited and their cognitive potentials are represented by individual partitions of the set of states of play. Given individual partitions, the set of states of play is partitioned at the societal level in such a way that each cell of the societal partition is the meet of individual information sets. Let us assume that each cell of this societal partition can be potentially indicated by a corresponding public indicator. Let us call such cells the *commonly-knowable (societal) states*.[21] Each of them represents a pattern of states of play such that, if an appropriate public indicator is provided, every agent can cognize it as well as infer that all other agents also cognize it. Further, assume that these public indicators somehow occur with some known frequencies and that every agent can regard it the best to follow the indicators over time (namely choose an action in the indicated states). This kind of equilibrium is known as correlated equilibrium (Aumann 1976, 1987).

In Chapter 3, Section 3.3, we observed that there is a form of the political state, called the correlated state, in which the government alternatively transfers benefits among private agents while absorbing rents for this intermediating function. In the same way, within an organization, the members may be playing the so-called game of the Battle of Sexes in which the members are mutually interested in overall coordination, but they are in conflict in choosing which type of coordination to take from the possible many. In that situation organizations may develop rules or conventions such that different types of coordination alternate depending on some indicators occurring at some frequencies. For example, management may treat favorably the investors or the workers in the distribution of organizational outcome, depending on the phase of the regular cycles of business. Gintis (2009) argues that social norms may be understood as a correlating device.

In correlated equilibrium, the equilibrium probability distributions of the commonly-knowable states are endogenous, but given to individual agents in a holistic manner (i.e. they are not individual strategic choices as in the case of mixed strategies). One may argue that it can be treated in this way if they have evolved through a cultural process (or, calculated by centralized calculations of the government or management but somehow accepted by all the players). However, in order to make such a conjecture more reasonable, let us consider the situation in which individual agents form their own beliefs represented by respective public indicators on the commonly-knowable states and ask under what conditions their beliefs become convergent and what implications this may have. Let us imagine the situation where agents' beliefs become identical: for each agent others' beliefs about his or her action become the same and every agent's choice expected by others with a positive probability is the one that would maximize his or her payoffs with respect to the prevailing belief. Let us refer to this situation as being in *cognitive Nash equilibrium* over commonly-knowable states.[22]

At first agents must form their own beliefs regarding others' choices under imperfect knowledge regarding others' preferences, cognitive patterns, beliefs, technology, and so on. It is customary in game theory to describe this situation by the device of probabilistically distributed types of agents. An overall probability distribution is called a common prior, if the individual belief of any agent about others' types is equal to its conditional distribution given his or her own type. Then, roughly translated, the following remarkable theorem—due to Aumann and Brandenburger (1995)—holds:[23]

If the agents share a common prior, they can share a behavioral belief up to the commonly cognizable states via convergent public indicators of their beliefs. Thus, a unique public indicator entails as a substantive form of institution. Conversely, a common prior is almost necessary for a shared belief to evolve.

The proposition proved by Aumann and Brandenburger (1995) was actually only a sufficiency part. But they suggest that the statement is very tight in the sense that there may be no equilibrium if any of the conditions is slightly weakened. As institutions are not to be thought of as something that can be reached without anybody knowing much of anything, the tightness may be regarded as indicating an "almost necessary" part as well.

To repeat, this is an equilibrium condition as regards beliefs. Given such equilibrium beliefs, each agent would choose a particular action and a particular commonly knowable state would result. But in order for cognitive Nash equilibrium to be sustained, the action choices of individual agents based on such beliefs should not generate surprise for anyone. That is, recursive states of play must confirm the common belief in the context of the societal game.

How does it become possible that a common prior exists and current beliefs become commonly known among agents? As previously stated, a common prior is about the joint distribution of types of individual agents in terms of preferences, cognitive patterns, and technology through which agents infer others' actual actions and beliefs. It is hard to imagine that such a common prior can develop in a vacuum or prior to a one-shot game. But it seems reasonable to assume in the context of a game recursively played in society that it is historically shaped and shared in society somewhat like coordinating devices in correlated equilibrium. It may be indicated by patterns of consumption across social classes, a distribution among a population of political orientation and emotional characteristics, prevailing technological paradigms, and so on, depending on the domains of the societal games to be played. They must have been experienced over time and came to be widely known; and similar inferences are drawn from them by agents. We may possibly identify a common prior as cultural belief. Culture is nothing but historically accumulated common knowledge.[24]

Individual agents update a common prior by individual information that can further refine their own partitions of the commonly knowable states. They would choose their actions to maximize their own payoffs (whatever they may be) against these individualized beliefs. These beliefs are different in detail, but they are in agreement up to the societal partition of possible states. In order to play the societal game and generate a stable societal order, agents thus need to share a certain degree of commonality of beliefs conditioned by culture and similar pattern recognitions induced by ongoing public indicators. Those beliefs are common in dual senses: they are commonly known as well as identical up to commonly knowable societal states. Such an epistemic (cognitive) Nash equilibrium is not constructed by the decentralized decisions of fictitious *Homo Economicus* who hold a priori beliefs and intentions in a purely individualistic manner. But it is not determined independently of individuated cognition either, because shared beliefs refer to the common characteristics of individual beliefs and the former cannot exist without the latter. Thus, both social cognitive categories and individual cognition are knitted together to generate a societal order. An understanding of this dualistic nature of the social order is the key to an analysis of the evolutionary process of societal rules. Both methodological individualism and holism cannot tell the complete story of society (Arrow 1994; Hodgson 2007).

The public indicators that generate a cognitive Nash equilibrium on the commonly knowable societal states provide common cognitive frames for individual agents, as institutions, regarding ways in which the societal games are played and are to be played. But they are not exogenously given only by the design of particular agents such as governments, political entrepreneurs, social engineers, and so on. Their basic structures are generated and sustained through the cognitive and physical actions of all the individual agents of the current generation. They are even partially impacted by those of the past generation in the form of culture, as well as those of the future generation in the sense that expectations of the current generations about the future may matter. Thus, institutional environments can be considered to constitute extended cognition of all the individual agents that they create together and share together. By extending cognitive resources and contents in this way, each individual agent can expand the horizon of cognition beyond his or her own skull and skin.

4.3 The co-evolution of the societal rules

This section tries to build a bridge from the preceding, theoretical discussion of what institutions are to the forthcoming, concrete discussions in the next chapter of how the contemporary corporate landscape evolves and what its nature can be. Namely, its task is to provide a conceptual framework for tracing and understanding the process for the societal rules to change. Figure 3.1 (page 69) was introduced to indicate the rules of the societal games, or institutions, as mediating between the equilibrium play of the game and individual belief in a snapshot; and the previous section of this chapter provided a theoretical background for the relationships. It was argued that for the rules of the societal games to be internalized by the agents as shared beliefs, the intermediary of domain-specific public indicators may play a crucial role, from which agents can infer more or less similarly the ways in which the game is to be played. As mentioned more than once, domain-specific, equilibrium-supporting public indicators may include such matters as constitutions, statutory laws, organizations of well-known specific public functions, social norms, symbolic public rituals (e.g. Chwe 2001), organizational rules and routines, and so on. These things are often thought to be institutions in themselves. My argument stressed, however, that, in order for them to be effective, they ought to be an equilibrium pattern-representation of recursive play of the societal game. It would induce the action-oriented internal representations (beliefs) within the agents, which would in turn reproduce the equilibrium patterns of play.[25]

Is it therefore the case that the equilibrium pattern of play of the societal game is induced by the shared beliefs, which are induced by the equilibrium pattern of play via corresponding public indicators, and so on ad infinitum? Are we not then trapped in a circular argument? Is it not possible for institutions as equilibrium patterns of play-cum-shared beliefs to endogenously change at all? I hope that the argument of the previous section provides a clue to expand on the circular flow and suggest a way to initiate discussions on the evolutionary change of the societal rules.

4.3.1 *Inter-domain interactions*

Consult Figure 4.2, which corresponds to Figure 3.1 in terms of the locations of the basic variables represented by shaded boxes, clockwise from the upper-left box: individual strategies, the state of play, public representations, and (individual) beliefs (internal representations), respectively. These variables are now not in stationary states, but in flux. Let us first start with the upper-left, shaded box that represents the individual strategies of agents. Here individual agents, including business corporations, face the shifting environments and attempt to respond strategically to them.

The environments of the strategic choices of individual agents may be divided into three sub-classes: natural environments, institutional environments, and neoclassical environments. Natural environments include such obvious items as the atmosphere, water, soil, forests, and so on. They are collective assets for aesthetic, consumptive, and productive actions of individuals and corporations; and to make explicit that their values are affected by those actions (and thus not purely environments), they may be referred to as the global commons. Institutional environments are the

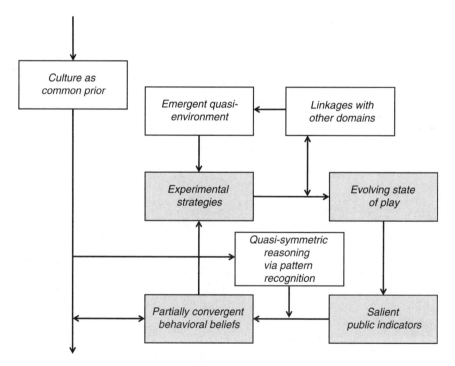

Figure 4.2. The evolving state of play and the emergence of societal rules

rules of societal games. They may be conceived as given to individual agents, including business corporations, beyond their immediate control. But, as has been stressed, they are actually endogenous outcomes of the recurrent play of societal games. Even those rules outside the economic-transaction domains, such as political and social ones, cannot be entirely independent of corporate actions. The neoclassical environments are comprised of the trilogy of the tastes of agents, technology, and initial endowments of resources to the agents that are treated as "data" in neoclassical economics.[26] But, needless to say, the parameters representing those data are also affected by agents' actions. For example, consumers' tastes may be affected by corporate products and advertisements; technology by cognitive activities in corporate laboratories; cognitive and physical assets by corporate investment and accumulation, and so on. Thus they are actually apt to be treated as "quasi-parameters" in studies of institutional changes, as suggested by Greif (2006: 159–60).

Individual agents perceive changes in these environments in the course of play and respond to them. They may experiment on new strategies or stick to old strategies. For example, on perceiving increasing global warming in the global commons, some business corporations may increase spending on the development of environmentally friendly technologies and corporate social responsibility (CSR) programs. They also react to changes in the "quasi-parameters" such as those relating to consumer tastes. A group of engineers who had worked in the corporate labs of a multinational may leave the organization and together with researchers from a university start up a new firm in an attempt to explore the possibility of new knowledge. All such individual actions generate a modicum of change in the state of play in each domain. However, as noted above, all changes in the environments are actually "quasi-endogenous." Action changes in one domain of the societal game may induce changes in other domains of the societal game, which in turn may have feedback effects on its own domain (indicated by the feedback loop starting from the upper-right box and returning to it via the box representing the quasi-environments). Among such feedback mechanisms, two are particularly noteworthy: the dynamic extensions of the strategic interactions across the multiple domain that we discussed in Chapter 3: the strategic complementarities and the linked games. Drawing some examples from organization fields, let me briefly describe the essence of these two mechanisms.[27]

The first is the dynamic extension of strategic complementarities (Section 3.3.4) that are induced by the strategic interactions of the agents across complementary domains, triggered by a change in the quasi-parameters in

one or both domains. Suppose for example that, prompted by the accumulation of a particular type of cognitive assets at the societal level, some
business corporations start to experiment on a new mode of architecture
for associational cognition. Then, some or all of the members of those
business corporations, the investors, the managers and/or the workers,
may begin to be motivated to play different strategies in the political-
exchange domain to create political environments in favor of the new
corporate development. This may in turn facilitate further development
in the corporate domain, thus creating momentum. Such a mechanism was
already implicit in the discussion of Section 3.3.5 "Evolutionary bifurcation
of the developmental state," but the implications of such a process can be
formally described and analyzed with the momentum theorem of Milgrom,
Qian, and Roberts (1991). This theorem is particularly useful for analyzing
dynamic interactions between strategies and quasi-parameters such as policy, quasi-endogenous technological change, asset accumulations, and so on.
Also, it provides a baseline to see how dynamic strategic complementarities
may sometimes incur prolonged uncertainty in the direction of institutional
transition because of a conflict of strategic interests among the agents.

Consider the domains X and Z where two states of play, x' or x'' and z' or
z'', can be alternative strategic equilibria (cf. Section 3.3.4. Recall that these
states are represented by vectors of individual strategies). Suppose further
that there are quasi-parameters ϑ and μ such that an increase in ϑ (or μ)
would increase the payoff difference $U(x', z: \vartheta) - U(x'', z: \vartheta)$ for all the players
in domain X (alternatively the payoff difference $V(x, z': \mu) - V(x, z'': \mu)$ for all
the players in domain Z). This is the condition called the uniform increasing difference with respect to the quasi-parameter. Note that it is not
assumed that the agents in either domain have the same payoff functions.
Only a uniform direction of payoff-differences with respect to a change in
the parametric value is assumed. Under this condition, if the value of ϑ and/
or μ increases over time, the relative attractiveness of x' and/or z' would be
improved, but assume that their impacts are not strong enough so that the
transition from the state of play x'' to another state x' (and/or z'' to z') would
not occur, if the domain X and Z remain separated. Suppose however that
x' and z', or x'' and z'', are mutually complementary in the sense defined in
Section 3.3.4. Then the effects of the increasing difference in respective
quasi-parameters may trigger mutually reinforcing changes in strategic
variables across domains. They may create a dynamic momentum, leading
to the co-evolution of new states of play from the combination (x'', z'') to
the alternative combination (x', z').

A static framework might hint that the presence of strategic complementarities make an institutional change more difficult and inertial, unless overall changes across domains occur all at once in the manner of a Big Bang. As discussed in Section 3.3.4 this is the view of the "varieties of capitalism" literature that does not explicitly take into account the strategic interactions of agents. However, the dynamic momentum theorem suggests that the very presence of strategic complementarities across domains may rather facilitate the co-evolution of societal rules, provided that right impetus is given initially by quasi-parameters in terms of the uniform increasing differences. On the other hand, even if a continued change in a quasi-parameter, say ϑ, is introduced in relative favor of a corresponding variable x', if the level of another parameter, say, μ remains low, then such dynamic change may not occur. For example, even though some statutory law is enacted in the polity domain with the intention of improving the efficiency of games in the economic-exchange domain, if appropriate cognitive assets in the economic domain and competences in legal enforcement in the public domain have not been accumulated, the intended outcome will not emerge. Also the emulations of good practice in other economies may not be workable for the intended structural change, for example if a bit of practice is borrowed from one country and another bit from another with no potential complementarities among them as well as without the accumulation of assets supporting them.

Institutional complementarities suggest that hybrids of institutions are not sustainable. In the next chapter, however, I discuss how the globalization of financial markets can lessen national constraints of institutional complementarities as discussed in Chapter 3, Section 3.3, leading to the emergence of some kind of organizational hybrids that are not possible in the closed economy. The logic of dynamic strategic complementarities can also identify an important factor for making the institutional transition rugged rather than smooth. It is the failure of the condition of uniform increasing difference to hold, that is, conflicts in marginal payoff among the agents with regard to a change in a quasi-parameter. Then, a certain policy change, or the endogenous accumulation of physical/cognitive assets, may create conflicting strategic responses among the agents in the domain in which it is occurring as well as in the complementary domain. Then, the process of strategic interactions may become complex and unpredictable. The next chapter discusses that such may indeed be the case in some national economies (e.g. Japan, France, and Germany).

Secondly, the social embeddedness introduced in Section 3.4.3 also evolve dynamically in the organizational field, as well as within each corporate organization. One of the fallacies frequently made with respect to the non-game-theoretic approach to social norms was to regard them as being exogenously fixed constraints on strategic choices for the economic domain, thus tending to deter institutional evolution/transition.[28] Or, even if social norms change, they do so more slowly than other institutions (e.g. Roland 2008). Such a difference in the speed of adjustment between social norms and organizational architecture would certainly leave some impact on the ways that the latter can evolve. For example, in Japan the practice of lifetime employment is changing only slowly and in a differentiated way, partly because some employers consider it a breach of the long-term commitment and mutual trust established between employers and employees and therefore not dignified.

However, it should also be noted that the initiative for co-evolution may occur on the side of the social-exchange domain. As discussed in Section 3.4.4, rising public concern over economic impacts on the quality of the global commons implies a de facto gradual transfer of environment rights from the corporate sector to the community at large. Thus, differentiated social capital begins to be endowed to business corporations, depending on their active engagement in environment-oriented CSR, the development of environmentally friendly technology and so on. Being embedded in such an evolving social milieu, the share markets may then start to internalize, albeit partly, differentiated corporate social capital into differences in share prices, which further motivates business corporations to re-orient their economic behaviors. Thus, evolving change in social value may have an impact, through the reshuffling of social capital allotted to individual business corporations, on the rules of the games, social and economic, that they play.

Another dynamic mechanism involving linked games is that a certain frame of the play of economic/organizational games induces a pattern of social capital distribution in the social-exchange domain, which in turn has positive or negative feedback impacts on the former. Chapter 3, Section 3.4.4 gave an example in which the piece rate payment scheme created a shopfloor norm that restricted a rat race developing among the workers. Under other circumstances, however, misaligned incentive contracts in the organization domain may create destabilizing competition among the workers via the induced distorted distribution of social capital. For example, in the process leading to the burst of the 2008 financial crisis, the supposedly best and brightest on Wall Street and in the City competed to achieve higher social status symbolized by the design of high-yield-generating derivative products. Their "greed" is often blamed for the eventual disastrous consequence. What did the greed mean in this case? The competition among financial engineers does not seem to have been simply an economic one of pursuing insatiable pecuniary payoffs, but also a social one in which they strived to exhibit their superior competence and intelligence that may have resulted in such emotional payoffs as a sense of prestige, being awed, envied, and so on. Thus, there was no ceiling to this social rat race, even though an extra million dollars might not have mattered to them for its own sake. The economic game and the social game were linked in such a way that the rules of the economic game, the reward to financial engineers according to their short-term financial performance, generated a rat-race culture among them in the social game, on one hand, and playing the social game encouraged them to take economic actions that generated economic risks endogenously, on the other. The primary fault may have been in the ways that incentive contracts were designed,[29] but it was the mind-sets of the people absorbed in that culture that eventually led to the spectacular failures of some major financial service houses. This is an example of unstable feedbacks, leading to the self-destructing effects on the stability of the game.

4.3.2 Organizations evolving

Generally, the state of play in each domain evolves through agents' adjustments of strategy to changes in the quasi-environments (indicated by the horizontal arrow from the upper-left box to the right box in Figure 4.2), amplified or dampened by the mechanisms of dynamic strategic complementarities and dynamic social embeddedness across domains. For example, a new design of organizational architecture starts competing with traditional ones in the organization field. If the new design is perceived as yielding (potentially) higher payoffs, it becomes a target for emulation. Distribution of social capital may start to be reshuffled, as new social sentiments transpire. In the political domain, the power balance of the agents may become tilted by the evolving state of play in the economic domain and the traditional coalition structure may become weakened, and so on.

Let me briefly mention two cases where the evolving states of play in the organization field eventually lead to a substantial reconfiguration of the field. One example may be interpreted as a case in which the activities internalized in old corporate architecture are dis-bundled and then re-bundled in new industrial architecture, and the other as a case in which the organization field evolves by incorporating new linkages among corporate organizations.

Experimental strategies adopted by the players of the organizational field may generally make the boundary of corporate domains and their linkages fluid. A classic example of this is the emergence of new intermediaries of various sorts, for example merchant houses, commercial banks, securities houses, venture capitalists, e-commerce vendors, etc., that bundle and mediate numerous bilateral private trading actions. Another mechanism could be conversely to branch out a single integrated corporate organizational domain into (possibly complementary) multiple corporate organizational domains, loosely linked. The emergence of the so-called Silicon Valley phenomena mentioned in Section 2.4.4 is a quintessential example of this: the R&D activities bundled under the integrated business corporation were disbundled partly by anti-monopoly regulations and partly through the voluntary exits of engineers. They were re-bundled more loosely as a cluster of small start-up firms with the intermediary of venture capital firms, to which essential cognitive assets were massively provided from the old corporate domain (Baldwin and Clark 2000). Then successful entrepreneurial firms are further re-bundled into an integrated corporation through acquisition by an established corporation in a niche market. If we view this process as the creative destruction of old combinations of cognitive assets, characterized as the classic *H*-model, to create new *RE*-mode combinations characterized by the reciprocal essentialities of cognitive assets between the management and the engineers, it can be reckoned as Schumpeterian innovation in the organization field of the commercialization of information technology.

However, the organization field of the commercialization of life science has been evolving somewhat differently, as Powell *et al.* (2005) described and depicted with massive data sets and novel analytical methods. In the 1980s hundreds of small science-based firms were established based on the scientific knowledge developed in university labs. Some of them matured into what Powell *et al.* called dedicated biotech firms (DBFs). In the early days, however, they did not necessarily have skills in marketing the drugs that they invented and often relied on pharmaceutical giants, while the latter lacked the new knowledge base in what were rapidly advancing life sciences. This situation did not lead to the acquisition of DBFs by the giants as in the information technology field, however, but complementary collaborations between them. The collaborative networks soon evolved to involve such diverse actors as universities, public research organizations, small start-up firms, as well as venture capital firms and organizations such as the National Institute of Health (NIH) as funding agencies. Since no single organization can develop a full range of scientific, developmental, and managerial cognitive assets to produce new medicines, organizations of various types diversified their connections with others in research collaboration and financial support. Career mobility back and forth between university and industry became commonplace (Owen-Smith and Powell 2004). Through all these, overlapping, multiple bundling of organizations, horizontal networks have been evolving with a small core of organizations at the center. The organizations in the central positions are there because of established reputations in terms of highly effective, differentiated connections to diverse partners but not simply by virtue of being large. Once such a pattern has evolved, Powell *et al.* found, it reinforces the value of "multipleconnectivity" further, pulling in promising new entrants and pushing out failed incumbents. This flexible bundling may be highly conditioned by the nature of the cognitive assets need to be organized in this industry. While the sources of scientific knowledge are widely dispersed and rapidly developing, the cognitive assets needed for the commercial development of new medicines are less broadly distributed.

In the next chapter I will discuss another possibility of evolutionary change in which some of the traditional architectural modes are being gradually transformed into what I refer to as the *RE*-mode in various path-dependent ways.

4.3.3 *Actions to beliefs to actions and so on*

Let us return to discuss the remaining part of the circular flow of Figure 4.2. The evolving state of each domain generates messages and symbols indicating possible directions of change in the pattern of play, even if they are still uncertain or incomplete. Then they are perceived by the players of the relevant domains of games and possibly beyond (this refers to the flow from the upper-right box to the lower-right box). Addresses made by political leaders, the campaign slogans of political parties, emergent social icons, new modes of organizational architecture, media reports, and many other events summarize and indicate possible new patterns. However, none of them may be immediately regarded as decisive, in which case pros and cons, for right or wrong, for various possibilities of change or the status quo would be debated to influence others' strategies and sentiments, to persuade or dominate public opinion, and so on. Statutory laws and regulations may be drafted and enacted in the political domain to anticipate, facilitate, or confirm a certain direction of change in the strategic choices of agents. Judges may make new interpretations of laws in the judicial domain. These public processes act together with the strategic play of the societal games and in fact they are a part of it.

Business corporations can be regarded as micro societies by themselves, embodying political-public processes of its own. Then, within the corporate domain as well, discussions and debates may take place regarding ways in which various cognitive assets are to be deployed, combined, motivated, and governed, involving management, boards, unions, dominant shareholders, consultants, analysts, and so on. Needless to say, business corporations are also one of the important agents dispatching symbols and messages toward society at large regarding their intended strategies in the form of, for example, a president's speech, corporate publicity, portfolio of new products, a CSR program, etc.

Individual agents, including business corporations as integrated entities, perceive the pattern of the evolving states of play of the societal games through their own play as well as through the interpretations of various public indicators that they choose to, or are induced to, perceive. This results in the reconfigurations of their world-views represented by the respective partitions of the set of states of play and subjective probability distributions on it (which is indicated by the arrow from the right-bottom to the left-bottom shaded boxes). At first, such cognition may appear to be individual action, taking place inside the skull and skin of the natural person or inside the boundary of an organization in the case of the corporate person. Individual persons certainly have varied orientations, dispositions, scope and depth in their cognitive assets as well as different experiences. Likewise, individual corporations are characterized by unique forms of architecture in organizing varied cognitive assets for associational cognition. They are imbued with a unique corporate legacy as well as a conscious managerial design. In spite of those individual characteristics, however, both individual and corporate cognitive processes are social ones as well. They have the same background information derived from shared experiences in relevant domains of games. Also, human cognitions, individual and corporate, are largely characterized by pattern recognition. If so, the role of public indicators in aligning individual cognitions would be considerable. Individual agents can offload a substantial amount of cognitive burdens to the socially-filtered, salient public indicators. Individual inference methods are also acquired and nurtured through common educational backgrounds and social experiences. In addition, as discussed in Chapter 2, Section 2.5 the frame of organizational cognition is conditioned by an organizational convention evolving in the embedding organizational field. And, culture, as the common knowledge that society has accumulated and inherited, provides a backdrop for individual cognitions.

Thus, the cognitions of the players in societal games are individuated as well as socially conditioned and anchored at the same time. Therefore their revision of behavioral beliefs about the patterns of play of the game more or less "meet" in the sense formally conceptualized in the previous section. Otherwise, the social order would be utterly chaotic. However, this does not necessarily imply yet that they can positively or normatively agree on the substance of their behavioral beliefs in detail or at ease. Also, their personal interests may shadow even the formation of behavioral beliefs, needless to say of normative beliefs. If no substantial agreement in behavioral beliefs is felt, they still need to experiment on their strategy based on their own behavioral and normative beliefs (indicated by the upward arrow from the left-bottom box to the left-upper box in Figure 4.2). Public debates never cease. Thus the circular process continues. From this perspective, the relationship between public indicators and beliefs are recursive and iterative, rather than linear, but they are not completely sealed off from each other's influence.

The evolutionary process of the rules of societal game is thus complex and fluid. A change in the societal rules cannot be simply designed, implemented, and enforced by statutory laws, nor by political entrepreneurs. It involves the process of actual playing the game as well as cognitive filtering, both individual and societal. Through this process, only if some public indicators gain the status of salience in that they appear increasingly persuasive, believable, and dominant, will players' behavioral beliefs become convergent, overlap and coordinate to a substantive degree. Only then may we say that new rules of societal games, or institutions, have emerged.

Even under a situation in which some new societal rules emerge in the sense described above, agents are still likely to have different opinions about them or value them. Some may not like them or may not believe in them in a normative sense, but simply ignoring them would not necessarily benefit them, although they may try to challenge those rules by experimenting with new strategies, or by engaging in public discourse to change others' opinions in the coming cycles of play. Meanwhile, aspects of evolved shared beliefs may be incorporated into the accumulated stock of common knowledge in society and update it. As suggested by Denzau and North, we may think of "culture as encapsulating the experiences of past generations of any particular cultural group" (1994: 15). This cultural process keeps going alongside rule-evolution processes over time and connect them, providing important inputs to the latter in future.

Thus the process of rule change may be regarded as being rather gradual. On one hand it involves the process of actual moves (physical actions) of play of societal games as indicated by the upper part of Figure 4.2. On the other hand, it involves the cognitive process as represented by the lower part. The former generates constantly moving states of play by comprising adaptive responses to changing quasi-environments, experiments, emulations, mistakes, as well as a result of the turnovers of the players due to various factors (e.g. demographic change, the exits and entries of business corporations and political organizations). The constantly moving states of play, however, need to be summarized by the construction of various public indicators and filtered through individual cognitive processes to generate shared behavioral beliefs. Therefore this process may be slower than the first to change. In some cases prevailing formal public indicators and/or societal cognitive categories, such as laws, regulations, rules, conventions, and so on, may even become misaligned with the evolving states of play. Such situations create social tension, inducing agents' motivations and actions in public and other domains to consciously change those unfit public indicators. Thus, the process of institutional evolution would be bound to take time and be gradual. Even in cases in which it appears to be punctuated with a sudden change in viable public indicators, they are often preceded by some play that anticipates their ascendance in embryo.

Notes

1. As a Russian-born, Polish-Jew who immigrated to the USA via Europe during the Second World War, Hurwicz had firsthand experiences of the oppression and inhumanity of various kinds of authoritarian regimes and ideologies, which undoubtedly formed the deep-seated basis of his life-long commitment to the scientific search for the possibility of a decentralized, efficient economic mechanism. He also had rare personal experiences of studying or working as a research assistant for Mises in Switzerland, Hayek in London, and Lange in Chicago, all of whom were major players on either side of the famous controversy of the possibility of centralized socialist planning (Hayek 1935; Lange 1938). His own contribution to this debate is Arrow and Hurwicz (1960), which evolved to a more general interest in the theory of mechanism design that treats the economic mechanism as a variable rather than a given (Hurwicz 1960, 1973, 2008).
2. Hurwicz also uses the terminology "incentive compatibility" (1973) instead of "privacy preserving." Also recent mechanism design theory uses the terminology "strategy proofness" when the rules of a mechanism are not to be violated by individual strategic behaviors.
3. Technically speaking this is the proof of the impossibility of Walrasian allocation satisfying the conditions of Pareto-efficiency, individual rationality, and strategy-proofness.
4. Maskin (1977/1999) proved that if a socially desirable state is achievable as a Nash equilibrium (Nash-implementable), then the social choice function needs to satisfy the so-called Maskin-monotonicity condition. This specifies that, if a

certain outcome is chosen by the social choice function under a certain profile of individual preferences, then that outcome is still to be chosen under any monotone transformation of the individual preference functions in such a way as not to change the relative position of that outcome. With an additional condition, it can be also a sufficient condition for Nash implementation.

5. For an introductory survey of matching, see Roth and Sotomayor (1992), Roth (2008). For auctions, see McAfee and MacMillan (1987), Milgrom (2004).

6. An attempt to explicitly integrate the spontaneous view of the societal rules with the norm-based design approach was proposed by Hayek (1973, 1979). He considered that the spontaneous order—endogenously created over time through the experiences, practices, and customs (*nomos* in classical Greek) of many generations without the imposition by political authority—represented their consensual wisdom. Thus he ascribed to this order the status of *kosmos* in classical Greek meaning "a right order in a state or a community." This highest order may be crystallized as the constitution that represents the basic make-up of societal order. Then, within such constitutional framework "the universal rules of just conduct" were to be derived to regulate the actions of agents. They are to be applied to an unknown number of cases in an object-free, consequence-free fashion, as well as in manners to be compatible with the mutual protection of the personal domains of individuals. On the basis of such universal rules, the rules to regulate government organizations and actions were further to be defined, which were in turn to construct societal "made order" (*taxis* in classical Greek).

   Notwithstanding the coherence of this top-down hierarchical construction, there appears to remain a tension between the spontaneous nature of *kosmos* (mainly expounded in Hayek 1973) and the norm-based design leading to *taxis* (mainly in Hayek 1979). Although the Hayekian principle for "the universal rules of just conduct" may be agreeable to many of us on ethical ground, it appears to have, unfortunately, been implemented not necessarily in every place and every time. Hayek argued that such rules needed to be "found" by the legislative assembly, the members of which were to be carefully selected according to individual merits, personal maturity, and so on. The *kosmos* in his scheme, therefore, seems to remain something in which the ideal rules are hidden, waiting to be found, implemented, and enforced by the selected elites of society.

7. It is well known that Max Weber distinguished two categories of rational action: Zweckrationalität (object-rationality) and Wertrationalität (value-rationality). The former is instrumental, while the latter is prescribed by some transcendent system of values.

8. Heath (2008) criticizes the game-theoretic orientation toward so-called consequentialism. That is, he argues that it is premised on the idea that players' exclusive interests are in an action's consequences so that it cannot deal with people's value judgments on one's own/others' actions themselves. However, the payoffs of the players in the game can be defined on the space of the profiles of players' choices (i.e. outcomes) so that this criticism does not seem to be warranted.

9. Binmore (2005) proved that a self-enforcing, stable Nash bargaining solution obtained in the original state is theoretically equivalent to the maximization of the weighted sum of individual utilities across all the social positions *à la* Harsanyi (1977). He argued that this fairness criterion may be more easily applied to situations where opportunities for society change in the short-run. In Chapter 2, Section 2.5, I developed a similar argument regarding the nature of corporate governance. Namely, a self-enforcing, three-way relationship between the investors, managers, and workers may evolve as a Nash solution, and it can be represented as the maximization of the weighted sum of their utilities.

10. One early pioneer of the equilibrium approach to institutions is Schotter (1981). Equilibrium concepts used by various authors include sub-game perfect (e.g. Milgrom, North, and Weingast (1990), Greif (1994, 2006), Greif, Milgrom, and Weingast (1995), Weingast (1997), Aoki (2001), Bicchieri (2006)); Nash (e.g. Basu (1998), Calvert (1995), Sened (1997), and Dixit (2004)); evolutionary (e.g. Sugden (1986), Young (1993, 1998), Aoki (1998), Matsui and Okuno-Fujiwara (1994), Bowles (2005)); super-modular (Milgrom and Roberts (1990), Aoki (1994*b*)); correlated (e.g. Gintis (2009)); among others. Also see a recent survey of institutional economics by Greif and Kingston (2008).

11. Technically speaking, the difference between the two may be captured in a game-theoretic framework as follows. Hurwicz identified the rules of the game (or the "mechanism" in his term) with the "game form" composed of the set of players, the set of admissible (legal) strategies for each player and the outcome function that assign a certain physical consequence to each of the possible profiles of players' choices (Hurwicz 1996, 2008). If the players choose strategies according to their own payoff evaluations of those consequences, the "game" results (the payoffs can be subjective so that they cannot be included in the rules). In contrast, the endogenous approach regards the players' strategic-choice-sets as including all possible choices, i.e., physically possible on the relevant domain and not limited to legal ones, and identify multiple equilibrium plays of the game as varieties of societal rules. Namely, the exogenous and endogenous approaches can be distinguished in identifying the societal rules either in the (designable) game-form or the endogenous outcome of the play of the game under relatively unspecified, exogenous game-form. However as discussed in the following text, the extent to which the game-form is free from human devices is limited. See Aoki (2001: 4–20). Basu (1998) also makes a similar point in terms of the comparison between the "law" game including the public enforcer under such name and the institution-free "anarchic game." Two games can generate the same outcome as "lawful equilibrium" in the former and "anarchic equilibrium," if the public enforcer is included as a player of each game (albeit anonymous in the latter game) rather than an external guardian of the rules. This suggests a way to resolve the difference between the institutions-as-law view and the institution-as-equilibrium view.

12. Lewis originally dealt only with coordination games that would give rise to conventions as a solution to the desideratum (Lewis 1969), but in fact his problem applies to any game (Lewis 1975). It became conventional among game theorists to identify the Lewisian convergent higher-order expectations among agents as common knowledge and, further, to consider that Nash equilibrium strategies ought to be common knowledge among the players in that sense. As Aumann and Brandenburger (1995) pointed out, however, if each player is rational, knows his or her own payoffs and knows the strategy choices of the others for certain, then players' choices constitute a Nash equilibrium by definition. Such first-order knowledge among the players is called "mutual knowledge" in theory, made distinct from the common knowledge defined as convergent higher-order knowledge. However, as we are concerned with conditions for the establishment of equilibrium rather than its static characterization, we need to attend to common knowledge here rather than only mutual knowledge.

13. This is analogous to the situation that Hayek described in his famous article on "[t]he Use of Knowledge in Society" (1945). Every individual has some advantage over all others in that "one can have the knowledge of the particular circumstances of time and place" (1945: 251). It may also be noted that Hayek's treatise on *The Theory of Sensory Order* (1952) is built on the premise that the human mental process can be principally understood as the process of a "classification" of events, and it anticipated the later development of the theory of knowledge as described below as well as that of cognitive neuro-science.

14. A function P that associates with every state a in the set A of states a nonempty subset $P(a)$ of A is called an information function for A, if it is exhaustive and consistent in the sense given in the main text. The information function induces a partition of the set A which we denote by $P(A)$. Then given any two partitions $P'(A)$ and $P''(A)$ on A induced by information functions $P'(.)$ and $P''(.)$, the partition $P'(A)$ is said to be finer than the partition $P''(A)$ (and $P''(.)$ is coarser than $P'(.)$), if $P'(a) \subseteq P''(a)$ holds for all $a \in A$. Intuitively the information sets induced by $P'(.)$ give at least as much information as the information sets given by $P''(.)$. The meet of any two information sets $P'(a)$ and $P''(a)$ is defined as the smallest set including both $P'(a)$ and $P''(a)$. If the meet of information sets $P_i(a)$ of all the agents in society is included in a subset E of A, then we say that E is their *common knowledge* at state a.

15. Any set E which includes the meet of the information sets of all the agents at a is said to be "self-evident" among the agents by Osborne and Rubinstein (1994: 73) and a "public event" by Milgrom (1981).

16. See Fagin *et al.* (1995), Proposition 2.5.1; Osborne and Rubinstein (1994), Proposition 74.2. See also Milgrom (1981).

17. The usual examples given in any text book to show the equivalence of the Aumann and Lewis definitions use the former type. See for example Fagin *et al.* (1995, ch. 2).

18. For recent attempts to resurrect Lewis' argument, see Vanderschraaf and Sillari (2001/2007), Cubbit and Sugden (2003), Gintis (2009).

19. The construct P^* may be regarded as akin to what Milgrom (1981) defined as "public events" and postulated as generating common knowledge. Together with other conditions, he derived the Aumann characterization of common knowledge from it.

20. Aoki (2001) identifies institutions with the "shared behavioral beliefs" essentially equivalent to the concept of "the rules of societal games" in this book. Then, I discussed the various "forms of their representation" essentially equivalent to the concept of equilibrium public indicators in this book (2001: 215–20). In that exposition, however, the relationships between behavioral beliefs and their representations are not sufficiently elucidated. I now consider that public indicators induce individual beliefs and, when they achieve the status of representing equilibrium states of play, may be called "(substantive forms of) institutions." As mentioned already, North (1990) identifies formal rules and social norms as institutions (but not organizations and beliefs). Greif (2006) identifies formal rules, norms, and organizations, together with behavioral (and internal) beliefs, as institutions that induce the regularity of behavior. The legal positivists identify statutory laws as institutions. As the issue of what institutions are is partly a semantic one, there should not be any strong case against those claims, as far as the roles of the public indicators are understood as mediating between behaviors and (behavioral) beliefs to create the societal order. For example, if those public indicators were not credible, then they would not effectively regulate agents' actions as intended via their beliefs, which would be counter to an intuitive notion of what institutions do. An insightful view into the nature of law, both civil and common, from a similar perspective as in this book is expounded in Deakin and Sarkar (2008).

21. Such collections of states are usually referred to as events in game theory. But as we are concerned with recursively played games rather than one-shot games, let us refer to them as societal states.

22. It is the interpretation of the mixed strategy equilibrium as the equilibrium of beliefs. See Aumann (1987). Aumann and Brandenburger (1995) refers to this equilibrium as "epistemic Nash equilibrium."

23. Precisely speaking, this proposition also requires the common knowledge of the rationality of the others and mutual knowledge of payoff functions.

24. For such a notion of culture, see Binmore (2005). Also see Guiso, Sapienz and Zingales (2006) for culture as a common prior.

25. Denzau and North described the result of a similar process as follows: "The mental models are the internal representations that individual cognitive systems create to interpret the environment: the institutions are the external (to mind) mechanism individuals create to structure and order the environment" (Denzau and North 1994: 4).

26. Cf. note 11 in this chapter.

27. For more elaborate arguments and examples for these two mechanisms, see Aoki (2001: Part II).

28. For example, many scholars, including economists and anthropologists, tend to draw a sharp distinction between the pre-modern, norm-based economy and the capitalist market economy (e.g. Polyani 1944; Geertz 1963; Hicks 1969), or between the norm-based and contract-based economies of the long distance trade in medieval times (Greif 1994). It is argued that the pre-capitalist community norms either deter the transition to a capitalist market economy, or are to be dismantled in order to allow the transition. However, there can also be cases in which pre-community norms play certain facilitating roles in the transition (Aoki and Hayami 2001, Greif 2006: ch. 10). It is because the social-exchange game may be linked with sequentially evolving domains of different types. For example, suppose that the pre-modern rural community that has developed a norm regulating members' economic activities in a manner as described in Section 3.5 encounters new transaction opportunities with outside merchants. Then they may emulate the same norm-based behavior as a means of controlling moral hazard behavior of their own as well as that of outside merchants in this new domain of transactions. To develop the market reputation of the community, the members of a community may exercise lateral monitoring over each other not to cheat outsiders, whereas possible cheating by outside merchants is punishable by the collective termination of further trading. However, as the social capital that can be accumulated from community-exchanges dwindles, together with the expanded trade relationship, the internal social norm gradually ceases to operate.

29. See endnote 5 in Chapter 1.

5

The Evolving Diversity of the Corporate Landscape

5.1 What happened to Japanese corporations in the "Lost Decade"?

Having developed a conceptual framework for the evolution of societal games, I now move on to apply it to an analysis and interpretation of contemporary situations. More specifically, the objective of this final chapter is to find out how the contemporary corporate landscape is evolving globally, what it implies, and what its major policy implications are. For this purpose, however, I will first examine specifically the case of Japan in some detail and then go on to discuss global situations generally [Those readers who are not particularly interested in Japanese case may wish to skip this section after the introduction and move on to Section 5.2.]. There are four reasons for this focus. First, there is an obvious personal reason: Japan is a case which I can speak of with greater confidence based on close personal observation, since I move frequently across the Pacific Ocean between there and Silicon Valley. Second, in spite of the fact that the Japanese economy has been hit as hard by the 2008 financial crash and its aftermath as other economies, it is still the second largest economy in terms of gross national product (GNP), although it is expected to be surpassed by the Chinese economy not before too long. It has the most egalitarian income distribution among OECD countries[1], while the stock values of Japanese corporations in the FT Global 500 make up 8 percent of the total value of that group, with comparable dispersion of share ownership to the USA and UK. So what is happening in her corporate economy may be of interest by itself.

In addition, there are two other reasons of more general relevance. As is well known, prior to the current worldwide crisis Japan experienced a decade of deflation, dubbed as the "Lost Decade," triggered by the burst of the bubble in the early 1990s and the subsequent financial crisis. Many people point out the similarity in the causes, events, and possible consequences of the two crises.[2] As the mists that overshadowed the decade more or less lifted in the early 2000s, the Japanese corporate landscape emerged with some considerable architectural restyling. Thus, knowing how this took place during that period may even be of interest to readers who are not particularly interested in Japan per se. In saying so, I am not referring to possible lessons from misplaced macro-economic engineering or the failure of financial policy under the liquidity trap and so on.[3] This does not belong to the realm of my expertise. I am referring to the possibility that it may provide an interesting case to enable us to learn how a "crisis" in terms of shared behavioral beliefs can be a symptom of institutional change and how it relates to the possible evolution of societal rules. The Lost Decade is considered to have begun sometime around 1992–3 when not only the asset value crashed but also the by-then taken-for-granted, one-party rule of the Liberal Democratic Party was demised. However, the seed of the crisis had already been sown in the previous decade, whereas during the Lost Decade substantial changes in the rules of societal games began to take place in a trial and error manner, particularly in the area of the corporate domain, although this process is still ongoing and far from complete.

This leads to the final reason for considering how the corporate landscape is evolving in Japan before looking at the global picture. The changing pattern of corporate organizational architecture (OA) and associated corporate governance structure (CG) in Japan, as identified below, may not just be specific to Japan. It may be suggestive of some generial trends taking place in the global corporate landscape, albeit in a path dependent and therefore nation-specific way. It was observed a few decades ago that there were national styles of CG, which might have been regarded as being particularly fitted to a traditional mode of OA as well as other social and political institutions with recognizable national characteristics. However since then the landscape of the corporate economy has been changing globally under the pressure of the global integration of financial markets and the multi-nationalization of corporations and so on. There is little doubt that the present crisis would induce further change in the global corporate economy. As shown below, evolving patterns in Japan may appear at first sight as the emergence of hybrids between the so-called S-mode and H-mode identified in Chapter 2, each representing the essential characteristics of the traditional Japanese and American corporate firms. Are these hybrids nothing but a transitory phenomenon of the convergent trend into the American model? In other words, will the global corporate landscape become increasingly flatter? Or, do they represent an important new niche in the evolving landscape? An application of the conceptual framework developed so far would tell us that the more interesting picture of the latter kind is likely to be the case. Further, observations of some stylized emergent facts from other developed economies appear to add strength to such reasoning. That is, a diversity of corporate architecture is becoming internalized more on a global scale than as a cross-national diversity that is emphasized by the "varieties of capitalism" literature.[4]

What makes the global corporate landscape more rugged and colorful is the ever-more visible presence of corporate architecture characterized by the increasing reciprocal essentialities of the cognitive assets of the management and the workers (the *RE*-mode as conceptualized in Chapter 2, Section 2.4.5). They are globally competitive in certain niche markets where the cognitive assets of engineers, workers, professionals and so on can play indispensable roles in implementing the innovative and competitive strategy envisioned by the corporate management. Further, we will see that this architectural mode co-evolves with organizations and markets served by labor with less-essential cognitive assets, because corporations of the former type becomes viable and competitive by spinning off less cognitive-intensive tasks to the latter, creating a kind of dual structure in the corporate sector. Thus, the evolving global diversity appears to present a partly old and partly new problem of widening disparity in incomes, financial and cognitive assets, and opportunities. As discussed below, an evolving variation of corporate organizational architecture can have bright prospects, but at the same time entail this uneasy phenomenon as well. The future of the corporate economy may crucially depend on how games in the corporate domain and the political and social domains interact nationally and globally to cope with this problem. This is one of the topics to be discussed toward the end of the book.

5.1.1 *Data: the emergence of hybrids*[5]

In order to identify the nature of change that the Japanese corporate sector underwent during the Lost Decade, I first reproduce the results of data analysis due to G. Jackson and H. Miyajima prepared for a project that we organized together (Jackson and Miyajima 2007; Chapter 1 of Aoki *et al.* 2007).[6] This analysis exhibits a clear pattern of variations in the linkage of organizational architecture (OA)-employment characteristics and corporate governance(CG)-finance characteristics among Japanese corporations. How

Table 5.1. Japan's emergent OA–CG linkages, by cluster

	J-firm			Hybrid			Total
				Type I		Type II	
	1a	1b	3a	2a	2b	3b	
Bond-asset ratio	0.01	0.02	0.01	0.06	0.10	0.03	0.03
Bank loan-asset ratio	0.20	0.14	0.21	0.06	0.14	0.17	0.16
Shares held by							
financial institutions	23.1	19.9	21.5	45.6	42.5	22.1	27.1
other firms	34.6	29.5	34.1	16.2	18.5	28.0	28.3
foreigners	2.0	3.6	3.1	18.3	12.2	4.6	6.0
individuals	39.5	46.2	40.7	19.2	25.9	44.6	37.9
Corporate governance index							
shareholders protection	3.4	4.7	5.1	7.8	6.8	5.7	5.2
board openess	9.4	9.6	10.5	13.9	13.6	10.6	10.9
transparency	7.1	9.2	9.3	19.7	17.1	11.0	11.2
Employment							
Union (%)	100	19	70	100	99	51	73
Lifetime employment (%)	100	100	100	84	100	29	84
Merit-based pay (%)	0	0	100	100	10	100	45
Stock options (%).	0	46	0	45	35	56	28
Additional information							
Employees per firm	940	718	1325	7574	5493	1030	2067
ROA	−0.72	1.22	−0.44	1.74	0.47	1.45	0.45
% of sample (firms)	26.2	15.8	13.0	9.4	14.7	21.0	100
% of sample (employees)	11	5	8	31	36	10	100

Source: Jackson and Miyajima (2007), Table 1.4:34. This table shows the results of a cluster analysis, using the log-likelihood method, applied to a group of 723 respondent listed corporations divided into distinct clusters that maximize the statistical differences between each group, while minimizing the variation within each group. Data were collected in 2002.

can this finding be interpreted? I try to offer a somewhat novel interpretation of the nature of the on-going change by applying the essentiality-based framework and typology developed in Chapter 2.

Table 5.1 depicts an inductively derived typology of the diverse CG–OA patterns among Japanese business corporations based on various financial, governance, and employment variables in 2002. A cluster analysis identified three broad clusters (clusters 1, 2, 3), and each was further subdivided into two sub-clusters (sub-clusters *a* and *b*) in order to capture any further heterogeneity within the initial groups.[7] The cluster analysis thus highlights the most common configurations of CG–OA variables within the sample of Japanese business corporations.

If the Japanese corporate economy has not changed in the last 20 years or so from the previous stylized characteristics, referred to as the 'J-firm' model (e.g. Aoki 1988, 1990), one may expect a strong co-variance between bank-oriented finance and governance characteristics, on one hand, and the lifetime employment practice for the core workers and associated incentive characteristics, on the other. It was considered that there existed strong complementarities between the two (e.g. Aoki 1988, 1990, 1994a, 1994b). However, the results of cluster analysis indicate the emergence of new combinations. They suggest that Japanese business corporations fall into three broad groups: traditional Japanese (J-firm) corporations with strong relational elements on all dimensions, and two types of "hybrid" corporation that combine either market-oriented finance with relational organizational architecture (type-I), or banking finance and insider boards with more market-oriented employment and incentive patterns (type-II). Next, I will describe these groups in some detail.

J-firm cluster. The first broad cluster, composed of three columns in Table 5.1 (1a, 1b and 3a), may be interpreted as comprising traditional J-firm type corporations with or without a slight reform in their respective internal characteristics. In terms of finance and ownership, these corporations use predominately bank finance rather than bonds and have high levels of inter-corporate shareholding, but low levels of ownership by foreigners or financial institutions. In terms of boards and management, corporations belonging to the subgroup (1a) have not undertaken reforms of their CG practices. These corporations have low scores across all aspects of the corporate governance index (CGI), reflecting low shareholder influence, few outsiders on the board, and low levels of transparency. In terms of employment and incentives, these corporations maintain lifetime employment norms and have not replaced seniority-based pay systems with merit-based pay. Only a small percentage adopted stock options as a form of managerial incentive and most of the corporations have enterprise unions. This sub-group contains a large number of firms from the construction, chemicals, apparel and textile industries, and small firms in the machinery and automotive sectors.

The external elements of corporations in subgroup (1b) are rather similar to those in subgroup (1a), but these corporations are more "independent" of traditional company groups, reflected in lower ratios of bank borrowing and inter-corporate shareholding. However, they have more "paternalistic" labor relations in that lifetime employment is maintained despite lower levels of unionization. These corporations are concentrated in less strongly unionized sectors, such as trading companies and lower-skilled service firms, and they also include some family-controlled companies in electrical machinery or foods. Finally, it is noted that subgroup (3a) is also very closely identifiable with the classic J-firm due to high inter-corporate ownership and persistent lifetime employment, despite being marginally "modified" through the stronger use of merit-based pay in firms such as retail establishments or the relatively smaller automotive firms in the Toyota group.[8]

Hybrid cluster of type-I: market monitoring of relational employment. The second broad cluster of listed corporations (columns 2a and 2b) displays a "hybrid" pattern that mixes market-oriented finance and ownership characteristics with relational OA characteristics. Let us refer to this cluster as type-I hybrids. These corporations make strong use of corporate bonds, and display high levels of ownership by foreign investors. The relatively high proportion of ownership by financial institutions are by trust banks and their investment and annuity trusts (essentially equivalent to mutual funds and pension funds in the USA), but not by commercial banks—ownership by that sector decreased substantially during the Lost Decade and afterwards (see Figure 5.1 in page 165). Notably, despite their strong capital market orientation, employment patterns remain relational based on the commitment to lifetime employment and very high levels of unionization.

Internally the type-I hybrid cluster is somewhat heterogeneous and suggests some distinct patterns of change. The first subgroup (2a) is distinguished by very high levels of transparency and foreign ownership, as well as the stronger use of merit-based pay systems. Although these corporations have not abandoned seniority payment schemes entirely, they have adjusted wages to reflect greater differentials within particular age cohorts based on the evaluation of individual performance or measures of group and corporation performance (Aoki *et al.* 2007, especially ch. 9 by Abe and Hoshi and ch. 10 by Jackson). This subgroup includes prominent Japanese blue chip companies such as Toyota, Canon, or Kao. The second subgroup (2b) has been more cautious in promoting transparency, and displays lower levels of foreign ownership but higher usage of corporate bonds. In parallel to these new elements, this subgroup also retains a greater number of traditional J-firm characteristics, such as a modest use of bank borrowing and a predominance of seniority-based pay. Well-known examples include Hitachi, NTT DoCoMo, some major utilities companies, and several Mitsubishi group corporations. On the whole, both type-I hybrid groups have a stronger economic performance, in terms of return on assets, than the J-firm groups, which suggests the potential competitiveness of hybrid forms of this type.

Hybrid cluster of type-II: bank monitoring of market-oriented employment. The cluster represented in column (3a) exhibits patterns asymmetric or inverse to type-I, and these we call type-II hybrids. It is the external elements of their CG that are more like the J-firm clusters, such as bank finance and inter-corporate ownership. The CG index scores are average. However, these corporations have distinctly more market-oriented or "adversarial" employment patterns with low levels of lifetime employment and unionization, as well as more frequent use of stock options. This group includes corporations from the IT or other high-tech service sectors, some retail establishments, general trading companies, or family-controlled companies. In these sectors, competitive advantage may be less dependent on firm-specific workers' cognitive assets (WCA), or firms may utilize a more mobile, occupational labor market, such as in IT services.

In sum, this analysis suggests the increasing heterogeneity of CG–OA linkage between those corporations maintaining J-firm characteristics and those changing toward hybrid patterns. In terms of mere numbers, the J-firm clusters still accounted for 55 percent of corporations compared to type-I hybrids that constituted roughly just one-quarter of Japanese listed corporations. However, type-I hybrid groups were actually becoming the dominant pattern, considering that this group included many of the largest Japanese corporations and thus accounted for 67 percent of total employment of the sample corporations. Only 10 percent of corporations fell into the type-II hybrid group with strongly market-oriented employment patterns. But as I will discuss shortly, the presence of this group may not be ignored as it appears an indispensable element of the emergent diversity.

In terms of economic performance, type-I hybrid groups achieved a significantly higher economic performance in terms of return on assets than tradition J-type corporations. This poses an interesting question regarding the potential effectiveness of the hybrid linkage. Meanwhile, traditional J-firm type corporations continue to struggle with stagnant or negative economic performance. Poor performance may reflect the weak CG role of the main banks at the time of the survey, as they themselves were struggling to emerge from the banking crisis at that time. The type-II hybrid also achieved an above-average performance, but interestingly exhibited a very high variance of ROA, suggesting its diversity.

We intend to do follow-up studies in the future to see how patterns are evolving further post 2002, a year after the world's economy was hit by the burst of the so-called dot.com bubble. But our hunch is that the basic evolutive patterns have not changed substantially since then. Given the patterns, therefore, an interesting question emerges as to what factors may influence whether a particular corporation falls into a J-firm, type-I hybrid or type-II hybrid pattern.

We note that the type-I hybrid corporations are much larger than the other groups, reflecting the importance of corporation size in determining finance and ownership characteristics in particular. Size is an important proxy for the degree of financial dependence on bonds for external finance (Arikawa and Miyajima 2007a: ch. 2 of Aoki *et al.* 2007), as well as whether corporations are attractive to foreign institutional investors, who seek a high degree of market liquidity and thus often limit their investment to the top 100 or so Japanese corporations (Ahmadjian 2007: chapter 3 of Aoki *et al.* 2007). However, if international bond-financing declines somewhat in response to the current crisis, given the relatively stronger position of Japanese major banks in comparison to the period when the dot.com bubble burst, we may not exclude the possibility that some of the less-competitive corporations of the subgroup (2b) may become more dependent on bank finance again and accordingly resume to some extent J-firm-like characteristics.

Meanwhile, employment characteristics appear to be closely related to a number of different factors, including industrial sector and corporate age, as well as other path dependent factors such as the degree of unionization and the prior establishment of a labor–management consultation process. We also note that more market-oriented employment in the type-II hybrid cluster is correlated with younger corporate age and particular sectors, such as high technology corporations or low-skill retail outlets, where firm-specific skills may be less relevant.

5.1.2 Interpretation: transitory phenomena or an emerging diversity?

Having recognized patterns of emergent diversity in the Japanese corporate landscape, the next questions are how to interpret the phenomena. Given that the J-firm cluster and type-I hybrid cluster differ widely in their business performance and the latter group includes most of the world-class business corporations of Japan, there must be some defining factors distinguishing them. What can it be? There may be two different interpretations: one is to view the type-I and type-II hybrids as a transitory phenomenon of convergence to the *H*-mode of the Anglo-American type characterized by the market-oriented features in CG and the hierarchical associational cognition in OA. An alternative is to take the view that some new relationships between the management and the workers of global relevance are emerging in some type-I hybrid corporations. I would like to argue that the latter hypothesis may be more likely for three reasons. First, the latter possibility may be generically captured as the emergence of a new mode somewhat reminiscent of the *RE*-mode that I introduced in Chapter 2. Recall that the model is characterized by the reciprocal essentialities of managements' and workers' cognitive assets (MCA and WCA). Second, given the institutional complementarities surrounding the traditional J-firm before the emergent change, the second view is more consistent with the path-dependent nature of institutional evolution. Third, in spite of the asymmetry existing between type-II hybrids and type-I hybrids in the form of their finance–employment combination, the two hybrids are dynamically complementary to each other in breaking the old institutional constraints that existed before the change.

We begin by examining the possible nature of the OA of the emergent type-I hybrids. Let us note the obvious facts that in the early 1990s Japanese corporations were forced to face unprecedented challenges in the aftermath of the euphoria of the infamous bubble of the late 1990s. Among them there were: (1) the impacts of IT that made obsolete some aspects of the traditional *S*-mode architecture of the J-firm, which had relied on implicit informtion assimilation as a primary source of competitive edge in some export industries, while the continuing practice of, as well as behavioral beliefs in, the commitment to long-term employment made it difficult to adapt to the situation by experimenting on the *SV*-mode of industrial architecture (cf. Section 2.4.4); (2) the loss of confidence in the traditional corporate governance structure which was based on shared beliefs in the commitment of relational banks to bail out corporations in trouble (cf. Section 3.3.5); (3) the challenges of the global integration of markets, for example the emergence of industrial China, reliant on an unlimited supply of labor from the rural sector, the rising wave of foreign portfolio investments, the prospects of increasing environmental problems and resource shortages and so on. The decade of the 1990s was characterized by diverse managerial responses in Japanese corporations to these emerging situations.

As noted already in Chapter 2 and elsewhere (e.g. Aoki 1988, 1990), in traditional J-firm corporations, the roles of the management and the workers, and thus the nature of the relationships between their respective cognitive assets, were not always strictly distinct from each other and well articulated. It was an accepted organizational convention among Japanese corporations that top management was recruited from the ranks of permanent employees and that this was considered to be the pinnacle of their career advancement. This practice facilitated the implicit cognition-sharing between the management and the workers, as well as the sharing of responsibilities for decision-making and its outcome. In such a setting, the autonomous role of management was somewhat blurred in comparison to the ways how it is manifest in traditional American corporations, where the allocation of cognitive assets is clearly and hierarchically ordered. The accumulation of management's cognitive assets (MCA) in Japan was geared more toward the ability to induce and support cognition-sharing and consensus-making among the members of the organization, as well as to stimulate workers' team-oriented incentives in pursuing the organizational goal.

However, in the wake of the evolving environments described above, the management of Japanese corporations seemed to be faced with the challenge of becoming more autonomous and distinctive in the use of their own MCA. MCA now needs to be directed more toward devising and implementing a distinctive business strategy to regain corporate confidence and competitiveness. In lieu of the ability to communicate effectively with various constituencies within OA and arbitrate their interests, it became more important for management to redesign the organizational architecture by such measures as modifying the traditional seniority wage system with a more explicit pecuniary incentive provision for workers' cognitive assets (WCA); reforming the board structure by adding outside voices and/or by scaling down its size to make it an effective and flexible decision-making organ rather than a consensus-making field; adopting a more differentiated and focused marketing strategy rather than competing over market share in familiar markets; engaging in corporate restructuring through merger and acquisition beyond the traditional boundaries of corporate grouping by taking advantage of the deregulation of the holding company, etc (Aoki *et al.* 2007; Milhaupt and West 2004). To implement such strategies, managements were often forced to face hard bargaining, implicitly as well as formally, with enterprise unions, in a number of different ways.[9] While retaining core workers within the framework of lifetime employment, the number of employed workers was substantially reduced through the provision of early retirement schemes and transfers to related businesses, the disinvestment of non-core business lines, an increasing reliance on agency labor or temporary employees, and so on.[10]

As a result of this process, an old conventional perception regarding the Japanese corporations became obsolete: the perception that Japanese corporations in export-oriented manufacturing industries were on a par with, or sometimes even excelled, their foreign competitors in terms of productivity, but that those corporations in regulated, domestic corporations were not so placed.[11] Now competitive, productive corporations co-exist with laggard ones across both export and domestic industries. A coherent combination of a distinct business strategy with a slimmer body of highly skilled and motivated workers as the core workforce appears to have become a decisive factor for improved business performance: an organizational architecture reminiscent of the *RE*-mode based on the reciprocal essentialities of MCA and WCA. Meanwhile those corporations that had not succeeded in realizing this combination and remained wedded to the old type of OA–CG linkage constituted the J-firm cluster as well as a fair portion of the (2b) cluster.

The question remains, however, why the type-I hybrids are not regarded as Japan's transitory phase to the Anglo-American model. This is question related to the second, path-dependence issue. Chapter 2 suggested that market-oriented, contract-based financing-cum-governance is complementary to a type of OA where hierarchical cognitive specializations are the norm (*H*-mode), whereas relational contingent governance by a main bank is complementary to cognition sharing under the system of lifetime commitment (*S*-mode). But the cluster analysis above appears to challenge such a prediction. The type-I hybrids combine market-oriented financing with a quasi-traditional employment system. The game-theoretic analysis suggests, however, that under institutional complementarities multiple equilibria are possible as the discrete value combinations of institutional variables (e.g. finance, employment), but a mixture of those equilibria cannot be in stable equilibrium.[12] This can only be a transitory phenomenon, even if it is observed.

Notwithstanding the general difficulty of a hybrid, however, it can be speculated that an institutional shift from the system of the J-firms to that of the Anglo-American type is less likely, if not impossible. Why? First, in this reasoning the concept of the essentiality of workers' cognitive assets (WCA) can play a crucial role. Recall that a critical factor distinguishing types of organizational architecture (OA) between the *H*-mode (the generic form of the Anglo-American firms) and the *S*-mode (the generic form of the J-firm) was the distinction of the unilateral vs. ambiguously symmetric nature of the essentialities of cognitive assets involved in each form of OA. Thus, if the needs for a more distinct and autonomous role of MCA are to be achieved merely by distancing MCA from WCA and reducing the essential role of WCA, then the process may eventually transit to the model of managerial unilateral essentiality (the H-mode). It is to be noted that the non-essentiality of WCA in the H-mode does not mean that they are not valuable. They can be firm-specific in cooperation with MCA or highly skilled and mobile through external markets. But it means that management can increase its own marginal productivity even with market-recruited workers by enhancing management prerogatives in the use-control rights to non-human assets (PHA), while the workers relinquish rights to participate in it. However, such a transition may not be readily achievable, at least for traditional corporations evolving from the J-firm.

From a practical point of view, the implied qualitative overhaul of the management–worker relationship may be costly, at least in the short run, because of the inherently inertial nature of the employment system in Japan. This inertia involves non-economic factors related to their social relationships as a quasi-community, as well as the role of the power and contention of unions of lifetime employees, in resisting a unilateral increase in management control.[13] Further, more fundamentally, depending on industrial market and technological characteristics, the substitution of a new standard technology, such as digital-based ICT, general-purpose-machine technology and so on, for certain cognitive skills of the workers (WCA) may be limited. Even if the use-control rights of those machines are retained by MCA, it may or may not enhance the productivity of MCA, or equivalently the effectiveness of management strategy, without the cooperation of WCA. If it does, management can certainly opt for the H-mode OA or type-II hybrid-like OA rather than the type-I hybrid. If not, however, MCA does need to provide some incentives to WCA to be cooperative, and a lifetime employment commitment to them with a suitable compensation scheme could be one such path-dependent solution.[14]

Of course, the validity of these reasons depends on the specifics of markets, as well as the judgment, orientation, and competence of management. However, taken together, these reasons may suffice to allow us to entertain the possibility of the following hypothesis: in those corporations that belong to the type-I hybrid cluster (particularly (2a)) some of the management bodies have been endeavoring to gain a competitive edge by reforming the traditional model (the J mode) in a path-dependent way. Its crux is that they are aware that a distinct, sharply focused business strategy can be important in responding to the above-mentioned challenges, but its effectiveness can only be enhanced by securing the cooperation of essential WCA. This shift in strategy may be characterized as a decoupling of MCA and WCA from what used to be an ambiguously-symmetric essentiality relationship and then re-coupling them as more distinct, yet reciprocally indispensable partners. It may be suggested therefore that, if they are successful in this respect, the core part of the Japanese corporate economy may evolve in such a way as to approximate the *RE*-mode of OA. Indeed, it is quite notable that no major cluster of business corporations has yet emerged in Japan with a combination of highly market-oriented finance with OA based on the hierarchical associational cognition reminiscent of the *H*-mode. While this possibility cannot be excluded in the future, the existing empirical evidence as well as the institutional-economics logic of path dependency does not suggest a strong pattern of convergence on this form of organization.

Thirdly, there is an issue of possible institutional constraints/complementarities on the organizational evolution of the type-I hybrid. That is, for path-dependent evolution of type-I hybrids to take place, how have the old institutional constraints imposed on the J-firm model been loosened? Or to rephrase this, how can the commitment of lifetime employment for both management and workers, albeit limited to the core workforce, be sustainable without the relational contingent governance of the main bank? Financing itself is not a problem, as better-run corporations do not have a difficulty in financing investment by themselves or relying on market financing if necessary. However, recall that the main bank used to provide dual, disciplinary/protective, CG roles. While it allowed the internal members of the J-firm to exercise de facto use-control rights over WHA in the good times, it committed to bail them out in the bad times, but threatened to terminate support in the case of the worst events. The fewer the outside opportunities for the permanently employed were, the stronger the latter disciplinary power of the threat would become (Section 2.4.4). Thus, as more firms practice lifetime employment, the main bank's role in this CG scheme becomes more effective. Also, if there were fewer outside opportunities, then valuable cognitive assets internal to the corporate team need to be protected from possible temporary corporate setbacks, particularly ones due to an external shock. Thus, the CG role of the main bank system went side-by-side with the absence of mobile external markets for quasi-essential cognitive assets.

However, the co-evolution of a type-II hybrid with a type-I hybrid implies that this situation is being transformed. Substantial numbers of workers voluntarily quit the old J firms or were discharged from them in the process of restructuring. They now form a non-negligible portion of the workforce in type-II hybrids, together with an ever larger portion of the new generation of the workforce who are not willing to commit to, or are denied, long-term employment. The co-emergence of type-II hybrids facilitates labor mobility, albeit to a limited degree, and thus eases the possible burdens of job-switching (I will discuss this in terms of its political implications later). This means that the gap between the continuation value of lifetime employment and the value of outside opportunities for the workers of type-I hybrids has been somewhat narrowed, which in turn reduces the value of the dual roles of the governance role of the main bank. Type-I hybrids do not need to rely on the bailing-out commitment of the main bank as before. In the emergent situation, the asymmetric hybrids of type-I and type-II may be complementary to each other's emergence.

Incidentally, this observation suggests another interesting point. As described type-II hybrid cluster, involving a more highly mobile workforce, contains corporations of diverse characteristics. Roughly speaking it contains two subgroups: relatively younger corporations in such industries as IT, and corporations relying on a relatively low-skilled workforce such as retail outlets. In the former, the workers may have been recruited from those leaving established corporations as well as new entrants to markets, and some of their WCA may potentially be essential. On the other hand, those corporations in the latter subgroup are generally not employing workers whose WCA is potentially essential. Both types of corporation in this cluster are basically reliant on banking finance, for obvious reasons. They are relatively young and have not yet established a reputation in the financial markets, etc. However, it may become possible for them to be financed from markets in the future, as they grow more mature and build a sound reputation. If this happens, can they be said to be evolving into something closer to the H-mode (on the high road or the low road)? Furthermore, although type-I and type-II hybrids are currently asymmetric in their form of hybridization, will some of them eventually converge to the same cluster characterized by the H-mode via asymmetric paths?

We may not exclude such a possibility. However, I speculate that even if some corporations in both hybrids become more like the H-mode in future, the type-I hybrid may continue to survive with the H-mode as possible complements for the same reason I explored above with respect to the Type-II hybrids. That is, the latter may serve as possible ports of entry of MCA and WCA out of the former. Or, in a better phase of the business cycle the latter may even serve as ports of departure to the former as well as entry from them. Possible competition for better human cognitive assets from the H-mode on the high road may discipline the management of type-I corporations to sustain effective linkages with essential WCA. A commitment to long-term employment by some corporations, on the one hand, and the voluntary and involuntary mobility of human cognitive assets outside of them, on the other, may thus not necessarily be mutually exclusive, but might be complementary in terms of competitive discipline.

However, all these do not seem to mean that the direction of corporate governance (CG) reform in Japan is clearly set or pursued. To evaluate the value of the internal linkage between the MCA that formulates business strategy and the WCA essential for its implementation, the product market evaluation (thus current profits) is fundamental. However, the product market can only evaluate the present outcome of the internal linkage, not its possible outcomes in the future. Also, a valuable internal linkage takes time to build. Furthermore, the product market may not be able to fully and effectively evaluate the external impacts of corporate behavior on the global commons and other social causes. The share market may thus potentially be in a better position to predict possible future outcomes of reciprocal linkages of MCA and WCA by aggregating dispersed information, expectations, and values prevailing in the economy, if they can filter noises to a reasonable degree.[15] Then a crucial question could be: to what extent can the share market become informative; and if it can be assumed to be reasonably so, then how can the share market evaluation of an individual business corporation be utilized effectively in the selection and possible replacement of management at the corporate level? I will take up these questions in a general context in Section 5.3. For now I only present data that may have bearings on the second question.

Figure 5.1 provides aggregated information on share ownership for all corporations listed on the Tokyo Exchange. First, we note that individual holdings are steady at around the 20 percent level throughout the period. Although it is not explicit in this data, it is a well known fact that, distinct from Continental European countries, there are no significant block-holdings by families in Japan except for a few cases so that there does not seem to be any serious issue of a possible distortion of the information or controlling bias by dynastic interests. Holdings by trust accounts at the trust banks and those by insurance companies are also fairly steady. They serve essentially the same function as that of mutual funds and pension funds in the USA or the UK. On the other hand, bank holdings have been significantly reduced during the past decade because of the unwinding of reciprocal holdings with business corporations, indicating the general decline of banks' role in relational contingent governance. The position lost by banks and non-financial inter-corporate holding is taken over by foreign investors, consisting mostly of funds of various kinds. Together with individual holdings, growing foreign holdings indicate the wide dispersion of share ownership. Indeed, a dispersion index of Japan is comparable to those of the UK and the USA (Japan 0.8, cf. the USA 0.9 and the UK 0.74) among the top 20 corporations in terms of capital values.[16]

From these observations, the following conjecture may be derived: for small and medium-sized business corporations or larger business corporations with bank loans in the J-firm clusters and possibly some of corporations belonging to (2b) clusters, we may not exclude the possibility that banks may resurrect themselves to perform major monitoring and disciplinary functions, although their effectiveness is yet to be seen. But for large business corporations with rather limited or even zero bank loans and widely dispersed ownership, the ability of the banks to correct poor management before a real crisis definitely appears to be limited. Instead, investors in the share market are becoming more diverse and sophisticated in their monitoring roles.[17] In particular, an active market for corporate control is emerging in Japan, and is playing an important role in corporate restructuring (Arikawa and Miyajima, 2007b: ch. 2 of Aoki *et al.* 2007). Poorly performing business corporations are being taken over at a higher rate, even in comparison with the USA. Yet Japanese merger and acquisition (M&A) deals remain more likely to be coordinated in the sense of being brokered through pre-existing inter-corporate networks and less open to "hostile" bids than in other countries (Jackson and Miyajima 2007b). For example, emerging private equity funds are often linked to banks and may utilize pre-existing social ties to promote trust.

For the time being, a variety of mechanisms are tried for using share market signals or their surrogates for the governance of individual corporations. One possible alternative to the traditional bank's disciplinary role would be to transform the board of directors from the traditional status of a management substructure into a quasi-independent body that could discipline top executive management in a critical corporate state. Some business corporations are taking a step in that direction by adopting a board structure with independent subcommittees or increasing the number of independent directors after an overhaul of the corporate law introduced in 2002 and 2005. How this will work has yet to be seen, but it would be worth observing experiments (Miyajima 2007: ch. 7 of Aoki *et al.* 2007; Gilson and Milhaupt 2005). In addition, in corporations where WCA are essential to the implementation of the business strategy constructed by MCA, the voice of the workers can also be of relevance as important inputs into the CG process; this could be achieved through their own organizations (unions) and/or their implicit influence on the insider-dominated board (Sako 2006). Thus the Japanese CG system is becoming more diverse in correspondence with the same trend in OA.

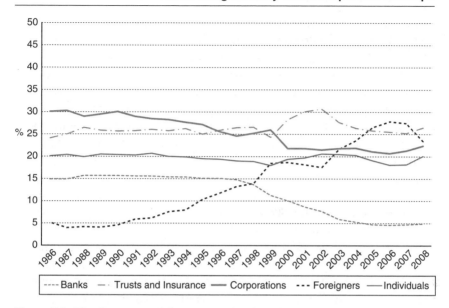

Figure 5.1. The dispersion of share ownership by value in Japan
Source: Tokyo Stock Exchange (2009). *2008 Share Ownership Survey,* Table 3.

5.1.3 *The co-evolving nature of the political state*

Having seen the evolving diversity of OA–CG combinations in the corporate organizational field, let us briefly look at the ways in which the changing rules of play in the corporate domain interact with those in the political domain. In Chapter 3, Section 3.3.5 and elsewhere,[18] I characterized the political state of Japan in the heyday of the J-firm as one type of the correlated state—the bureaucracy-mediated pluralist state (cf. Sections 3.3.2 and 3.3.5). In those times each corporation competed for larger shares in their respective markets, but their common industry-specific interests were aggregated, and differences among them were arbitrated, within their respective industrial associations. Retired bureaucrats from relevant ministries often occupied important executive positions in these associations. The political economy agenda of each interest group was then to be input into the relevant bureaus of administration, with possible help from allied politicians dubbed as *zoku* (tribal) politicians, for potential legislation, fiscal subsidies, entry regulations, the-so-called administrative guidance as a device for enforcing intra-industrial agreements, and so on. At the pinnacle of these relationships, there was the iron triangle of the Ministry of Finance (MOF), major city banks and influential politicians. All their interests were

165

intricately and opaquely entangled and mutually dependent. In this political state, even the opposition Socialist Party played a complementary role by representing and mediating the economic interests of their own constituent interest group, labor unions, into the public policy-making process.

As the Japanese corporate sector started to drift away from the ubiquitous J-firm style of OA–CG linkage toward the described diversity, this mode of political state also started to undergo a significant change. One of the most dramatic events was the separation of banking and securities supervision from the MOF in 1997, which subsequently led to an arm's length relationship between the financial regulator and the industry. The MOF was forced to accept this change in order to preserve its own legitimacy after having blundered in the enormously unpopular bailout of agricultural interests in the post-bubble liquidation of the *Jusen* (Housing-Loan Corporations) in 1995, reminiscent of the 2008 US sub-prime loan crisis.[19] Having lost the symbiotic protection of the MOF, the main banks' ability to perform the role of relational contingent governance vis-à-vis business corporations was decisively put into question. Major corporations had already drifted away from the orbit of the main bank system since the late 1980s, while non-advantageous corporations of the J-firm type lost their protective umbrella. As the interests and strategies of business corporations became diverse, the roles of industrial associations, as well as the ability of administrative bureaus to mediate their constituent interest groups and realize their political agenda, were also substantially weakened, except for less competitive industries such as the local construction industry and retail.

There was also a unique event in the political domain that was to accelerate the demise of the political order of the bureaucracy-mediated state. This was the shift from multiple-seat to single-seat representation in the Parliamentary electoral system, introduced in 1992 after the fall of the one-party rule of the Liberal Democratic Party (LDP) that had lasted for more than three decades. This change has made the electability of *zoku*-politicians representing special interest groups increasingly less likely, and has led to a decline of their agency roles in the bureaucracy-mediated state. All these evolving situations contributed to the growing uncertainties of behavioral beliefs among people as well as the sense of a loss of definitive societal direction. It may even be said that a major reason why the phrase "Lost Decade" captured the minds of so many was not so much materialistic as psychological. Taken-for-granted individual beliefs were shaken. The enormous political popularity of then-Prime Minster Koizumi,who exclaimed in 2002 "Reform! Otherwise I will destroy my Party," owed to a public perception that he created as a reformer. After his retirement in 2007, three LDP politicians succeeded him as Prime Minister, all with extremely low levels of public support because of the lack of clear leadership, and resulting in extremely short tenure. Finally, the Democratic Party of Japan (DPI) captured power from the LDP through their breakthrough victory in general election of the Lower House in August 2009, in which they had campaigned for the transforming the "bureaucracy-led" political regime to the "polity-led" one based on the electoral choice of the public. This is the first time for Japan since the 1920s that the workable competitive electoral representation system has led to a change in the government.

I posit that the emerging diversity in the corporate domain and the gradual demise of the bureaucracy-mediated state in the political exchange domain are mutually complementary and reinforcing of each other. Thus neither of the trends is likely to be reversed back toward the old systems. Their future will not be independently shaped, either. But, what will come next? I would consider that the market force driving the corporate domain toward diversity is strong enough not to be reversed. However, it has brought in a new political economy phenomenon: a growing public perception of a widening division within the workforce and consequently the population as a whole between those with relatively secure employment positions (as in the type-I hybrid cluster) and those without. As discussed above, some aspects of this division may be considered as inherently complementary, but it may be hard to swallow as an inevitable reality by those who are accustomed to the behavioral beliefs that while inequality existed, it was mildly gradational. A large majority of the Japanese used to believe that they belonged to the middle class. Such beliefs were nurtured by the bureaucracy-mediated state, while they contributed to the relative stability of society. Now, the question of how to deal with perceived disparities in income, job security, accessibility to the accumulation of cognitive assets (education, on-the-job or formal training) and so on are becoming one of the most important issues in the public discourse of Japan today. Probably the political agenda of the emergent competitive electoral representation state will hover around this issue as one focal point. The ways by which this issue will be resolved (or will not be resolved) will have significant impacts not only on the shape of the coming political state but also on the future path of the corporate domain as well.

Since what lay at the core of the mutually complementary institutional arrangements of Japan in the past was the so-called lifetime employment system in a broad sense that there was only limited individual mobility across organizations in every profession and job, I would predict therefore that, for new institutional arrangements to evolve in a clearer form, it will take a period equal to one generation. Given that the current institutional transition was triggered in the early 1990s, it may be reckoned that Japan is mid-way through the transition. However, the changes that have occurred so far are already significant. The new government who won a public mandate to experiment on changes in the government-bureaucracy relationships may facilitate further mutual adaptations between the polity, on one hand, and corporate and societal domains, on the other. I would conjecture that some aspect of the bureaucracy-mediated, correlated state may remain in future as an element of consensus-making institutional arrangements in a path-dependent manner, even though the bureaucrats therein will be forced to be more responsive to electoral choices and their rent-seeking opportunities will be further reduced. In other words, some kind of hybrid between the bureaucracy-mediated state and the competitive electoral representation state may be in the making (either in the form of a two-party alternate system, one party rule complemented with an effective opposition party, or a grand coalition of multiple parties) in parallel to the described evolving diversity of the corporate institution.

5.2 Global convergence to diversities?

The previous section suggests that the emerging hybrids in the corporate sector of Japan may be interpreted as an emergent case of the architectural mode of associational cognition in which the cognitive assets of management (MCA) and those of the workers (WCA) are reciprocally essential. Theoretically, the reciprocal essentialities (RE) of both kinds of assets refer to the relationship such that, without their mutual association, neither of them can increase their marginal products simply by substituting the use-control of non-human, physical assets (PHA) to the other. Roughly speaking, such a situation arises where specific WCA become indispensable for operating PHA or the value of PHA itself declines. This concept may sound similar to that of the complementarities between MCA and WCA, or that of the firm-specificity of WCA. But as discussed in Chapter 2, Section 2.4, they are not precisely identical. Differing from firm-specific assets, reciprocal essentialities may be created in some cases even without any in-house training of the workers, although it may often be helpful for their creation (as in the case of Japan's type-I hybrids). The complementarities in the normal state of cooperation between MCA and WCA are somewhat ubiquitous in any organizational architecture, but it does not explicitly refer to the limited role that PHA may have to play for the productivity of

MCA and WCA in the hypothetical state of their non-cooperation and thus as a determinant of their relative bargaining power.

Thus, the *RE*-mode can be regarded as a unique class of organizational architecture. I submit that this mode manifests itself in diverse substantive forms in various places and that it increasingly does so. I am not going to argue that the global corporate economy would uniformly converge to such mode. However, it does occupy some significant segments of the corporate landscape today, side by side with other modes of architecture, some traditional and some relatively new. It represents one important way for some business corporations to respond to ever-more competitive markets and an evolving technological as well as social and political milieu. If this is indeed the case, then the evolving diversity would necessarily anticipate the roles of shareholding, financial markets, and nation states that are somewhat different from what the premise of the exclusive dominance of the *H*-mode may imply. But the latter is often taken for granted in orthodox economics.

It is easy to see first of all that the said condition favoring the *RE*-mode can arise in human-asset intensive industries like professional services. The celebrated example of Saatchi and Saatchi by Rajan and Zingales illustrates this case:

In 1994, Maurice Saatchi, Chairman of Saatchi and Saatchi, proposed for himself a generous option package. The US fund managers, who controlled 30 percent of the shares, became furious.... [S]o the shareholders voted down the proposal at the general shareholders' meeting. This opposition led to the departure of Maurice Saatchi, quickly followed by the resignation of several key senior executives. [They] started a rival agency (M and C Saatchi) that in a short period of time captured some of the most important accounts of the original Saatchi and Saatchi. The original firm, which later changed its name to Cordiant, was severely damaged. (Rajan and Zingales 2000: 1641)

As they argued, in those industries, the exercise of residual rights of control over PHA, essentially the rights of their withdrawal, may not be as effective as the property-rights theory (Hart 1995) predicts. Share-ownership is not beneficial without allowing for cooperative relationships among the essential human cognitive assets to create the value of the firm.

The *RE*-mode may be productive even in industries where the systems of PHA are substantial, if their uses require a high degree of coordinated efforts of specific cognitive assets of the workers to use them as cognitive tools at the operational level of hierarchy. For example, consider the development of the next-generation automobile based on renewable energy technology. It requires large-scale physical investment in equipments and space, experimental models, rare earth materials, and so on, amounting to billions of dollars. However, without a coordinated effort among the holders of cognitive assets across such varied disciplines as mechanical engineering, manufacturing engineering, chemical engineering, material science, information technology, industrial design, and so on, there cannot possibly be any promising outcome. This is a very different situation from the one where the centralized design and control of communications networks (the H-mode) can improve on organizational effectiveness and productivity such as in retail, and mass production industries.

Further, recall that in the classification of generic organizational architectural (OA) mode the words "management" and "workers" are used as the generic denominations referring to any two classes of agents that are in mutual relationships of strategy-making and its implementation respectively. Then, the RE-mode can be found not only within single corporate organizations but also in their linkages. For example, take the computer software industry or the electronic-game industry in which core corporations (e.g. Microsoft, Nintendo, NTT DoCoMo) provide platforms for software development through the design of OS or operating hardware devices (e.g. game-playing machines, cellular phones), while many other firms are specialized in the development of specific application software or games that can be operated on that hardware. Then, the role of the generic "management" is embodied in the platform providers and that of the generic "workers" in satellite firms. OS or material devices in which the platform providers' designs are embodied cannot be operated with end-values without the availability of diverse application software, while innovative software design cannot be automatically generated only by non-human assets such as computers, software and the like without human cognitive assets at the level of satellite firms (e.g. the ability to perceive, conceptualize, create something new). To the degree that this is so, the latter's cognitive assets are indispensable and become essential to this type of industrial architecture.

Recall also that the SV-mode is architecture internalizing the cluster of entrepreneurial start-up firms as described in Chapter 2, Section 2.4.4. Those firms compete with one another in the design of new products that may constitute modular parts of a larger product system. They are like the satellite firms in the previous example in that their cognitive assets are used in encapsulation within the overall architectural frame. But their essentialities remain only as potential until their development efforts prove to be promising or successful. Successful start-up firms will be acquired by established firms (e.g. Google, Cisco Systems), if their cognitive assets are deemed as essential by the latter. In this way, the *SV*-mode may be interpreted as providing a process for creating the *RE*-mode within the integrated corporations through so-called A&D (i.e. acquisition and development) or the intial public offering (IPO). This possibility also shows that the notion of reciprocal essentialities is not identical with the traditional notion of firm-specificity, because the linkage of reciprocally essential cognitive assets can be created through markets. However, it also indicates the difficulty of sustaining the linkage after the creation, because the cognitive assets of the acquired firm can be mobile and may exit if the provision of proper incentives is not made.

An obvious reason for the rising importance of the *RE*-mode is that knowledge creation is becoming an ever-more important source of competitive edge for business corporations. However, as the knowledge to be created becomes more complex and requires collaborations among WCA specialized in different disciplines and expertise, it may become increasingly difficult to pursue fully within the frame of a single corporation. The *SV*-mode of architecture is one way to cope with this need, and the network collaboration among biotech corporations characterized by a diverse array of connectivity is another important phenomenon (e.g. Powell *et al.* 2005). As discussed in Chapter 4, Section 4.3.2, in the biotech industry, universities and public and private research organizations also play a pivotal role in the network, and career mobility back and forth between them and industry is now commonplace (Owen-Smith and Powell 2004). These phenomena also suggest the growing importance of the essentialities of WCA that cannot be understood in terms of the traditional concepts of firm-specificity.

Various examples as given above point to the obvious fact that the increasing presence of the *RE*-mode correlates with the rising importance of non-management cognitive assets (WCA) vis-à-vis management's control rights over physical assets. I submitted the hypothesis that the relatively-better performance of type-I hybrids in Japan may be due to the productivity of the internalized hardcore labor force. There seems to be some circumstantial evidence indicating similar trends in other developed economies as well. France is distinct among Continental European countries in that the ownership of large corporations shifted remarkably from domestic concentration to more dispersed institutional shareholders just like in Japan. Accordingly, France's FT Global 500's share of world stock market capitalization increased from 3.9 per cent in 1999 to 6.7 per cent in 2007, while that of the UK declined from 11.9 per cent to 9.5 per cent and that of Germany from 5.2 per cent to 3.9 per cent.[20] The change was largely brought on by an increase of foreign ownership from 24.9 per cent of market capitalization in 1996 to 39.6 per cent in 2004. A recent empirical study by Deakin and Rebérioux (2009) found that French corporations under such strong financial market pressure tend to expand expenditure on the training of core workers, provide more flexible and higher remuneration to them, while reducing the size of the core workforce by utilizing agency workers and subcontracting peripheral jobs. This is contrary to the prediction of the so-called Low Road that predicts that higher financial market pressure will be accommodated by sacrificing labor interests in general. But it is similar to the Japanese trend in that a highly qualified workforce is retained, while relying on an external, more insecure workforce for non-essential tasks. But the authors did not find a similar trend for the UK.

Deakin and Rebérioux's interpretation of the phenomenon is rather that "In France, labor law is far stronger and appears to operate as a 'beneficial constraint' on management: so negotiated shareholder value, based on rent sharing between shareholder and the core workforce, is the predominant pattern." But another intepretation, albeit not necessarily incompatible, could be that some of the better-run French companies are trying to remain competitive in global markets by relying more on the cognitive assets of the core workers, while corporations in the UK tend to stick to the traditional *H*-mode architecture either because of inertia or because the *H*-mode remain competitive in industries such as finance and the service industry. As discussed further below, if the observed trend in France were only due to rent-sharing by the intervention of the "social democratic state," it might undermine the very nature of that state, because it could eventually weaken the competitiveness of the rent-sharing corporations without the accumulation of workers' cognitive assets on the one hand and increase the politically troublesome income disparity between the core workers and the working poor on the other hand.

As indicated above, Germany's share of world stock market capitalization has declined as a whole, but there is quite a bit of diversity in corporate reactions to market pressure. Höpner (2001) constructed an index of the shareholder orientation of large corporations summarizing such items as "information quality of annual report, investor relations, implementation of profitability goals, and incentive compatibility of management compensation" for the late 1990s and found a large variation across its values with Bayer AG, VEBA AG, SAP AG ranking at the higher end. The shareholder orientation of those corporations is linked to the rise of institutional investors as their shareholders, as it is in Japan and France. Although those large corporations largely remain within the framework of industrial wage agreements, better-performing corporations supplement their wage agreements with plant-level pacts. It is often observed in market-oriented corporations that institutional shareholders put pressure on management, with the cooperation of the workers, toward more professional performance. This trend also induces a long-term shift in relations between unions and works councils. The works council that was originally a "quasi-public organization" to monitor and enforce industrial agreements increasingly takes on the role of "co-management" in supporting the adjustment of firm strategies in ways that promote and draw upon essential WCA. Works councils help to protect skilled workers in terms of employment and arrange firm-specific rewards, but the use of "voice" is also key to maintaining trust and the smooth cooperative organizational processes that allow essential WCA to thrive within the emergent OA (Jackson 2005; Streeck 2009).

On the other hand, an increasing number of less competitive corporations have been dropping out of the industry level contract altogether to undercut industry rates, and rely more strongly on contingent and low skilled labor, including immigrant workers. The renowned vocational training system is somewhat declining at plant level as well as the school level, while it is becoming more flexible and customized with an emphasis on "more theoretical skill profiles" (Thelen 2007), suggesting the rising importance of WCA attuned to new technology. Although some authors, like Gazier (2008), characterize these phenomena of disparities as an instance of the "Low Road," it may be the case that the traditional G-mode OA, embedded in the symmetric essentialities of MCA and WCA at the industrial level (cf. Section 2.4.2), has started to be transformed at least partially, just as some of the traditional J-firm have in Japan (Thelen and Kume 2006, Streeck 2009). One of the outcomes of this gradual process could be a partial transition of the traditional G-mode corporations to something reminiscent of the RE-mode, where the reciprocal essential linkage of MCA and WCA is monitored, but not dominated, by institutional shareholders. Indeed, the legacy of co-determination at the corporate level is not a deterrent to such a transition, but it may facilitate the transition to some extent for corporations that aspire to be competitive in human-asset intensive industries. Unions and investors are cooperative in the supervisory board in setting executive remuneration. Despite the growth of stock options and a mini "explosion" of pay levels to top management, the performance criteria set in German corporations for exercising options seem to be rather stringent. Once again, it seems to be the case that labor does not "veto" the measures, so much as their implementation is designed to avoid some perverse incentives on them (Fiss and Zajack 2004; Buck and Shahrim 2005; Sanders and Tuschke 2006).

Having emphasized the rising importance of the *RE*-mode of OA, however, I would not claim that the global corporate landscape will be completely painted by its variations alone. Needless to say, there are industries where non-human, physical assets (PHA) can still play decisive productive roles in the context of *H*-mode OA incorporating standardized workers' cognitive assets (WCA). They include not only physical assets-intensive industries, but also data-intensive industries, like large-scale retail outlets, retail banking, and so on, that can rely on computer networks with standard software applications. The *H*-mode OA always exists almost everywhere, albeit that it tends to bifurcate into two directions: one characterized by distinct strategic-making by agile management and the deployment of a workforce skilled, but attuned to standardized tasks; and the other with a heavyweight management and a less trained workforce. Further, as the emergent situations from Japan, France, Germany, and elsewhere suggest, the *RE*-mode of architecture is built around a relatively limited core group of workers. Its competitiveness is complemented by the presence of asymmetric OA modes served by less cultivated cognitive assets, to which it can throw peripheral tasks or redundant employment (e.g. some segments of the type-II Hybrid cluster in the case of Japan, agency workers in the case of France, workers not protected by industrial-level agreements in Germany). In addition, rising social concerns with the quality of life and the global commons may mean that products made with traditional materials and tools are more appreciated in certain segments of niche markets (e.g. furniture, food-processing). In the production of such goods, the dexterous use of the tools by the workers constitutes the integrated part of architecture, which would be only possible in small or medium-sized firms.

These factors together contribute to the evolution of diverse forms of organizational architecture and corporate strategy. Some modes (like the one just mentioned at the end of the last paragraph) are bound to be local, while others can spread beyond national boundaries and become globalized by the increasing activities of transnational corporations as well as cross-national emulation by nation-based corporations. Such evolutive diversity will therefore not be delineated by national characteristics alone to the same extent as a few decades ago. As repeatedly said, the national legacies of institutional-complementarities are still there and are certainly impacting on the ways in which individual corporations act and organize themselves in the evolutionary process. But there are also ubiquitous factors, such as mutual fits of technologies and markets, that shape this process. An aspect of the evolutive process may therefore be characterized as a process of *gradual convergence to diversities*, even though the speed, range, and content of the process may differ across countries, depending on the national make-up of industries, development stage, nature of the political state, social milieu, historical legacies, and so on (e.g. Bloom and Reenen 2007).

Inevitably, there are bright sides, as well as shadowy ones, to this process. First, diversities may allow the technology- and market-fitting selection of OA portfolios to be increasingly feasible on a global scale. As discussed in Chapter 2, Section 2.4, if the organization fields characterized by the types of available cognitive assets are separated from each other by national or regional boundaries, then particular organizational conventions tend to evolve regardless of technological and market suitability. The globalization process can ease such constraints. Second, the general insight of the evolutionary theory teaches us that diversities in general could make the economic system as a whole more adaptable to environmental change as well as robust to external shocks. For example, imagine a situation in which all the financial institutions in the world were uniformly architected and strategized just like Wall Street and the City. Then the magnitude of the impacts of the current financial crisis would have been much more serious. Third, diversities in OA and associated corporate strategies as a whole may be also fit for the diversities of market demands generated by cultural and social differences across regions and nations as well as by a rising assertion of individuality on a global scale.

However, together with this kind of positive potential, there are also some alarming aspects and/or unsettled political and social issues within the evolving diversity. First, there appears to be a problem of widening disparities of income, wealth, and opportunity across individuals, across corporations, as well as across nations. As already mentioned, from the organizational architectural perspective, this problem is related to the tendency that the growing importance of the workers' cognitive assets in the emergent *RE*-mode and sophisticated *H*-mode anticipate, as its complements, the presence of other architectural modes; particularly ones absorbing less skilled human assets, and even perhaps some skilled ones among those workers excluded from the ever slimmer core workforce of the elite organizations. From the political-economy perspective, this tendency manifests itself as the increasing presence of the working poor, a voice against the violation of the principle of equal-treatment-for-the-same-work, the inadequacy of safety-net provisions for a redundant workforce, discriminating treatments of immigrant workers, and so on. As Deakin and Rebérioux (2007) pointed out for France vs. the UK, Gazier (2008) for Social Democratic countries vs. Germany, and myself for Japan, each political state begins to respond to this problem in different ways, ranging from public transfers and regulations, state-level negotiations among interested groups, benign neglect, and so on with different consequences. This political economy process is bound to be a trial-and-error one within the frame of a nation state and beyond, but will undoubtedly have feedback implications for national competitiveness, the international division of jobs and so on. It is beyond the scope of this book to discuss these issues, but one thing seems to be clear: although equalizing the quality, level, and orientation of cognitive assets across populations in absolute terms is obviously impossible for any economy, it is still desirable for assuring opportunities for as much upward mobility as possible across different classes of cognitive assets for the sake of societal stability, upgrading of technology and organizational architecture, individual development, and so on. For this, the ways in which public and corporate sectors interact will have obvious impacts, and trial and error processes in this respect may eventually lead to a substantial adaptation even of the nature of a nation state itself as illustrated above for Japan in Section 5.1.3.

There is also the unsettled issue of how financial regulations are to be designed in a way compatible with the emergent diversities of corporate architecture and to exploit possible benefits from them. A positive aspect of the current crisis is that this problem is now widely recognized as the acute agenda of the global political economy and this urges the international community to search earnestly for a solution to it, even if it may not be easy to discover in the short term. Until the burst of the 2008 crash, it was almost taken for granted among the dominant constituents of the financial community, media, and even academia that, the freer the financial markets were from regulations and the stronger the shareholders' governing power was over business corporations, the more efficient and prosperous the global economy would be. This ideology, as well as practices legitimized by it, had not only distorted financiers' incentives (cf., Chapter 4, Section 4.3), but even more importantly pressurized non-financial business corporations to look for short-term share-value gains, which might have been less productive and/or counter to the nurturing of human cognitive assets and their best uses in the corporate economy.

Then, what should a proper relationship be between non-financial corporations on one hand and financial markets and financial corporations on the other? Before discussing the nitty-gritty on this issue, however, it is desirable to go back to the basics. The discussion in Section 2.4.5 clarified the reasoning that in the *RE* (reciprocal essentialities) mode of organizational architecture (OA) the control of physical assets (PHA) alone does not increase the management bargaining position, and thus its incentives to accumulate its own cognitive assets (MCA). Securing the cooperation of the workers' cognitive assets (WCA) to operate PHA is necessary. In the case of the separation of (ownership) control and management, its corollary is: even if the shareholders directly attempt to control the use of PHA through so-called asset restructuring (or enforce management to act in their interests), it would not be value-enhancing without the linked accumulation and cooperation of WCA. In other words, MCA and WCA are not precisely the agents (thus the instruments) of the owners of PHA for their share value gains, but rather PHA is provided as the tools (thus as the instruments) of associational cognitions of MCA and WCA, of which gains are to be distributed among the three. Of course this does not mean that WCA and MCA can abuse the use of PHA in any way. The shareholders can exercise their own governance roles by making the insiders credibly believe that PHA would be withdrawn once the state of corporate business became in a critical condition.

Given this fundamental power of shareholders, the primary role of share markets vis-à-vis *RE*-mode corporations in the normal state of affairs would be an informational one. That is, diverse investors can monitor the effectiveness of the internal linkage of reciprocally essential cognitive assets and the share markets aggregate their opinions about it to share prices as summary statistics. In that sense, share markets can remain as a crucial cognitive infrastructure for the emergent *RE*-mode OA. The insiders can cognize through the movement of share prices how their activities are evaluated in the corporate economy and society at large, and be induced to respond to them. The expected threat of a withdrawal of PHA in the case of a critical event can certainly provide ultimate incentives for the insiders to do so.

However, when there appears to be increasing signs of consensus in informative share markets such that a listed corporation is losing the essential internal linkage between MCA and WCA, how can such critical information be utilized? In this regard, there seems to be no unique, novel solution. It can be used in various forms depending on the situation, including open takeover bids, friendly acquisitions, Chapter 11-like bankruptcy procedures, bail-out by the banks, de-listing and restructuring by private equity funds, management or employee buyouts, and so on. These activities can be productive, as far as some cognitive assets are potentially valuable in the future and can be re-made as essential by the linkage to new MCA partners. Although failed management needs to be decisively driven out of this loop, an attempt of restructuring agents, whoever they may be, would be futile, if they try to maximize just short-term share values by ignoring the incentives of potentially essential cognitive assets (particularly WCA).

Institutionalized rules regarding the market for corporate control as well as bankruptcy procedures would then become crucial factors in determining whether or not potentially valuable cognitive assets are preserved, re-linked, or destroyed. Thus, a question arises as to how a proper line can be drawn between a short-term share-price maximizing strategy and a long-term "corporate-value" maximizing strategy, and between management's self-serving attempt to entrench themselves from outside monitoring and its legitimate attempt to insulate valuable systems of associational cognitions from possible destruction by selfish outsiders. While these issues are empirical and political ones and are often controversial, the important theoretical point is that market valuations and their use for corporate control are to be aligned with the fundamental nature of business corporations as systems of associational cognitions.

5.3 Summing-up: no "end of history"

As already mentioned in Chapter 1, at the beginning of this millennium, Hansmann and Kraakman, Professors of Yale Law School and Harvard Law School respectively, published a soon-to-be-well-cited article entitled "The End of History for Corporate Law" (2001). In that paper they argued that the best form of organization for large corporations is the shareholder-oriented model and that practice and law are convergent on this model. They claimed, "since the dominant corporate ideology of shareholder primacy is unlikely to be undone, its success represents the 'end of history for corporate law.'" This book is dedicated to challenging such orthodox views theoretically, methodologically, and empirically. I may add "ideologically" as well.

From an economic-theoretic perspective, the orthodox view of corporate governance is built on the following contractual premise: the firm is composed of a nexus of contracts among resource holders contributing to its activities and anything that cannot be specified *ex ante* in those formal contracts ought to be prescribed on behalf of the shareholders as the accrual of the "residual rights of control" of physical assets (Hart 1995) and the status of "residual claimants."[21] Good corporate law is to be written on this principle with those rights to be allocated to a single class of shareholders with no discrimination. This shareholder-oriented model is assumed to be efficient if the management of the corporation is duly disciplined to act as the agent of the shareholders to maximize their values.

To examine if such a claim can be universally right, let us make clear a distinction between the "value of the firm" as the total value created by the firm and the "shareholders' value" as the shareholders' share in it (Aoki 1984, Zingales 1990). On the orthodox view, the shareholders' value is composed of the "normal rate of returns" to their contributions of non-human assets (financial assets) plus the residual surplus. Why are residuals to be attributed to the shareholders? This idea is derived from two premises: (1) individual contributions of employed members of the firm to its value are at least theoretically identifiable and good contracts may be written to elicit and reward their contributions (even in the second best manner); but (2) practically individual contributions of human assets may not be completely controllable after contracting, however, without proper monitoring (whereas non-physical assets do not shirk or tell a lie by their own will). Therefore, the shareholders would be hurt and may not be able to get even the proper rate (normal rate) of return, if they are not empowered and motivated to do monitoring through residual rights of control and residual claimant status (Alchian and Demsetz 1972).

These presumptions appear innocuous and irresistible, if we do not question a basic methodological stance prevailing in economics orthodoxy: methodological individualism. That is to say that any social constructs such as business corporations and their behavior can be, and ought to be, explained by the actions of the individuals composing them and, furthermore, their tastes, attitude toward risk and effort, expectations for the future, cognitive orientations and competences and so on are all individual.[22] Throughout the book, I have been questioning such premises generally as well as in the contexts of business corporations and the corporate economy in particular. I have submitted, hopefully consistently with recent views of other disciplines such as cognitive neuro-sciences, that human beings can be engaged in associational cognitive activities with the aid of a system of tools in certain social contexts and that one of the essential aspects of business corporations is precisely to organize group-level cognitions as formal systems (cf. Sections 2.2 and 2.3). Furthermore, I have submitted, on the basis of recent achievements of epistemic game theory, that stable social constructs and orders, including business corporations, and their evolution cannot be possible without social cognitive categories such as share prices, law, social norms, culture etc., together with individual beliefs and actions (cf. Section 4.2).

If we broaden our theoretical perspective in this direction, then a completely different picture of the corporate economy would emerge in front of us. The corporate architecture of associational cognition can take various forms, depending on the cognitive relationships among the members as well as their relationships to a system of tools of cognition. And there are correspondingly discrete forms of governing it that can become shared frames within which the corporate members play the intra-organization game as a team (cf. Section 2.4). Particular modes of organizational architecture, or their mixtures, can evolve as self-governing conventions over time (cf. Section 2.4), although at the substantive level they co-evolve with social and political institutions in a mutually fit and reinforcing manner (cf. Sections 3.3 and 3.4). The legal system can mediate the process, but the law alone cannot design and implement societal rules for this process at will. As a result of the evolutionary nature of the institutional process and complementarity relationships among economic, social, and political institutions, any mode of corporate architecture and its governance, including the shareholder-oriented model celebrated by Hansmann and Kraakman, cannot be superior independently of the social and political milieu, history, technology, available individual cognitive assets, and so on.[23] Rather, varieties of organizational forms may better serve society.

Until a generation or so ago, organizational conventions and associated governance structures tended to be more nation-specific, reflecting the stage of development and historical legacy of each nation. However, through the remarkable process of the globalization of markets, information, and organization since then, the global corporate landscape now emerges as internalizing architectural variations that cross national borders. One of the conspicuous elements visible in this picture is the growing importance of human cognitive assets, not limited to those of the management, but also including those of the core workforce. The book has captured this phenomenon as the *RE*-mode architecture, referring to the nature of the reciprocal essentialities of management's and the workers' cognitive assets (cf. Section 2.4). It has suggested that this mode of architecture is evolving, alongside other traditional modes, in many places of the world economy in varied substantial forms (cf. Sections 5.1 and 5.2).

There are positive aspects to this development, particularly in terms of the increasing possibility of a better use of human cognitive assets as well as exploiting the gains to be made from diversity. However, it also generates perceived realities of widening disparities in income, financial and cognitive assets, and opportunity between individuals, organizations, and nation states. Furthermore, the current status of financial regulations does not match the evolving diversities of corporate architecture (cf. Section 5.2). The 2008 financial crisis exposed these situations to the limelight. Although the shareholder-oriented model can be theoretically and practically a right one under certain conditions, it has been utilized for legitimizing the interests of financial intermediaries seeking immediate financial gains. As Simon Johnson (2009) sharply put it, the excessive de-regulations of financial markets in the last two decades were ardently pushed by those "financial oligarchies" in Wall Street and the City. Non-financial business corporations were placed under tremendous pressure for short-term share price gains. Some corporate management colluded with short-term financial interests, negligent of nurturing the long-term corporate competence reliant on cognitive assets at the grassroots levels. To remedy these situations and make a better societal use of human cognitive assets, the dominance of the financial oligarchy in the corporate sector needs to be held in check.

Perhaps, for that purpose, walls are to be resurrected again between commercial banks, investment banks, private equity funds, insurance companies, and so on in such a way that each of them are to be made specialized in respective, socially beneficial roles and kept from short-term speculative activities such as the short selling of shares, credit default swaps (CDS), etc.[24] The latter kinds of activities may play certain useful information roles under the proper rules of play among a specific set of players (e.g. hedge funds to operate in the centralized clearing markets). However, betting money to profit from corporate failure without substantive engagement is not to be confused with basic financial support for making a productive corporate association sustainable. If public and private regulations support the service infrastructure for share markets to process relevant corporate information more accurately, it would certainly be helpful to make the advanced *RE*-mode organizational architecture more viable. Such information ought to include not only financial valuations but a broad disclosure of forward-looking business reviews and narrative forms of reporting, including on employment relationships, corporate social responsibility programs, technological development efforts, and so on.

The viability of the *RE*-mode may depend on a number of conjectures about how and under what type of regulations financial markets are to operate, whereas, empirically, market processes are also a medium of power shaped by diverse players. Furthermore, financial markets are intimately interconnected in an irreversible manner on the global scale, and information and assets are almost instantly mobile across them through the actions of financiers, while formal regulations have been designed and enforced within the frames of nation states or, at most, of regional unions of them. On the other hand, the expertise of existing international organizations such as the International Monetary Fund (IMF) and the World Bank have been basically built around the inter-governmental coordination of currency control and development financing so that the abilities to regulate complex private financial transactions in globalized markets are yet to be test. Global diversities of OA also imply diversities of interests in regulatory forms and substances. Therefore, it does not seem to be particularly hopeful that an ideal global regulatory framework can be immediately designed and implemented only through formal international agreements enforced by international organizations. Thus we cannot dismiss the importance of the force of the self-governance of corporations. It is to be remembered that some financial and non-financial corporations that behaved wildly prior to the crisis have indeed vanished or have survived only with the help of public assistance.

In addition to financial regulations, rising public concern with environmental issues makes corporate investment in social capital in the form of voluntary action one of their important strategic variables. As noted in Chapter 3, Section 3.4.3 there is a sign that share markets are beginning to internalize the value of corporate social capital in share valuations. It is not unanticipated if we note that de facto property rights over the global commons (the environment) are being transferred at a rapid pace from the corporate sector to the global community. And, as argued in Section 3.3.4, there are also private activist NGOs trying to overcome the limit of nation states in controlling the global commons. Individual business corporations react differently, either by self-regulating their actions *ex ante*, by resisting NGOs' demands, or by accommodating them. Through this "private" politics, governments may eventually discover that it is appropriate to emulate and/or enforce certain outcomes of private negotiations by subsequent legislation. Thus, in this domain as well, we cannot, and need not, rely exclusively on the possibility of formal international agreements.[25] The voluntary actions of business corporations, private politics between them and private agents, as well as forums and negotiations among nation states and within international organizations, can all be significant factors in the evolutive processes of environmental regulations.

In the world of increasing diversities, rule-making games are bound to be played on various dimensions and interrelated domains. A single centralized mechanism can hardly exist for that (cf. Chapter 4, Section 4.3). Various experiments, proposals and designs are to be proposed, tested, scrutinized, and selected through private practice as well as public discourse. In this process, business corporations will undoubtedly be important players. But what we can expect of them depends on our understanding of the nature and workings of business corporations in societal processes. This book is designed to offer a humble contribution to such an understanding.

The world is full of uncertainties and we never know for sure how business corporations are to cope with them. However, uncertainty is also the source of creativity. We are thus not at the end of history, fortunately!

Notes

1. The Gini coefficient for Japan is 24.9, for Germany 28.3, for the USA 40.8, and for Hong Kong 43.4. *Human Development Report 2007/2008*, UNDP (2009).
2. For the cause and nature of the crisis in Japan in the 1990s, see Aoki (2001: 340–5), Krugman (1999), Allen and Gale (2009).
3. See Krugman (1999, 2008) for this.
4. The sustainability of cross-national corporate diversities as emphasized by the "Varieties of Capitalism" literature is also questioned by Streeck (2009) and Carlin (2009).
5. This section draws on Jackson and Miyajima (2007) and Aoki and Jackson (2008). I am extremely grateful to Gregory Jackson and Hideaki Miyajima for allowing me to do so and to liberally interpret their empirical results.
6. In the first half of the 2000s I had an opportunity to organize, together with Professors Gregory Jackson and Hideo Miyajima, a collective research project on the evolving state of corporate governance in Japan, the members of which were drawn from diverse fields such as economics, business studies, law, and sociology. Intensive research continued for a few years and the final report was published as *Corporate Governance in Japan: Institutional Change and Organizational Diversity* (edited by M. Aoki, G. Jackson, and H. Miyajima and published by Oxford University Press in 2007, referred to below as Aoki *et al.* 2007).
7. The data were originally collected by Miyajima as part of a research project at the Policy Research Institute, Ministry of Finance in December 2002 and supplemented by financial data from the Nikkei database. The survey was sent to all listed non-financial business corporations and received a response rate of

34 percent. A detailed description of the survey and data items is provided in Jackson and Miyajima (2007: ch. 2 of Aoki *et al.* 2007) and Miyajima (2007: ch. 12 of Aoki *et al.*, 2007). For a detailed explanation of the methods of cluster analysis, see Jackson and Miyajima (2007). The analysis highlights only those variables that have statistically significant different means across groups at a 95 percent confidence level.

8. Although this group is statistically similar to subgroup 3b in having some market-oriented pay elements, I view it as having more substantive commonality with the J-firm pattern due to the essential retention of lifetime employment.

9. For an excellent study regarding the intra-organizational bargaining as a major determinant of the boundary of restructuring corporations (i.e. the problem of which activities are to be integrated, which are to be spun-off and so on) see Sako (2006).

10. Thus, the proportion of temporary employees in the total workforce, which was 17 percent in 1985 and 20 per cent in 1995, increased to 34 percent in 2007.

11. For example, see a McKinsey Global Institute study on Japan's productivity cited in Lewis (2005).

12. If complementarities exist between strategic variables, the outcome possibility set will exhibit non-convexity so that multiple corner equilibria are likely to exist, while their linear combinations cannot be in stable equilibrium. If institutional arrangements are identified with the equilibria of strategic games, this implies that diverse clusters of institutions are possible but their mixture cannot constitute viable institutional arrangements. See Aoki (2001, ch. 8).

13. The role of organization conflict in corporate change is examined in Sako and Jackson (2006) in the case of NTT.

14. There is a suggestive anecdote in this regard: in the late 1990s when some of the top Japanese business corporations were making earnest efforts toward reform of their traditional business model along the line of the Type-I hybrid, Moody's Investor Services downgraded Toyota's long-term debt ranking from Aaa to Aa1 on the ground that they were trying to retain the lifetime employment system that would hamper its competitiveness. Toyota made vociferous protests, arguing for the merits of the lifetime employment system (actually a commitment to long-term employment) as an advantage in the effort to remain competitive. After one decade (as of April 2009) they are enjoying the highest market valuation in the global auto industry in spite of serious sales setbacks caused by the global crisis.

15. Share markets cannot generate completely efficient prices, however. If all information available in the economy can be immediately and efficiently reflected in market prices, then nobody would be motivated to collect information (Grossman and Stiglitz 1980).

16. See note 8 in Chapter 3. However, two cautions are due. First, the Japanese index may overestimate the overall degree of dispersion since together the smaller

firms have a higher ownership concentration. Second, Japan is somewhat hard to represent by a dispersion measure, since "stable shareholding" is held in small blocks on a group basis and accounts for 20 percent of holdings in 2007, although it has been steadily declining in the last two decades.

17. For start-up business corporations which are not yet mature enough for a stock market valuation, venture capital firms that act as a sort of market surrogate in a relational manner are gradually gaining visibility (Hata *et al.* 2007: ch. 5 of Aoki *et al.* 2007).

18. See also Aoki (1998: ch. 7) and (2001; ch. 11).

19. See Toya (2006) for an excellent institutional analysis of this process.

20. In the same period, Japan's share increased from 6.8 to 8.0, while that of the USA declined from nearly 60 percent to 40 percent. Half of this large decline of the US share was eaten up by the emergent corporations from the so-called BRIC countries.

21. For example, see Alchian and Demsetz (1972), Jensen and Meckling (1976), Hart (1995).

22. See Hodgson (2007) for the various meanings of methodological individualism.

23. For long-term evidence refuting the supremacy of the shareholder-oriented model, see Acemoglu and Johnson (2005). For a survey of recent debate and evidences on this issue, Carlin (2009) is informative.

24. A credit default swap (CDS) is a credit derivative contract between two parties, say, hedge fund A and insurance company B. The buyer, A, makes periodic payments (premia) to the seller, B, and in return receives a payoff if an underlying financial instrument defaults. CDS contracts looks like ordinary insurance. However, the buyer, A, of a CDS does not need to own the underlying securities. For example, A can buy a CDS contract from insurance company B with reference to some debt with corporation C, without actually owning any C corporation debt. This may be done for speculative purposes, to bet against the solvency of C corporation in a gamble to make money if it fails. The lack of centralized clearing markets for such contracts and the resulting murky information involving contract design is considered to be one of the greatest sources of the 2009 financial crisis, particularly the failure of the AIG Group.

25. It is widely believed that immediate international agreements on emission control are vital for controlling global warming. However, I am largely persuaded by the telling argument of Thomas Schelling (2002, 2007) that commitment to results—such as emission rates that were to be measured only after a decade or more—but not to actions lacks the power of self-enforcement. He argues further that there are problems of disparities between the developed economies and the developing economies regarding the current levels of carbon emissions, the technological abilities to control emissions, the sense of fairness involved in the assignments of emission rights, the possible magnitude of damages due to global warming, and so on. He is therefore more in favor of international cooperation, particularly among developed economies, in research and

development in geo-engineering to make severe reductions of CO_2 feasible. He argues that even if there is no central coercive authority to enforce an agreement, the process of reciprocal scrutiny and cross-examination of efforts by individual nations to restrain emissions may be workable. He cites experiences of "burden-sharing" in NATO as an example of the effectiveness of such cooperation among nation states that have similar interests.

References

Abe, M. and T. Hoshi (2007). 'Corporate finance and human resource management in Japan,' chapter 8 in Aoki *et al.* (2007): 257–81.

Acemoglu, D. and S. Johnson (2005). 'Unbundling institutions,' *Journal of Political Economy*, 113: 949–95.

Adolphs, R. (2003). 'Cognitive neuroscience of human social behavior,' *National Review of Neuroscience*, 4: 165–78.

Ahlering, B. and S. Deakin (2007). 'Labor regulation, corporate governance, and legal origin: A case of institutional complementarities?' *Law and Society Review*, 41: 865–908.

Ahmadjian, C. (2007). 'Foreign investors and corporate governance in Japan,' Chapter 4 in M. Aoki *et al.* (2007): 125–50.

Aklerlof, G. (1976). 'The economics of caste and of the rat race and other woeful tales,' *Quarterly Journal of Economics*, 90: 599–617.

Alchian, A. and H. Demsetz (1972). 'Production, information costs, and economic organization,' *American Economic Review*, 62: 777–95.

Allen, F. and D. Gale (2009). *Understanding Financial Crises* (Clarendon Lectures in Finance), New York and Oxford, UK: Oxford University Press.

Alonso. R., W. Dessein, and N. Matouschek (2008). 'When does coordination require centralization?' *American Economic Review*, 98: 145–79.

Amable, B. (2003). *The Diversity of Modern Capitalism*, Oxford, UK: Oxford University Press.

Aoki, M. (1980). 'A model of the firm as a stockholder-employee cooperative game,' *American Economic Review*, 70: 600–10.

—— (1984). *The Co-operative Game Theory of the Firm*, Oxford, UK: Clarendon Press.

—— (1986). 'Horizontal and vertical information structure of the firm,' *American Economic Review*, 76: 971–83.

—— (1988). *Information, Incentives, and Bargaining in the Japanese Economy*, Cambridge, UK and New York: Cambridge University Press.

—— (1990). 'Toward an economic model of the Japanese firm,' *Journal of Economic Literature*, 28: 1–27.

—— (1994a). 'Monitoring characteristics of the main bank system: An analytical and developmental view,' in M. Aoki, H. Patrick, and P. Sheard, (eds.), *The Japanese Main Bank System*, Oxford, UK: Oxford University Press: 109–40.

—— (1994b). 'The contingent governance of teams: Analysis of institutional complementarity,' *International Economic Reviews*, 35: 657–76.

—— (1994c). *Corporate Governance in Transitional Economies: Insider Control and Roles of Banks*, Washington, DC: World Bank Institute.

—— (1996). 'Toward a comparative institutional analysis: Motivations and some tentative theorizing,' *Japanese Economic Review*, 1–19. Reprinted in C. Menard (ed.), *The Foundations of the New Institutional Economics, The International Library of the New Institutional Economics*, Vol. 1, Cheltenham, UK: Edward Elgar, 477–95.

—— (1998). 'The Evolution of organizational conventions and gains from diversity,' *Industrial and Corporate Change*, 7: 399–431.

—— (2001). *Toward a Comparative Institutional Analysis*, Cambridge, MA: MIT Press.

—— (2007). 'Endogenizing institution and institution change,' *Journal of Institutional Economics*, 3: 1–31.

—— and Y. Hayami (eds) (2001). *Communities and Markets in Economic Development*, Oxford, UK: Oxford University Press.

—— and G. Jackson (2008). 'Understanding an emergent diversity of corporate governance and organizational architecture: Essentiality-based analysis', *Industrial and Corporate Change*, 17: 1–27.

—— —— and H. Miyajima (eds) (2007). *Corporate Governance in Japan: Organizational Diversity and Institutional Change*, Oxford, UK: Oxford University Press.

—— and H.-K. Kim (eds) (1995). *Corporate Governance in Transitional Economies: Insider Control and The Role of Banks*. Washington, DC: World Bank.

—— and H. Takizawa (2002). 'Information, incentives, and option value: The Silicon-valley model,' *Journal of Comparative Economics*, 30: 759–86.

Arikawa, Y. and H, Miyajima (2007a). 'Relationship banking in post-Bubble Japan: Coexistence of soft- and hard-budget constraints,' in M. Aoki *et al.* (2007): Chapter 2: 51–78.

—— (2007b). 'Understanding the M&A boom in Japan: What drives Japanese M&A?', *RIETI Discussion Paper*, June 2007 07-E-042.

Aristotle. (1955). *Ethics*, translated by J. A. K. Thompson (rev. trans. by H. Tredennick), Harmondsworth: Penguin Classics.

Armour, J., S. Deakin, P. Lele, and M. Siems (2009a). 'How do legal rules evolve? Evidence from a cross country comparison of shareholder, creditor and worker protection,' American *Journal of Comparative Law*. In process.

——, ——, P. Sarkar, M. Siems, and A. Singh (2009b). 'Shareholder protection and stock market development: An empirical test of the legal origin hypothesis,' *Journal of Empirical Legal Studies*, 6: 343–81.

Arrow, K. J. (1962). 'The economic implications of learning by doing,' *The Review of Economic Studies*, 29: 155–73.

—— (1967). 'The place of moral obligation in preference systems,' in S. Hook (ed.), *Human Values and Economic Policy*, New York: New York University Press.

Reprinted in *Collected Papers of Kenneth J. Arrow*, Vol. 1. Cambridge, MA: Harvard University Press, 78–80.

——(1994). 'Methodological individualism and social knowledge,' *American Economic Review*, 84 (May): 1–9.

——(1999). 'Observations on social capital,' in P. Dasgupta and I. Serageldin (eds) (1999): 3–5.

——and L. Hurwicz (1960). 'Decentralization and computation in resource allocation,' in R. W. Pfouts (ed.), *Essays in Economics and Econometrics*, Chapel Hill: University of North Carolina Press, 34–104. Reprinted in K. J. Arrow and L. Hurwicz (1977). *Studies in Resource Allocation Processes*, Cambridge, UK: Cambridge University Press: 41–95.

——and R. Lind (1970). 'Uncertainty and the evaluation of public investment decisions,' *American Economic Review*, 60: 364–78.

Aumann, R. J. (1976). 'Agreeing to disagree,' *Annals of Statistics*, 4: 1236–39.

——(1987). 'Correlated equilibrium as an expression of Bayesian rationality,' *Econometrica*, 4: 1236–40.

——and A. Brandenburger (1995). 'Epistemic conditions for Nash equilibrium,' *Econometrica*, 63: 1161–80.

Austin, J. L. (1962), *How to Do Things with Words*, New York: Oxford University Press.

Axelrod, R. (1986). 'An evolutionary approach to norms,' *American Political Science Review*, 80: 1095–111.

Bacharach M. (2006). *Beyond Individual Choice: Teams and Frames in Game Theory*, Princeton, NJ: Princeton University Press.

Baldwin, C. Y. and K. B. Clark. (2000). *Design Rules: The Power of Modularity*, Vol. 1. Cambridge, MA: MIT Press.

Bardhan, P. (2005). *Scarcity, Conflicts and cooperation: Essays in the Political and Institutional Economics of Development: Some General Reflections*. Mimeo, University of California, Berkeley.

Barkaw, H., L. Cosmides, and J. Tooby, (eds) (1993). *Adaptive Mind: Evolutionary Psychology and the Generation of Culture*, New York: Oxford University Press.

Barnard, C. (1938). *The Functions of the Executive*. Cambridge, MA: Harvard University Press.

Baron, D. P. (2007). 'Corporate social responsibility and social entrepreneurship,' *Journal of Economics & Management Strategy*, 16: 683–713.

——and D. Diermeier (2007). 'Strategic activism and nonmarket strategy,' *Journal of Economics & Management Strategy*, 16: 599–634.

Basu, K. (1998). 'Social norms and the law,' in P. Newman (ed.), *The New Palgrave Dictionary of Economics and the Law*. London: Macmillan, 476–80.

Battigalli, P. and M. Dufwenberg (2009). 'Dynamic psychological games', *Journal of Economic Theory*, 144: 1–35.

Berle, A. (1931). 'Corporate powers as powers in trust,' *Harvard Law Review*, 63: 853–70.

References

—— (1959). Forward to E. Mason, *The Corporation in Modern Society*, Cambridge, MA: Harvard University Press, ix–xv.

—— and G. Means (1932). *The Modern Corporation and Private Property*, New York: Macmillan.

Becht, M. and C. Mayer (2001). 'Introduction' to F. Barca and M. Becht (eds), *The Control of Corporate Europe*, Oxford, UK: Oxford University Press.

Belloc, M. and S. Bowles (2009). 'International trade and the persistence of cultural-institutional diversity,' in process.

—— and U. Pagano. (2009). 'Co-evolution of politics and corporate governance,' *International Review of Law and Economics*, 29: 106–14.

Benabou, R. and J. Tirole (2006). 'Incentives and prosocial behavior,' *American Economic Review*, 96: 1652–78.

Berger, P. and T. Luckmann (1966). *The Social Construction of Reality: A Treatise in the Sociology of Knowledge*, New York: Doubleday Anchor.

Berman, H. J. (1983). *Law and Revolution*, Cambridge, MA: Harvard University Press.

Bicchieri, C. (2006). *The Grammar of Society: The Nature and Dynamics of Social Norms*. Cambridge, UK and New York: Cambridge University Press.

Binmore, K. (1994). *Game Theory and the Social Contract*, Vol. 1: *Playing Fair*, Cambridge MA: MIT Press.

—— (1998). *Game Theory and the Social Contract*, Vol. 2: *Just Playing*, Cambridge MA: MIT Press.

—— (2005). *Natural Justice*, New York: Oxford University Press.

Blackstone, W. (1765–9/2005). *Commentaries on the Laws of England*, LawMart.com.

Blair, M. and L. Stout (1999). 'A team production theory of corporate Law,' *Virginia Law Review*, 85: 247–327.

Blau, P. (1964/1998). *Exchange and Power in Social Life*, with new introduction, Brunswick, NJ: Transaction Publishers.

Bloom, N. and J. Van Reenen (2007). 'Measuring and explaining management practices across firms and countries,' *Quarterly Journal of Economics*, 122: 1351–408.

Botero, J., S. Djankov, R. La Porta, F. Lopez-De-Silanes, and A. Shleifer (2004). 'The regulation of labor,' *Quarterly Journal of Economics*, 119: 243–77.

Bourdieu, P. (1983). 'The forms of capital,' in J. G. Richardson (ed.), *Handbook of Theory and Research for the Sociology of Education*, New York: Glenwood Press: 241–58.

Bourdieu, P. and L. Wacquant (1992). *An Invitation to Reflexive Sociology*, Chicago, IL: University of Chicago Press.

Boycko, M., A. Shleifer, and R. W. Vishny (1996). 'A theory of privatization,' *Economic Journal*, 106: 309–19.

Boyd, R. and P. J. Richerson (1985). *Culture and the Evolution Process*, Chicago, IL: University of Chicago Press.

Bowles, S. (2005). *Microeconomics: Behavior, Institutions, and Evolution*, Princeton, NJ: Princeton University Press.

Bratman, M. E. (1993). 'Shared intention,' *Ethics*, 104: 97–113.

Braudel, F. (1969/1980). *On History*, translated by S. Matthews, Chicago, IL: University of Chicago Press.

Buck, T. W. and A. Shahrim (2005). 'The translation of corporate governance changes across national cultures: The case of Germany,' *Journal of International Business Studies*, 36: 42–61.

Buller, D. J. (2006). *Adapting Minds: Evolutionary Psychology and the Persistent Quest for Human Nature*, Cambridge, MA: MIT Press.

Burawoy, M. (1979). *Manufacturing Consent*, Chicago, IL: University of Chicago Press.

Burt, R. S. (2005). *Brokerage and Closure: An Introduction to Social Capital*. Oxford, UK: Oxford University Press.

Calvert, R. L. (1995). 'Rational actors, equilibrium, and social institutions,' in J. Knight and I. Sened (1995): 57–93.

Carlin, W. (2009). 'Ownership, corporate governance, specialization and performance: Interpreting recent evidence for OECD countries,' in J.P. Touffut (ed.), *Does Company Ownership Matter?* Cheltenham, Glos, UK: Edward Elgar Publishing Ltd.

Chandler, A., Jr. (1977). *The Visible Hand: The Managerial Revolution in American Business*, Cambridge, MA: Harvard University Press.

—— (1990). *Scale and Scope: The Dynamics of Industrial Capitalism*, Cambridge, MA: Harvard University Press.

Charness, G. and M. Dufwenberg (2006). 'Promises and partnership', *Econometrica*, 74: 1579–601.

Chiao, J. Y., T. Harada, H. Komeda, A. Li, Y. Mano, D. Saito, T. B. Parrish, N. Sadato, and T. Iidaka (2009). 'Neural basis of individualistic and collectivist views of self,' *Human Brain Mapping*, in process.

Chwe, M. S. (2001). *Rational Ritual: Culture, Coordination, and Common Knowledge*, Princeton, NJ: Princeton University Press.

Clark, A. (1997). *Being There: Putting Brain, Body and World Together Again*, Cambridge, MA: MIT Press.

—— (2008). *Supersizing the Mind: Embodiment, Action, and Cognitive Extension*, Oxford, UK: Oxford University Press.

Coase, R. (1937). 'The nature of the firm,' *Economica*, 4: 386–405.

—— (1960). 'The problem of social cost,' *Journal of Low and Economics*, 3: 1–44.

Coleman, J. (1988). 'Social capital in the creation of human capital,' *American Journal of Sociology* 94 (supplement): 95–120.

—— (1990). *Foundations of Social Theory*, Cambridge, MA: Harvard University Press.

Cosmides, L. and J. Tooby (1994). 'Better than rational: Evolutionary psychology and the invisible hand,' *American Economic Review*, 84: 327–32.

—— (2004). 'Social exchange: The evolutionary design of a neurocognitive system,' in M. S. Ganzzaniga (ed.), *The Cognitive NeuroSciences*, 3rd edn, Cambridge, MA: MIT Press: 1208–95.

191

References

Cremer, J. (1990). 'Common knowledge and the co-ordination of economic activities,' in M. Aoki, B. Gustafsson, and O. E. Wiliamson (eds), *The Firm as a Nexus of Treaties*. London: Sage, 53–76.

Crouch, C. *et al.* (2005). 'Dialogue on institutional complementarity and political economy,' *Socio-Economic Review*, 3: 359–82.

Cubbit R. P. and R. Sugden (2003). 'Common knowledge, salience and convention: A reconstruction of David Lewis' game theory,' *Economics and Philosophy*, 19: 175–210.

Dasgupta, P. (2000). 'Economic progress and the idea of social capital,' in P. Dasgupta and I. Serageldin (eds), (2000): 325–424.

—— and I. Serageldin (eds) (2000). *Social Capital: A Multifaceted Perspective*, Washington DC: World Bank Publication.

Dasgupta, S., J. H. Hong, B. Japlante, and N. Maminge (2004). 'Disclosure of environmental violations and the stock market in the Republic of Korea,' *World Bank Policy Research working paper* 3344.

—— B. Laplante, and N. Maminge (2001). 'Pollution and capital markets in developing countries,' *Journal of Environmental Economics and Management*, 42: 310–35.

Davis, J. P. (1905/2000). *Corporations: A Study of the Origin and Development of Great Business Combinations and of their Relation to the Authority of the State*. Reprinted by Beard Books, Washington, DC.

Deakin, S. and A. Reberioux (2008). 'Corporate governance, labour relations and human resource management in Britain and France: Convergence or divergence?' in J. P. Touffut (ed.), *Does Company Ownership Matter?* Cheltenham, Glos, UK: Edward Elgar Publishing Ltd.

—— and P. Sarkar (2008). 'Assessing the long-run economic impact of labour law systems: A theoretical reappraisal and analysis of new time series data,' *Industrial Relation Journal*, 39: 453–87.

Demsetz, H. (1967). 'Towards a theory of property rights: A review of evidence.' *Research in Law and Economics*, 2: 1–47.

Denzau, A. T. and D. North (1994). 'Shared mental models: Ideologies and institutions,' *Kyklos*, 47: 3–31.

DiMaggio, P. and W. W. Powell (1983). 'The iron cage revisited: Institutional isomorphism and collective rationality in organizational fields,' *American Sociological Review*, 48: 147–60.

—— (eds) (1991). *The New Institutionalism in Organizational Analysis*, Chicago, IL: University of Chicago Press.

Dixit, A. K. (2004). *Lawlessness and Economics*, Princeton, NJ: Princeton University Press.

Dodd, E. M. (1932). 'For whom are corporate managers trustees?' *Harvard Law Review*, 45: 1145–63.

Doeringer, P. B. and M. J. Piore (1971). *Internal Labor Markets and Manpower Analysis*, Lexington, MA: D.C. Heath and Company.

Dowell, G., Hart, S., and B. Yeung (2000). 'Do corporate global environmental standards create or destroy market value?' *Management Science*, 46: 1059–74.

Drucker, P. (1946/1972). *Concept of the Corporation*, rev edn, New York: Mentor Books.

Durkheim, E. (1893/1984). *The Division of Labor in Society*, New York: Free Press.

—— (1901/1950). *The Rules of Sociological Method*, Glencoe IL: Free Press.

Elster, J. (1989). 'Social norms and economic theory,' *Journal of Economic Perspectives*, 3: 39–117.

Elster, J. (1998). 'Emotions and economic theory,' *Journal of Economic Literature*, 36: 47–74.

Fagin, R., J. Y. Halpern, Y. Moses, and M. Y. Vardi (1995). *Reasoning about Knowledge*, Cambridge, MA: MIT Press.

Fehr, E. and C. F. Camerer (2007). 'Social neuroeconomics: The neural circuitry of social preferences,' *Trends in Cognitive Sciences*, 11: 419–27.

—— and S. Gächter (2000). 'Fairness and retaliation: The economics of reciprocity,' *Journal of Economic Perspectives*, 14: 159–81.

—— —— (2002). 'Altruistic punishment in humans,' *Nature* 415: 137–40.

Field, A. J. (1981). 'The problem with neoclassical institutional economics: A critique with special reference to the North-Thomas model of pre-1500 Europe,' *Explorations in Economic History*, 18: 174–98.

Fiske, S. T. and M. A. Pavelchak (1986). 'Category-based versus piece-meal based affective responses; developments in schema-triggered affect,' in R. M. Sorrentino and E. T. Higgns (eds), *Handbook of Motivation and Cognition: Foundations of Social Behavior*, New York: Guilford, 167–203.

Fiske, A. P., S. Kitayama, H. R. Marcus, and R. E. Nisbett (1998). 'The cultural matrix of social psychology,' *Handbook of Social Psychology*, 4th edn New York: McGraw-Hill: 915–81.

Fiss, P.C., and E. Zajac (2004). 'The diffusion of ideas over contested terrain: The (non)adoption of a shareholder value orientation among German firms,' *Administrative Science Quarterly*, 49: 501–34.

Fogassi L, P. Ferrari, B. Gesiercih. *et al.* (2005). 'Parietal lobe: From action organization to intention understanding,' *Science*, 308: 662–7.

Franks, J. and C. Meyer (2001). 'The ownership and control of German corporations,' *Review of Financial Studies*, 14: 943–77.

Franks, J., C. Mayer, and H. F. Wagner (2005). 'The origins of the German corporation – finance, ownership and control,' *ECGI- Finance Working Paper, Working Paper No.110/2005*.

Friedman, M. (1970). 'The social responsibility of business is to increase its profits,' *The New York Times Magazine* (13 September). Reprinted in T. Donaldson and T. P. H. Werhane (eds) (2007). *Ethical Issues in Business: A Philosophical Approach*, Englewood Cliffs, NJ: Prentice Hall: 217–23.

Fujii, N., S. Hihara, and A. Iriki (2007). 'Social cognition in premotor and parietal cortex,' *Social Neuro Science*, 3: 250–60.

Gavetti, G. and D. Levinthal (2000). 'Looking forward and looking backward: Cognitive and experimental search,' *Administrative Science Quarterly*, 45: 113–37.

References

——and J. W. Rivkin (2007). 'On the origin of strategy: Action and cognition over time'. *Organization Science*, 18; 420–39.

Gazier, B. (2008). 'Why contemporary capitalism needs the working poor,' *Prisme* No. 14, Paris: Cournot Centre for Economic Studies.

Geanakoplos, J., D. Pearce, and E. Stacchetti (1989). 'Psychological games and sequential rationality,' *Games and Economic Behavior*, 1: 60–79.

Geertz, C. (1983). *Peddlers and Princes*. Chicago, IL: University of Chicago Press.

Genka, T. (2009). 'Hierarchie der texte, hierarchie der autoritäten: Zur hierarchie derRechtsquellen bei gratian,' *Zeitschrift der Savigny-Stiftung für Rechtsgeschichte, Kanonistische*. (Read in Japanese version).

Ghemawat, P. (1997). *Games Businesses Play: Cases and Models*, Cambridge, MA: MIT Press.

Gilbert, M. (1989). *On Social Facts*, Princeton, NJ: Princeton University Press.

Gilson, R. J. and C. J. Milhaupt (2005). 'Choice as regulatory reform: The case of Japanese corporate governance,' *American Journal of Comparative Law*, 53: 343–77.

Gintis, H. (2007), 'A framework for the unification of the behavioral sciences,' *Behavioral and Brain Sciences*, 30: 1–61.

——(2009). *The Bounds of Reason: Game Theory and the Unification of the Behavioral Sciences*, Princeton, NJ: Princeton University Press.

——, S. Bowles, R.T. Boyd, and E. Fehr (eds) (2006). *Moral Sentiments and Material Interests: The Foundations of Cooperation in Economic Life*, Cambridge MA: MIT Press.

Glaeser, E., D. Laibson, and B. Sacerdore (2002). 'An economic approach to social capital,' *Economic Journal*, 112: 437–58.

Gower, B., LCB (1969). *Principles of Modern Company Law*, 3rd edn, London: Stevens & Sons.

Graff Zivin, J. and A. Small (2005). 'A Modigliani–Miller theory of altruistic corporate social responsibility,' *Topics in Economic Analysis & Policy*, 5, Article 10.

Granovetter, M. (1985). 'Economic action and social structure: The problem of embeddedness,' *American Journal of Sociology*, 91: 480–510.

Greif, A. (1994). 'Cultural beliefs and the organization of society: A historical and theoretical reflection on collectivist and individualist societies,' *Journal of Political Economy*, 102: 912–50.

——(1997). 'Micro theory and recent developments in the study of economic institutions through economic history', in D. Kreps and K. Wallis (eds), *Advances in Economics and Econometrics: Theory and Applications*, Vol. 2, New York: Cambridge University Press: 79–113.

——(2006). *Institutions and the Path to the Modern Economy: Lessons from Medieval Trade*. New York, and Cambridge, UK: Cambridge University Press.

——(2008). 'Why did Europe Differ? Corporatism and Institutional Development', Stanford University, processed.

——and C. Kingston (2008). 'Institutional and organizational design,' forthcoming in *Handbook of Rational Choice Social Research*.

—— P. Milgrom, and B. Weingast (1994), 'Coordination, commitment and enforcement: The case of the merchant guild,' *Journal of Political Economy*, 102: 745–76.

Greve, H. R. and A. Taylor (2000). 'Innovation as catalysts for organizational change: Shifts in organizational cognition and search', *Administrative Science Quarterly*, 45: 54–80.

Grossman, S. and J. Stiglitz (1980). 'On the impossiblity of informationally efficient markets,' *American Economic Review*, 70: 393–408.

Guiso, L., P. Sapienza, and L. Zingales (2006). 'Does culture affect economic outcomes?' *Journal of Economic Perspectives*, 20: 23–48.

Hall, P. and D. Soskice, (eds.) (2001). *Varieties of Capitalism: The Institutional Foundations of Comparative Advantage*, Oxford, UK: Oxford University Press.

Hannah, L. (1976). *The Rise of the Corporate Economy*, London: Methuen.

Hansmann, H. and R. Kraakman (2001). 'The end or history for corporate law,' *Georgia Law Journal*, 89: 439.

Harding, G. (1968). 'The tragedy of the commons,' *Science*, 162: 1243–8.

Harsanyi, J. (1977). *Rational Behavior and Bargaining Equilibrium in Games and Social Situations*, Cambridge, UK and New York: Cambridge University Press.

Hart, O. (1995), *Firms, Contracts, and Financial Structure*, Oxford: Clarendon Press.

—— and J. Moore. (1990). 'Property rights and the nature of the firm,' *Journal of Political Economy*, 98: 1119–58.

—— —— (2005). 'On the design of hierarchies: Coordination versus specialization,' *Journal of Political Economy*, 113: 675–702.

Hata, N., H. Ando, and Y. Ishii (2007). 'Venture capital and its governance: The emergence of equity financing conduits in Japan,' in M. Aoki *et al.* (eds) (2007), ch. 7: 151–78.

Hayami, Y. (2006). 'Social capital, human capital and community mechanism: Toward a consensus among economists' draft.

Hayashi, K. (2000), 'Reform of the Islamic law: On the birth of the institutions of new lease contracts under the Ottoman Empire (Isuramuhou no tanjo: Osumanchou ni okeru shin chintai keiyaku seido no tanjo wo megutte,' (in Japanese) in *Iwanami Lectures on the World History*, Vol. 14: *Islamic and Pan-Indian Oceanic World*, Iwanami Publishers: Tokyo: 169–92.

Hayek, F.A. (ed) (1935). *Collectivist Economic Panning*, London: Routledge.

—— (1945). 'The use of knowledge in society,' *American Economic Review*, 35: 519–30.

—— (1952). *Sensory Order*, Chicago, IL: University of Chicago Press.

—— (1973). *Law, Legislation and Liberty*, Vol 1: *Rules and Order*, Chicago, IL: University of Chicago Press.

—— (1979). *Law, Legislation and Liberty*, Vol 3: *The Political Order of a Free People*, Chicago, IL: University of Chicago Press.

—— (1988). *The Fatal Conceit: The Errors of Socialism. The Collected Works of F.A. Hayek*, Vol. 1., Chicago, IL: University of Chicago Press.

References

Heal, J. (2005). 'Corporate social responsibility: An economic and financial framework,' *The Geneva Papers*, 30: 387–409.

—— (2009). *When Principles Pay: Corporate Social Responsibility and the Bottom Line*, NY: Columbia University Press.

Heath, J. (2001). *Communicative Action and Rational Choice*, Cambridge, MA: MIT Press.

—— (2008). *Following the Rules: Practical Reasoning and Deontic Constraint*, Oxford, UK: Oxford University Press.

Hicks, J. (1969). *A Theory of Economic History*, Oxford, UK: Oxford University Press.

Hodgson, G. M. (2004). 'Opportunism is not the only reason why firms exist: Why an explanatory emphasis on opportunism may mislead management strategy,' *Industrial and Corporate Change*, 13: 401–18.

—— (2006). 'What are Institutions?' *Journal of Economic Issues*, 40: 1–25.

—— (2007). 'Meanings of methodological individualism,' *Journal of Economic Methodology*, 14: 211–26.

Hoffman, A. J. (2001). *From Heresy to Dogma: An Institutional History of Corporate Environmentalism*. Stanford CA: Stanford University Press.

Holmström, B. (1979), 'Moral hazard and observability,' *Bell Journal of Economics*, 10: 74–91.

—— (1982). 'Moral hazard in teams,' *Bell Journal of Economics*, 10: 324–40.

Höpner, M. (2001). 'Corporate governance in transition: Ten empirical findings on shareholder value and industrial relations in Germany,' *MPIfG Discussion Paer* 01/5.

Huizinga, J. (1938/1950). *Homo Ludens: A Study of the Play Element in Culture*, Boston, MA: The Beacon Place.

Hume, D. (1739/1992). *Treaties of Human Nature*, Buffalo: Prometheus Books.

Hurley, S. (2008). 'The shared circuits model (SCM): How control, mirroring, and simulation can enable imitation, deliberation, and mindreading,' *Behavioral and Brain Sciences*, 31: 1–58.

Hurwicz, L. (1960). 'Optimality and informational efficiency in resource allocation processes,' in K. J. Arrow, S. Karlin, and P. Suppes (eds), *Mathematical Methods in the Social Sciences*, Stanford CA: Stanford University Press. Reprinted in K. J. Arrow and L. Hurwicz (1977). *Studies in Resource Allocation Processes*, Cambridge, UK: Cambridge University Press: 393–412.

—— (1972). 'On informationally decentralized systems,' in R. Radner and C. B. McGuire (eds), *Decision and Organization: A Volume in Honor of J. Marschak*, Amsterdam: North-Holland. Reprinted in K. J. Arrow and L. Hurwicz (1977). *Studies in Resource Allocation Processes*, Cambridge, UK: Cambridge University Press: 425–59.

—— (1973). 'The design of mechanisms for resource allocation', *American Economic Review*, 63: 1–30.

—— (1993). 'Toward a framework for analyzing institutions and institutional change' in S. Bowles, H. Gintis, and B. Gustafsson (eds), *Market and Democracy: Participation, Accountability and Efficiency*, Cambridge, UK and New York: Cambridge University Press: 51–67.

—— (1996). 'Institutions as families of game-forms', *Japanese Economic Review*, 47: 13–132.

—— (2008). 'But who will guard the guardians?' *American Economic Review*, 98: 577–85.

—— and S. Reiter (2006). *Designing Economic Mechanisms*, Cambridge, UK and New York: Cambridge University Press.

Hutchins, E. (1996). *Cognition in the Wild*, Cambridge, MA: MIT Press.

Iacoboni, M., I. Molnar-Szakacs, V. Gallese, G. Buccino, J.C. Maziotta, *et al.* (2005). 'Grasping the intentions of others with one's own mirror neuron system,' *PLoS Biology*, 3: e79.

Ikegami, E. (1995), *The Taming of the Samurai: Honorific Individualism and the Meaning of Modern Japan*, Cambridge, MA: Harvard University Press.

Izuma, K., D. N. Saito, and N. Sadato (2008). 'Processing of social and monetary rewards in the human striatum,' *Neuron*, 58: 284–94.

Jackson, G. (2001). 'The origins of nonliberal corporate governance in Germany and Japan,' in W. Streeck and K. Yamamura (eds) (2001). *The Origins of Nonliberal Capitalism: Germany and Japan in Comparison*. Ithaca, NY, Cornell University Press: 121–70.

—— (2005). 'Contested boundaries: Ambiguity and creativity in the evolution of German codetermination,' in W. Streeck and K. Thelen (eds), *Beyond Continuity: Explorations in the Dynamics of Advanced Political Economies*, Oxford: Oxford University Press, 229–54.

—— (2007). 'Employment adjustment and distributional conflict in Japanese firms,' in M.Aoki *et al.* (eds) (2007). ch. 10: 282–309.

—— and H. Miyajima (2007a). 'Introduction,' in M. Aoki *et al.* (eds) (2007). ch. 1: 1–47.

—— —— (2007b). 'Varieties of capitalism, varieties of takeover markets: A comparison of five countries,' *RIETI Discussion Paper*, 07-E-054.

Jensen, M. and W. Meckling (1976). 'Theory of the firm: Managerial behavior, agency costs, and capital structure,' *Journal of Financial Economics*, 3: 305–60.

Johnson, S. (2009). 'The quiet coup,' *The Atlantic Online*, http://www.theatlantic.com/doc/print/200905/imf-advice. (accessed on August 8, 2009).

Kahneman, D. (1994). 'New challenges to the rationality assumption." *Journal of Institutional and Theoretical Economics*, 150: 18–36.

Kandori, M. (1992). 'Social norms and community enforcement,' *Review of Economic Studies*, 59: 63–80.

Kaneko, M. and A. Matsui (1999). 'Inductive game theory: Discrimination and prejudices,' *Journal of Public Economic Theory*, 1: 101–37.

Kaplan, S. N. and P. Strömberg (2003). 'Financial contracting theory meets the real world: An empirical analysis of venture capital contracts,' *Review of Economic Studies*, 70: 281.

Kasaya, K. (1988). *Shukun Oshikome no Kozo: Kinsei Daimyo to Kashindan (The Structure of Forced Early Retirement of Lord: Daimyo and His Retainers)*, in Japanese, Tokyo: Heibonsha.

Katzenstein, P. J. (1985). *Small States in World Markets: Industrial Policy in Europe*, Ithaca, NY: Cornell University Press.

References

Kim, H. and H. R. Marcus (1999). 'Deviance or uniqueness, harmony or conformity? A cultural analysis,' *Journal of Personality and Social Psychology*, 77: 785–800.

King, A. A. and Lennox, M. J. (2001). 'Does it really pay to be green? An empirical study of firm environmental and financial performance,' *Journal of Industrial Ecology*, 5: 105–16.

Kitayama, S., and H. R. Markus (eds) (1994). *Emotion and Culture: Empirical Studies of Mutual Influence*, Washington, DC: American Psychological Association

——— H. R. Markus, H. Matsumoto, and V. Norasakkunikit (1997). 'Individual and collective processes in the construction of the self: Self-enhancement in the United States and self-criticism in Japan,' *Journal of Personality and Social Psychology*, 72: 1245–67.

Knight, J. and I. Sened (eds) (1995). *Explaining Social Institution*, Ann Arbor, MI: University of Michigan Press.

Krugman, P. (1999). *The Return of Depression Economics*, New York: W.W. Norton.

——— (2008). *The Return of Depression Economics and the Crisis of 2008*, New York: W.W. Norton.

Kuran, T. (2005). 'The absence of the corporation in Islamic law: Origins and persistence,' *American Journal of Comparative Law*, 53: 785–834.

Lange, O. (1938). *On the Economic Theory of Socialism*, Minneapolis, MN: University of Minnesota Press.

La Porta, R., F. Lopez-de-Silanes, A. Shleifer, and R. Vishny (1998). 'Law and finance,' *Journal of Political Economy*, 106: 1113–55.

——— ——— ——— ——— (1999). 'Corporate ownership around the world,' *Journal of Finance* 54: 471–517.

——— ——— ——— ——— (2008). 'The economic consequences of legal origins,' *Journal of Economic Literature*, 46: 285–332.

Lehmbruch, G. (1999). 'The rise and change of discourses on 'embedded capitalism in Germany and Japan and their institutional setting,' Mimeo. Universitat Konstantz.

Lewis, D. (1969). *Conventions*, Cambridge, MA: Harvard University Press.

——— (1975). 'Languages and language,' in K. Grunderson (ed.), *Language, Mind and Knowledge*, University of Minnesota Press. Reprinted in H. Geirsson (ed.), *Reading in Language and Mind*, Sommerset NJ: Wiley and Blackwell: 134–54.

Lewis, W. W. (2005). *The Power of Productivity: Wealth, Poverty, and the Threat to Global Stability*. Chicago, IL: University of Chicago Press.

Makdisi, G. (1981). *The Rise of Colleges: Institutions of Learning in Islam and the West*, New York: Columbia University Press.

Markus, H. and S. Kitayama (1991). 'Culture and the self: Implications for cognition, emotion and motivation,' *Psychological Review*, 98: 224–53.

Marris, R. (1964), *The Economic Theory of Managerial Capitalism*, London: Free Press and Macmillan.

Marschak, J. and R. Radner (1972). *Economic Theory of Teams*, New Haven, CT: Yale University Press.

Marx, K. (1844/1992). *Economic and Philosophical Manuscripts of 1844*. Translated by G. Benton and included in *Early Writings by K. Marx*, Harmondsworth: Penguin Classics.

Maskin, E. (1977/1999). 'Nash equilibrium and welfare optimality,' *Review of Economic Studies*, 66: 23–38.

Matsui, A. and M. Okuno-Fujiwara (1994). *Evolution and Interaction of Cultures*, Mimeo, Universities of Pennsylvania and Tokyo.

McAfee, R. P. and J. McMillan (1987). 'Auctions and Bidding,' *Journal of Economic Literature*, 25: 699–738.

McDonald, I. and R. Solow (1981). 'Wage bargaining and employment,' *American Economic Review*, 71: 896–908.

McMillan, J. (2002). *Reinventing the Bazaar: Natural History of Markets*, New York: W.W. Norton.

McWilliams, A. and D. Siegal (2000). 'Corporate social responsibility: A theory of the firm perspective,' *Academy of Management review*, 26: 117–27.

——— and C. M.Wright (2006). 'Corporate social responsibility: Strategic implications,' *Journal of Management Studies*, 43: 1–18.

Meijers, A. W. M. (2003). 'Can collective intentionality be individualized,' *American Journal of Economics and Sociology*, 62: 167–83.

Micklethwait, J. and A. Wooldridge (2003). *The Company; A Short History of a Revolutionary Idea*, Modern Library Chronicle Book, New York: Random House.

Milgrom, P. (1981). 'An axiomatic characterization of common knowledge,' *Econometrica*, 49: 219–22.

—— (2004), *Putting Auction Theory to Work*, New York: Cambridge University Press.

—— D. North, and B. Weingast (1990). 'The role of institutions in the revival of trade: The Law Merchant, private judges, and the Champagne Fairs,' *Economics and Politics*, 2: 1–23.

—— and J. Roberts (1990). 'The economics of modern manufacturing: Technology, strategy, and organization, *American Economic Review*, 80: 511–28.

——— (1992), *Economics, Organization and Management*, Englewood Cliffs, NJ: Prentice Hall.

—— Y. Qian, and J. Roberts (1991). 'Complementarities, momentum, and the evolution of modern manufacturing,' *American Economic Review*, 81: 84–181.

Milhaupt, C. and M. D. West (2004). *Economic Organizations and Corporate Governance in Japan: The Impact of Formal and Informal Rules*, New York: Oxford University Press.

Miyajima, H. (2007), 'The performance effects and determinants of corporate governance reform,' in M.Aoki *et al.* (eds) (2007). ch. 12: 330–69.

—— and F. Kuroki (2007), 'The unwinding of cross-shareholding in Japan: Causes, effects, and implications,' in M. Aoki *et al.* (eds) (2007), ch. 3: 79–124.

Monderer, D., and L. S. Shapley (1996). 'Potential games,' *Games and Economic Behaviour*, 14: 124–43.

References

Montague, P. R. and G. S. Berns (2002). 'Neural economics and the biological substrates of valuation,' *Neuron*, 36: 265–84.

Murakami, T. (1984, 1985). '*Ie* society as a pattern of civilization,' *Journal of Japanese Studies*, 10 and 11.

Nash, J. (1953). 'Two-person cooperative games,' *Econometrica*, 21: 128–40.

Nelson, R. R. and S. G. Winter (1982). *An Evolutionary Theory of Economic Change*, Cambridge, MA, Harvard University Press.

Neumann, J. von and O. Morgenstern. (1944). *Theory of Games and Economic Behavior*, Princeton, NJ: Princeton University Press.

Nonaka, Y. (1991). 'Knowledge creating company,' *Harvard Business Review*, 69: 96–104.

——and H. Takeuchi (1995). *The Knowledge Creating Company: How Japanese Companies Create the Dynamics of Innovation*, NY: Oxford University Press.

——R. Toyama and H. Hirota (2005). *Managing Firms: A Process Theory of the Knowledge-Based Firm*, London: Palgrave MacMillan.

North, D. C. (1990). *Institutions, Institutional Change and Economic Performance*, Cambridge, UK and New York: Cambridge University Press.

——(1995). 'Five propositions about institutional change,' in J. Knight and I. Sened (eds), (1995): 15–26.

——(2005). *Understanding the Process of Economic Change*, Princeton, NJ: Princeton University Press.

——J. J. Wallis, and B. R. Weingast (2009). *Violence and Social Order: A Conceptual Framework for Interpreting Recorded Human History*, Cambridge, UK and New York: Cambridge University Press.

OECD (2004). *Institutional Investors Yearbook* (final issue), Paris: OECD.

Ohmoto, Y., K. Ueda, and T. Ohno (2008). 'Enhancement of people's lie detection ability by showing the mechanically measured nonverbal information,' *Proceedings of Social Intelligence Design*, 2008 (SID2008).

Osborne, M. J. and A. Rubinstein (1994). *A Course in Game Theory*, Cambridge, MA: MIT Press.

Ostrom, E. (1990). *Governing the Commons*, Cambridge, UK and New York: Cambridge University Press.

——(2005). *Understanding Institutional Diversity*, Princeton, NJ: Princeton University Press.

——(2007). 'Developing a method for analyzing institutional change,' Bloomington: Indiana University Press.

——and J. Walker (1994). *Rules, Games, and Common-Pool Resources*, Ann Arbor: University of Michigan Press.

Owen-Smith, J. and W. W. Powell (2004). 'Knowledge networks as channels and conduits; the effects of spillovers in the Boston biotechnology community,' *Organization Science*, 15: 5–21.

Oyserman, D., H. M. Coon, and M. Kemmelmeier (2002). 'Rethinking individualism and collectivism: Evaluation of theoretical assumptions and meta-analyses,' *American Psychological Bulletin*, 128: 3–72.

Pagano, M. and P. Volpin (2005). 'The political economy of corporate governance,' *American Economic Review*, 95: 1005–30.

Parkinson, J. (2003). 'Models of the company and the employment relationship,' *British Journal of Industrial Relations*, 41: 481–509.

Parsons, T. (1951). *The Social System*, New York: Free Press.

Penrose, E. (1959). *The Theory of the Growth of the Firm*, Oxford, UK: Oxford University Press.

Plato (2000), *Laws*, translated by B. Jowett, New York: Prometheus Books.

Podolny, J. M. (2001). 'Networks as the pipes and prisms of the market,' *American Journal of Sociology*, 107: 33–60.

Polanyi, K. (1944). *The Great Transformation*, New York: Farrar Rinehart.

Porter, M. (1985). *Competitive Advantage: Creating and Sustaining Superior Performance*, New York: Free Press.

Powell, W. W., D. R. White, K. W. Koput, and J. Owen-Smith (2005). 'Network dynamics and field evolution: The growth of interorganizational collaboration in the life sciences,' *American Journal of Sociology*, 110: 1132–205.

Pratt, A. (1996). 'Shared knowledge vs. diversified knowledge in teams,' *Journal of the Japanese and International Economies*, 10: 181–95.

Putnam, R. D. (1993). *Making Democracy Work*, Princeton, NJ: Princeton University Press.

Rabin, M. (1993). 'Incorporating fairness into game theory and economics,' *American Economic Review*, 83: 1281–302.

—— (1998). 'Psychology and economics', *Journal of Economic Literature*, 36: 11–46.

Rajan, R. G. and L. Zingales (2000). 'The governance of the new enterprise,' in X. Vives (ed.), *Corporate Governance: Theoretical & Empirical Perspectives*, Cambridge, UK and New York: Cambridge University Press: 201–32.

—— —— (2003). *Saving Capitalism from the Capitalists: Unleashing the Power of Financial Markets to Create Wealth and Spread Opportunity*, New York: Crown Business.

Rawls, J. (1955). 'Two concepts of rules,' *The Philosophical Review*, 64: 3–32.

—— (1971). *Theory of Justice*, Cambridge, MA: Harvard University Press.

Rilling, J. *et al.* (2002) 'A neural basis for social cooperation', *Neuron*, 35: 395–405.

Rizolatti, G. and C. Sinigaglia (2008). *Mirrors in the Brain — How Our Minds Share Actions and Emotions*, translated by F. Anderson from Italian, Oxford, UK: Oxford University Press.

Roberts, J. (2004). *The Modern Firm: Organizational Design for Performance and Growth*, Oxford, UK: Oxford University Press.

Roe, M. (2003). *Political Determinants of Corporate Governance: Political Context, Corporate Impact*, Oxford, UK: Oxford University Press.

—— (2006). 'Legal origins, politics, and modern stock markets,' *Harvard Law Review*, 120: 462–527.

References

Roland, G. (2008). 'Fast-moving and slow-moving institution,' in J. Kornai, L. Matyas, and G. Roland (eds), *Institutional Change and Economic Behaviour*, IEA Conference Volume No. 144, Hampshire: Palgrave Mcmillan, 134–59.

Rosenberg, N. and L. E. Birdzell (1986). *How the West Grew Rich: The Economic Transformation of the Industrial World*, New York: Basic Books.

Roth, A. E. (2008). 'What have we learned from market design?' *Economic Journal*, 118: 285–310.

——and M. A. Oliveira Sotomayor (1992). *Two sided Matching: A Study in Game-Theoretic Modeling and Analysis*, Cambridge, UK and New York: Cambridge University Press.

Rubinstein, A, (1982). 'Perfect equilibrium in a bargaining model,' *Econometrica*, 50: 97–109.

Sacconi, L. (2010). 'A Rawlsian view of CSR as an extended model of corporate governance and the game theory of its implementation,' in L. Sacconi, M. Blair, R. E. Freeman, and A. Vercelli (eds), *CSR and Corporate Governance: the Contribution of Economic Theory and Related Disciplines*, Hampshire: Palgrave Mcmillan.

Sako, M. (2005). 'Does embeddedness imply limits to within country diversity?' *British Journal of Industrial Relations*, 43: 585–92.

——(2006). *Shifting Boundaries of the Firm: Japanese Company—Japanese Labour*, Oxford: Oxford University Press.

——and G. Jackson (2006). 'Strategy meets institutions: The transformation of management—labor relations at Deutsche Telekom and NTT,' *Industrial and Labor Relation Review*, 59: 347–66.': ':

Samuelson, P. (1947). *Foundations of Economic Analysis*, Cambridge, MA: Harvard University Press.

Sanders, W. G. and A. C. Tuschke (2006). 'The adoption of institutionally contested organizational practices: The emergence of stock option pay in Germany,' *Academy of Management Journal*, 50: 33–56.

Saxenian, A. (1994). *Regional Advantage: Culture and Competition in Silicon Valley and Route 128*, Cambridge, MA: Harvard University Press.

Schank, R. C. and R. P. Abelson (1977). *Scripts, Plans, Goals, and Understanding*, Hillsdale, NJ: Lawrence Erlbaum.

Schelling, T. C. (2002). 'What makes greenhouse sense?' *Foreign Affairs*, 81(3): 2–9.

——(2007). "Climate change: The uncertainties, the certainties and what they imply about action," *The Economists' Voice*, 4: Issue. 3, Article 3. Available at: http://www.bepress.com/ev/vol4/iss3/art3 Accessed on December 1, 2009.

Schotter, A. (1981). *The Economic Theory of Social Institutions*, Cambridge, UK and New York: Cambridge University Press.

Schumpeter, J. (1934). *The Theory of Economic Development*, Cambridge, MA: Harvard University Press.

Scott, W. R. (1994). 'Conceptualizing organizational fields: Linking organizations and societal systems,' in H. Derlien *et al.*, (eds), *Systemrationalität und Partialinteresse*, Baden-Baden, Germany: Nomos Verlagsgesellschaft: 81–99.

—— (1995). *Institutions and Organizations*, Thousand Oaks, CA: Sage Publications.

Searle, J. R. (2005). 'What is an institution?' *Journal of Institutional Economics*, 1: 1–22.

Seiyama, K. (1995). *Seido-ron no Kozu (A Frame of Theory of Institutions)*, Tokyo: Sobunsha.

Sened, I. (1997). *The Political Institution of Private Property*, Cambridge, UK and New York: Cambridge University Press.

Shleifer, A. and R. W. Vishny. (1997).'A survey of corporate governance,' *Journal of Finance*, 52: 737–87.

Siegel, D. S. and D. F. Vitaliano (2007). 'An empirical analysis of the strategic use of corporate social responsibility,' *Journal of Economics & Management Strategy*, 16: 773–92.

Simon, H. A. (1957). *Administrative Behavior*, 2nd edn, New York: Free Press.

Smith, A. (1759/1976). *The Theory of Moral Sentiments*, Oxford, UK: Oxford University Press

Sperber, D. and D. Wison (1986/1995). *Relevance: Communications and Cognition*. Oxford UK: Blackwell.

Solow, R. (1999). 'Notes on social capital and economic performance,' in P. Dasgupta and I. Serageldin (eds) (1969): 6–9.

Streeck, W. (1992). 'Social institutions and economic performance,' in *Studies of Industrial Relations in Advanced Capitalist Economies*, London: Sage Publications.

—— (1995). 'Community building in industrial relations: Creating conditions for workplace participation' in D. Sciulli (ed.), *Macro Socio-Economics: Form Theory to Activism*, Armonk, NY: M. E. Sharpe: 184–94.

—— (2009). *Re-Forming Capitalism: Institutional Change in the German Political Economy*, Oxford, UK: Oxford University Press.

Sugden, R. (1986). *The Economics of Rights, Co-operation and Welfare*, Oxford: Basil Blackwell.

—— (1993). 'Thinking as a team: Towards an explanation of nonselfish behavior,' *Social Philosophy & Policy*, 10: 69–89.

—— (1995). 'A theory of focal point,' *Economic Journal*, 105: 533–50.

—— (2003). 'The logic of team reasoning,' *Philosophical Explorations*, 6: 165–81.

Sugeno, W. (1931/1966). *Nihon Kaisha Kigyo Hasseishi no Kenkyu (Study of a History of the Emergence of Japanese Business Corporations)*, Tokyo: Keizai Hyoronsha.

Svejnar, J. (1982). 'On the theory of a participatory firm,' *Journal of Economic Theory*, 27: 313–30.

Teranishi, J. (1997), 'Sectorial resource transfer, conflict, and macrostability in economic development: A comparative analysis,' in M. Aoki, H. Kim, and M. Okuno-Fujiwara (eds), *The Role of Government in East Asian Economic Development: Comparative Institutional Analysis*, Oxford, UK: Oxford University Press: 279–311.

Thelen, K. (1999). 'Historical institutionalism in comparative politics,' *American Review of Political Science*, 2: 369–404.

References

—— (2004). *How Institutions Evolve: The Political Economy of Skills in Germany, Britain, the United States, and Japan*, Cambridge UK and New York: Cambridge University Press.

—— (2007). 'Contemporary challenges to the German vocational training system,' *Regulation & Governance*, 1: 247–60.

Thelen, K. and I. Kume (2006). 'Coordination as a political problem in coordinated market economies,' *An International Journal of Policy, Administration, and Institution*, 19: 11–42.

Tindale, R. S., Kameda, T. and Hinsz, V. (2003). 'Group decision making: Review and integration' in M. A. Hogg and J. Copper (eds), Sage *Handbook of Social Psychology*, London: Sage 381–403.

Tirole, J. (2001). 'Corporate governance,' *Econometrica*, 69: 1–35.

Tokyo Stock Exchange (2009). *2008 Share Ownership Survey*, Tokyo: TSE.

Tomasello M, M. Carpenter, J. Call, *et al.* (2005). 'Understanding and sharing intentions: The origins of cultural cognition,' *Behavioral and Brain Science*, 28: 675–735.

Topkis, D. (1978). 'Minimizing a submodular function on a lattice,' *Operations Research*, 26: 305–21.

—— (1998). *Supermodularity and Complementarity*, Princeton, NJ: Princeton University Press.

Toya, T. (2006). *The Political Economy of the Japanese Financial Big Bang: Institutional Change in Finance and Public Policymaking*. Oxford, UK: Oxford University Press.

Ui, T. (2009). 'Bayesian potentials and information structures: Team decision process revisited,' *International Journal of Economic Theory*, 51: 271–91.

Ullman-Margalit, E. (1977). *The Emergence of Norms*, Oxford, UK: Oxford University Press.

UNDP (2009). *Human Development Report 2007/2008*, New York: United Nations.

Vanberg, C. (2008) 'Why do people keep their promises? An experimental test of two explanations,' *Econometrica*, 76: 1467–80.

Vanderschraaf, P. and G. Sillari, (2001/2007). 'Common Knowledge', *Stanford Encyclopedia of Philosophy*. http://plato.stanford.edu/entries/common-knowledge/. Accessed on April 1, 2008.

von Thadden, E. L. (1995). 'Long-term contracts, short-term investment and monitoring,' *Review of Economic Studies*, 62: 557–75.

Weingast, B. (1997). 'The political foundations of democracy and the rule of law,' *American Political Science Review*, 91: 245–63.

Williams, R. (1976/1983). *Keywords: A Vocabulary of Culture and Society*, rev edn, Oxford UK: Oxford University Press.

Williamson, O. E. (1964). *The Economics of Discretionary Behavior: Managerial Objectives in a Theory of the Firm*, Englewood Cliffs, NJ: Prentice Hall.

—— (1975). *Markets and Hierarchies: Antitrust Implications*, New York: Free Press.

—— (1996). The *Mechanisms of Governance*, Oxford, UK: Oxford University Press.

—— (2000). 'The new institutional economics: Taking stock, looking ahead,' *Journal of Economic Literature*, 38: 595–613.

Witt, U. (1998). 'Imagination and leadership: the neglected dimension of an evolutionary theory of the firm', *Journal of Economic Behavior and Organization,* 35: 161–77.

—— (2000). 'Changing cognitive frames—changing organizational forms: an entrepreneurial theory of organizational development,' *Industrial and Corporate Change:* 733–55.

Wu, J. (2005). *Understanding and Interpreting Chinese Economic Reform,* Mason, OH: Thomson.

Yamagishi, T., K. S. Cook, and M. Watanabe (1998). 'Uncertainty, trust, and commitment formation in the United States and Japan,' *American Journal of Sociology,* 16: 161–97.

—— H. Hashimoto, and J. Schug (2008) 'Preferences versus strategies as explanations for culture-specific bahavior,' *Psychological Science,* 19: 578–83.

Young, H. P. (1991). 'An evolutionary model of bargaining,' *Journal of Economic Theory,* 59: 145–68.

—— (1993). 'The evolution of conventions,' *Econometrica,* 61: 57–84.

—— (1998). *Individual Strategy and Social Structure: An Evolutionary Theory of Institutions,* Princeton, NJ: Princeton University Press.

Zingales, L. (1998). 'Corporate governance', *in the New Palgrave Dictionary of Economics and the Law,* London: Macmillan: 497–503.

—— (2000). 'In search of new foundations,' *Journal of Finance,* 55: 1623–53.

Zucker, L. G. (1977). 'The role of institutionalization in cultural persistence,' *American Sociological Review,* 13: 443–64.

Index

Index